WINNING POWER

Winning Power

Canadian Campaigning in the Twenty-First Century

TOM FLANAGAN

McGill-Queen's University Press

Montreal & Kingston · London · Ithaca

© McGill-Queen's University Press 2014

ISBN 978-0-7735-4331-7 (cloth)
ISBN 978-0-7735-9036-6 (ePDF)
ISBN 978-0-7735-9037-3 (ePUB)

Legal deposit first quarter 2014
Bibliothèque nationale du Québec

Printed in Canada on acid-free paper that is 100% ancient forest free
(100% post-consumer recycled), processed chlorine free

McGill-Queen's University Press acknowledges the support of the
Canada Council for the Arts for our publishing program. We also
acknowledge the financial support of the Government of Canada
through the Canada Book Fund for our publishing activities.

Library and Archives Canada Cataloguing in Publication

Flanagan, Thomas, 1944–, author

   Winning power : Canadian campaigning in the twenty-first
century / Tom Flanagan.

Includes bibliographical references and index.
Issued in print and electronic formats.
ISBN 978-0-7735-4331-7 (bound). – ISBN 978-0-7735-9036-6 (ePDF). –
ISBN 978-0-7735-9037-3 (ePUB)

   1. Political campaigns – Canada. 2. Campaign funds – Canada.
3. Political campaigns – Technological innovations – Canada.
4. Political campaigns – Alberta – Case studies. I. Title.

JL193.F53 2014   324.70971   C2013-907147-4
                                   C2013-907148-2

Typeset by Jay Tee Graphics Ltd. in 10.5/14 Sabon

Contents

Figures and Tables

WINNING POWER

Introduction

Political campaigns are major events: almost fifteen million people voted in the 2011 Canadian general election. Candidates with any reasonable chance of winning typically report that they are helped by hundreds of volunteers. Even fringe candidates and also-rans may have a few dozen volunteers. No one has ever done a national tally, but with 308 federal constituencies, the total number of volunteers might be over 200,000, maybe even approaching 300,000. And a similar number of people are recruited by Elections Canada for relatively little pay in order to man the voting booths on election day.[1] That's a lot of people to be actively involved in a single project, especially one that goes on for thirty-six days, sometimes even longer.

Considering the number of people involved and the duration of the event, national political campaigns are probably the largest participatory exercises in Canadian life outside of wartime. Provincial and local campaigns are just as intense relative to the size of the jurisdiction in which they take place. And even for many of those not actively participating, a campaign is a crucial event because it dominates all news media, not only during the campaign but for weeks before and after.

So campaigns are a big deal. Beyond that, they are intrinsically important because they determine who will control the machinery of government for the next few years. Except in the special case of referendums, campaigns do not decide questions of public policy, but they lead up to the choice of the representatives who will make those decisions. Campaigns, therefore, are absolutely central to the practice of modern democracy.

Political campaigning is important in every democracy, but it has been on particular display in Canada in the new millennium. We have seen national elections in 2000, 2004, 2006, 2008, and 2011, as well as leadership races for the Canadian Alliance, Progressive Conservatives, Conservative Party of Canada, Bloc Québécois, Liberals (3), New Democrats (2), and Greens (2). There have been so many campaigns that Canadians may have become tired of them, and perhaps a bit cynical. This book goes back to basics to explain to jaded observers what campaigns are and why they are so important.

Also, it is not just a question of the number of campaigns. The whole environment for national campaigning in Canada has changed significantly in the past decade in at least four areas:

- the identity of the major players, including not just new political parties but organized labour, which now plays a major role in several provinces
- the legislated rules, especially the financial rules of the game
- the ever-growing importance of new communications media
- the rise of the "permanent campaign," with new tactics such as large-scale negative advertising in the pre-writ period

The change in the players is little short of remarkable. In 2000, the Liberal Party of Canada beat back a challenge from the newly formed Canadian Alliance, and the conventional wisdom was that the Liberals would be in power for the foreseeable future. All observers agreed that the Liberals were the pace-setters in Canadian campaigning – in fundraising, technology, and message discipline. The enduring primacy of Liberal campaigning was reflected in the title of Stephen Clarkson's book *The Big Red Machine*, which chronicled Liberal campaigns from 1974 through 2004. But Stephen Harper replaced Stockwell Day as leader of the Canadian Alliance, talked the Progressive Conservatives into a merger to form the Conservative Party of Canada, and started chipping away at Liberal support. These steps led to the Conservative minority governments of 2006 and 2008, and then the sweeping changes of 2011 – a Conservative majority government, replacement of the Liberals by the NDP as official opposition, decline of the Bloc Québécois to insignificance, and entry of the Greens into the House of Commons.

Changes at the provincial level have also been remarkable. A new conservative party – the Saskatchewan Party – won the government of that province in 2007. Another new conservative party – Wildrose – gave the ruling Alberta Progressive Conservatives a scare in 2012 before having to settle for official opposition status. In British Columbia, a revived provincial Conservative party challenged the Liberals for dominance of the non-socialist vote in 2010 and 2011, though the Conservatives faded badly afterwards and the Liberals were re-elected in 2013. Ontario has not seen the rise of any new parties, but organized labour, through shrewd use of "third-party" advertising, has become the kingmaker of Ontario politics. The Action Démocratique du Québec surged to become the official opposition in 2007, then collapsed and merged with another new party to form the Coalition Avenir Québec, which won 27 per cent of the popular vote and nineteen seats in the 2012 provincial election. The New Democrats formed the government of Nova Scotia in 2009, the first time that party had won an election in Atlantic Canada. It seems that the identity of the major players in Canadian politics has been changing more frequently than ever.

The fiscal regime for federal political parties has changed three times: first in 2003, when the Liberal government enriched the rebates for campaign expenses, limited personal contributions to $5,000, banned corporate and union donations to national parties, and introduced quarterly allowances as a replacement; second in 2006, when the new Conservative government banned corporate and union donations to local constituency associations and reduced the limit for personal contributions from $5,000 to $1,000 (adjusted annually for inflation); and then in 2011, when the Conservative government announced the gradual termination of the quarterly allowances over a three-year period running from 2012 to 2015. The rule changes made before 2011 put more money into the system, thereby making it easier for parties to start campaigning more intensively in the pre-writ period. The changes also shifted the balance of power among the parties, favouring the Conservatives and harming the Liberals, even though it was the Liberals who introduced the first round of changes. ("Those whom the gods would destroy, they first drive mad.")

Before the turn of the century, the Internet existed but was barely a factor in Canadian campaigns. But new communications media have been prominent in each recent federal election as well as in provincial campaigns – cell phones in 2000, the BlackBerry in 2004, blogging in 2006, YouTube in 2008, and Twitter in 2011.[2] Although these and other innovations have speeded up the news cycle, they really haven't changed the nature of campaigning. A much greater impact has come from older and less visible database technology, which the Conservatives have been able to harness to build an advantage over all other parties in grassroots fundraising. This extra fundraising capacity has paid for the Conservative adoption of the permanent campaign model, especially the very expensive pre-writ television ads used to define Stéphane Dion and Michael Ignatieff even before they could define themselves in the public mind as new Liberal leaders.

This book shows how all these factors are intertwined. New financial regulations nullified the traditional Liberal advantage in corporate and high-end individual donations and allowed the Conservatives to forge ahead, using their database superiority in grassroots fundraising to build an advantage over all other parties. The Conservatives then used that advantage to make a fundamental change in campaign methods, becoming the first party in Canadian history to adopt a permanent campaign model and make full use of the pre-writ period to undermine their opponents. These innovations in fundraising and campaigning didn't lead to immediate victory, but over a decade they wore down the Liberals and led to the Conservative majority elected in 2011.

And yet, *plus ça change, plus c'est la même chose*. No matter how much methods of campaigning change, campaigning always remains basically the same thing – building a coalition of supporters to win control of the government. The basic strategy for winning power remains what it always been – a triage of voters. Keep your core supporters loyal, ignore hard-core opponents, and concentrate your resources to appeal to soft supporters who need to be reassured and to soft opponents who can be won over. And the mechanism of coalition-building remains fundamentally the same – rhetoric. Voters in a democracy cannot be forced into a coalition: they must be persuaded. Campaigning is a celebration of political freedom and rationality, because it eschews the force of arms and uses the force of argument to help citizens choose their government.

My earlier book, *Harper's Team*, chronicled the Conservative rise to power, providing narrative accounts of Stephen Harper's leadership campaigns as well as the federal elections of 2004, 2006, and 2008. This book, in contrast, is organized thematically. It examines Canadian political campaigning in three parts. Part I looks at what is relatively permanent in campaigning: coalition-building, rhetoric, the rules of engagement, positioning, and campaign strategy. Part II takes up the new developments that have characterized the new millennium, especially changes in the fiscal regime, new technologies of persuasion, and the rise of the permanent campaign. Part III provides a case study of the 2012 Alberta provincial election, in which I was involved as Wildrose campaign manager. It provides concrete illustrations of the themes discussed throughout the book. Finally, an appendix discusses campaign strategy in by-elections, which are from time to time of considerable practical importance in Canadian politics.

The information base for the book is a combination of the literature on campaigning and my own practical experience as a campaign manager for the federal Conservatives and the Wildrose Party of Alberta. That unique combination is this book's comparative advantage. Few other Canadian academics who study campaigning have had this kind of practical experience, and few practising campaigners have a theoretical background in political science. I hope the reader finds the combination rewarding.

This book won't make you a winning political campaigner – it takes years of experience (and good luck) to do that. But it will make you a more informed observer of Canadian elections and campaigns. You will have a better idea of why campaign teams do what they do and why their efforts produce success or failure. Maybe you'll even become a better citizen by having an improved understanding of the central process by which we choose our rulers.

PART I

The Permanent Reality
of Campaigning

1

Fundamental Concepts

THE CHIMPANZEE WAY

Frans de Waal is an international celebrity, second only to Jane Goodall as a world-famous primatologist. In 1982, he published his first book, *Chimpanzee Politics: Power and Sex among Apes*, based on six years of studying a chimpanzee colony at the Arnhem Zoo in the Netherlands.[1] It is the most important book on politics since Machiavelli's *Prince*. I first read it in the early 1990s, around the time that I went to work for Preston Manning and the Reform Party. I have been drawing upon it ever since in order to get a better understanding of human politics in general, and Canadian politics in particular.

In de Waal's portrait of chimpanzee society, rank is all important. The adult males sort themselves out in a strict dominance hierarchy, or pecking order – alpha, beta, gamma ... omega. Each male has to salute those above him in the hierarchy with certain marks of respect, bowing low to the ground and making a sound known as the "pant-grunt." And it is not just about signs of respect: higher-ranking males sit where they want and grab food when they want it. Above all, they copulate more frequently with the more desirable females when they are at the peak of their fertile period. In the world of chimpanzees, a more desirable female is likely to be older, with previous experience in raising infants. Being a chimpanzee mother is not easy, and experience leads to success. Thus higher-ranking males, who prefer these experienced mothers as sexual partners, increase their odds of fathering offspring who will grow to maturity. Successful pursuit of dominance has a reproductive payoff, which tends to entrench this behavioural characteristic in the gene pool.

Some mammal species have male-dominance hierarchies based on iterated contests between individuals. For example, bull elk or sea lions take on all comers one at a time in order to establish control over a harem. But chimpanzees, like other primate species, establish dominance through coalition formation. Male chimpanzees differ in size and strength, but not so much that one individual can by his own efforts lord it over all the others. Two adult males can generally take down any other single male, no matter how strong and ferocious he is. So the key to "climbing the greasy pole" is to build a coalition of males, held together by occasional food-sharing, frequent grooming, and mutual support in case of conflicts. Achievement of rank requires not only individual prowess in threatening and fighting but also social skills to keep allies happy.

These male coalitions are strategic in nature. That is, they serve the purpose of attaining rank; they are not friendships. Hence they are prone to breaking up and re-forming as part of the ongoing struggle for dominance. Some of the most interesting parts of *Chimpanzee Politics* describe how a coalition that has brought Alpha to the top is threatened as Gamma starts to make nice with Beta. In human terms, he is suggesting to Beta that he will support him for Alpha and become Beta himself, while the current Alpha, whom they both supported in the past, will be forced downwards to Gamma or even lower. A male chimp takes years to climb to the top of the dominance hierarchy, where he will remain for a longer or shorter period of time, depending on his *virtù* and his social skills. Once overthrown, he may form a new coalition of support and get back to the top, because chimpanzee life is long and the males never lose their desire for dominance. One is tempted to quote the philosopher Thomas Hobbes about "the perpetual and restless desire for power after power, that ceaseth only in death."[2]

Females have their own ranking system, though it is not as strictly defined as the male hierarchy. Females do not form, break, and re-form strategic coalitions as the males do. Their alliances seem to be more like long-term friendships, based on cooperation in protecting their infants. All females are lower in rank than all the adult males and must acknowledge that dominance with marks of respect. Yet females sometimes also get involved in the male striving for rank. They don't join the male coalitions as such, but they may weigh in during disputes, helping to tip the balance to one side or the other. In that way, female preferences can help to determine who will be Alpha. The Alpha, however, will always be a male – unless, as sometimes happens in small groups in zoos, there are no adult males. In that case, an older female may play the Alpha role, though in the instance that de Waal observed, it was an uneasy situation and did not last once an adult male entered the scene.

De Waal's original research was done in the artificial situation of a zoo, but his basic findings have been repeatedly confirmed by African field studies, which have also added another dimension to our understanding of chimpanzee politics. In a pattern first described by Jane Goodall, chimpanzee bands engage in a kind of low-intensity warfare against each other. A group of males, occasionally including a female, will go off to patrol the boundaries of their band's territory. If they find a member of another band, they will attack with lethal force.[3] This type of fighting is very different from the noisy internal dominance struggles, in which participants may be wounded but are seldom killed. These border attacks are more like hunting, in that killing is the obvious purpose. Over time, a larger or more aggressive band may annihilate or drive another band away, and then take over its feeding territory. This pattern is highly reminiscent of the human quest for *Lebensraum*, geographical space in which the society can find resources to support demographic expansion.

Another dimension of chimpanzee coalitional behaviour has been highlighted by anthropologist Christopher Boehm, who has done field studies of chimpanzees as well as human beings. He notes that "subordinate coalitions" sometimes emerge in chimpanzee communities to punish oppressive Alpha males.[4] Such subordinate coalitions may consist of small groups of rival males who attack the Alpha, killing him or driving him out of the community (close to a death sentence, because solitary adult males are usually killed by the males of other bands). Groups of females also sometimes come together to punish Alpha males who abuse a female more than usual.

An observer of human politics cannot help but notice the striking similarities with chimpanzee behaviour:

- existence of a dominance hierarchy with privileges for those at the top
- male obsession with attaining rank
- coalition formation as the means of ascending the hierarchy
- formation of subordinate coalitions to fight back against overly dominant Alpha figures
- relative restraint in internal conflicts in contrast to lethal coalitional violence against outsiders

To make things even more complicated, another species of chimpanzees demonstrates quite different political behaviour. The bonobo, or *Pan paniscus*, lives south of the Congo River in the Democratic Republic of the Congo. Bonobos are slightly smaller and less aggressive than the better-known chimpanzee, *Pan troglodytes*. The males do less hunting, and violent clashes between bands, of the type reported for chimpanzees by Jane Goodall, have not been observed. Moreover, males do not dominate females in *troglodytes* fashion. Males struggle for dominance as individuals, but females build their own coalitions, which are much stronger than female chimpanzee coalitions and serve to protect female bonobos against bullying by the larger and stronger males.

Primatologists speculate that bonobos evolved in a unique direction because there are no gorillas in their forest homeland south of the Congo River. Bonobos are thus able to forage on the forest floor, whereas chimpanzees are forced into the treetops whenever gorillas are present. The greater abundance of food sources for bonobos allows females to spend more time together and build stronger coalitional bonds, as compared to female chimpanzees, who must fan out through the treetops to feed themselves and their infants.

Bonobos appear to have separated from the main chimpanzee line about a million years ago. The two species can still interbreed, though they do not do so in the wild because they are separated by the Congo River. Though bonobo behaviour has some interesting resemblances to human behaviour (less absolute male dominance, as compared to chimpanzees, for example), bonobos are not genetically closer to humans and do not furnish a better overall model than chimpanzees for human behaviour. But they do illustrate the plasticity of our primate heritage, which also shows up in human behaviour.

In any event, bonobos and chimpanzees are the closest relatives of human beings. It is generally thought that the human and chimpanzee lines diverged between five and seven million years ago, in a dry period when the African rainforest was receding. To oversimplify quite a bit, humans are chimpanzee cousins who became bipedal as we adapted to life on the treeless savannahs, while chimpanzees continued to brachiate through the rainforests. Whatever the details of the split, this close relationship means that our two species have an enormous amount in common, including a basic behavioural template for what in human language is called politics: coalitional striving to achieve rank, with reproductive benefits for success, as well as to combat exploitation by those who hold rank. As Aristotle said, man is truly a "political animal."[5]

HUMAN DISTINCTIVENESS

That we are closely related to chimpanzees and bonobos does not mean we are the same. We are different species, with lots of species-specific behaviour. Not surprisingly, human politics is unique in a number of ways.

Above all, the human use of language means that coalitions can be formed and broken up through verbal persuasion, as well as food-sharing, grooming, and fighting. Human politics depends crucially upon rhetoric, the art of persuasion. Also, human politics is deliberative. We engage each other in debate and make collective decisions about what to do – decisions that are then enforced upon community members, with sanctions if necessary. Human politics is not just about achieving dominance; it is also about policy – what should the community do? Chimpanzee politics, in contrast, is all about dominance. Those who achieve higher rank obtain reproductive advantages, but they don't enforce collective decisions upon their communities. Similarly, those who form subordinate coalitions to fight back may displace the Alpha, but they don't enact new policies, because chimpanzees don't have policies.

Our greater intelligence, as expressed in language, also means that human politics can be about abstractions. We can form coalitions that are held together by belief in religion, ideology, and national identity, as well as loyalty or opposition to an Alpha figure. Chimpanzee coalitions, on the other hand, are purely personal. The males struggle to achieve dominance, not to implement some imagined policy based on a set of abstract principles.

The earliest human communities were probably similar in size to chimpanzee bands, with a few dozen members; but intelligence, language, and the use of abstract symbolism has enabled human beings to create enormous communities several orders of magnitude larger than the milieux in which chimpanzees and bonobos live. One consequence is the coexistence of multiple dominance hierarchies. In Canada, for example, we have many political systems – federal, provincial, and local – each with its own hierarchy. We also have vast numbers of corporations, schools, universities, hospitals, voluntary organizations, and private clubs with their own governance systems that involve the attainment of rank. Almost every Canadian can find a forum in which to satisfy the human desire for attaining rank, even if that just consists of being elected president of a sewing circle, attaining a university degree, or getting promoted at work.

Another consequence of community size is the way in which human coalitions compete against each other for dominance. In the much smaller chimpanzee society, coalitions form to promote some individuals at the expense of others, or to oppose an oppressive Alpha figure, but there is nothing like a contest of opposing coalitions. Even in chimpanzee "warfare," groups of males go on patrol to discover, attack, and kill isolated individuals from other bands; they do not engage in pitched battles with armies from the other side.

Human beings form chimpanzee-style coalitions to create or oppose a dominance hierarchy of individuals, but human coalitions also struggle with each other – lethally in warfare, and not so lethally in domestic politics. This tendency is undoubtedly the root of the human fascination with team sports like soccer, football, baseball, and hockey. They appeal to some of the deepest drives of our primate heritage: the desire to bond with others, to attain dominance, and to vanquish other groups as groups.

Human politics, then, is certainly different from chimpanzee politics, but not categorically different. It is not like saying A is different from B. It is more like saying A plus B is different from A. That is, human politics includes everything that is in chimpanzee politics but overlays it with other layers of complexity. Like chimpanzees, human beings form coalitions to achieve dominance because of the benefits that come with dominance. These benefits may be sexual in the direct sense (think of the sexual adventures of American president Bill Clinton, International Monetary Fund managing director Dominique Strauss-Kahn, and Italian prime minister Silvio Berlusconi), but more often they are indirect. Greater control over resources (salaries, perks of office, prestige) leads to more numerous reproductive opportunities as well as better life chances for one's offspring. At that level, human politics really is like chimpanzee politics: A = A.

But then we rise to the second, strictly human level. We use language to build coalitions and to deliberate about public policy. We pursue abstract goals, not just personal advantage. And we often pit team against team rather than organizing coalitions to dominate outnumbered individuals. A + B > A.

CAMPAIGNING

Although the topic of political campaigns has not been mentioned yet, the reader should be able to sense where this is going. An electoral campaign is an organized attempt to put someone in a high public office – to make that person an Alpha figure – by building a coalition of support, or to remove someone by building an opposition coalition. In a modern democracy, electoral campaigns have multiple levels of participation. At the outer level are those whose only contribution is the minimal but still essential task of voting on election day. Within that large group are concentric circles of volunteers who distribute literature, knock on doors, organize events, and give money. At the centre is the tightly bonded face-to-face group of the leader's close advisers, who organize and direct the entire effort.

Of course, the campaign is carried out in a human way, with competing teams using intelligence, speech, and rhetorical persuasion; but at the most fundamental level, the reality is very chimpanzee-like – building a coalition that will bestow or remove dominance. Chimpanzees do it by hitting and biting their opponents, or perhaps showering them with feces, while grooming their supporters, plucking lice and other parasites from their fur. Human politicians abuse their opponents, showering them with metaphorical feces (negative ads), while flattering their supporters ("hard-working Canadian families") and promising to provide them with benefits (tax cuts, public daycare, infrastructure projects).

Political campaigning has a strong military flavour. The word "campaign" is derived from the Latin *campus*, through the Italian *campagna* and French *campaigne*, all meaning "field." When "campaign" entered the English language in the seventeenth century, it at first referred to a tract of open country, then to military activity carried out "in the field." By the late eighteenth century, a "campaign" could refer to almost any kind of organized activity carried out over extended space and time. In the late nineteenth century, with the expansion of the franchise and the growth of popular democracy, the word started to take on its modern political sense of an organized effort to elect candidates to public office.[6]

Other military terminology and metaphors abound in the world of campaigning. Campaigns are directed from a "war room," and they involve both a "ground war" (contacting voters in person) and an "air war" (persuasion through the mass media). They demand "message discipline" as rigid as military discipline. Campaigners talk about "carpet-bombing" the opposition with negative ads, about "intel" and "black ops." Maybe it's just playing at soldiers, but it helps to justify the effort and intensity necessary for a successful campaign. Campaigning demands total commitment, dedicating every waking hour to defeating your opponents. You can't do it half-heartedly, any more than you can successfully conquer an enemy on the battlefield by fighting 9 to 5, Monday through Friday.

Indeed, campaigning is a kind of domesticated civil war, harnessed for the purpose of peacefully changing governments. Given the sorry record of political bloodshed over the centuries, it is no small achievement for democracies to have evolved this method of peaceful alternation in power. But the military spirit is still strong. We don't call it a "campaign" for nothing. High-minded intellectuals and pundits like to pretend that campaigns should be about policy, but a moment's reflection shows the fallacy. Campaigns result in the choice of people to fill positions, not ideas to be implemented. Policies are props, useful to demonstrate the worthiness of people and parties but useless on their own.

I regret to say that when I was younger, I shared the typical intellectual's fascination with policy and cared little for politics. I rather disdained political campaigns, regarding them as vulgar exercises in pleasing the mob. I was far more interested in legislation or judicial decisions, because those directly determine public policy. But legislation and judicial decisions are bloodless exercises, whereas campaigning involves large numbers of real people struggling with each other to determine who comes out on top. It is a primal, elemental reality, almost on a par with finding a mate and raising children. Campaigning speaks to the very depth of our primate being, because it involves following a leader, picking sides, and fighting against enemies ("opponents" in the more civilized setting of today's democracy) – all activities for which human beings have an evolved inclination. Because of the way campaigning appeals to the core of our nature, it is not surprising that it arouses so much interest and participation in modern democracies. Governance – statecraft – is difficult, technical, and often obscure. Campaigning – stagecraft – is hard to produce but, when done well, seems easy to appreciate. Governance is dull; campaigning is fun (for primates like us!).

RHETORIC

Historically, campaigning has often involved actual, not just metaphorical violence. In the nineteenth century, it was not unusual for gangs of toughs to break up political meetings held by opponents and to burn the offices where their newspapers were printed. In the 1920s and 1930s, elections in many European countries saw street battles staged by the militias of extremist parties – fascists, militarists, communists, socialists, and anarchists. Violence still erupts in

Third World election campaigns, sometimes in an extremely frightening way, in terrorist attacks and suicide bombers. But in Western Europe and North America, democratic battles today are fought with arguments, not bombs or bullets. Rhetoric has replaced violence.

However, the triumph of rhetoric does not mean an intellectual utopia where abstract argumentation rules supreme. Indeed, Aristotle, the founder of political science, did not fall prey to the intellectual's fallacy of thinking that persuasion in public affairs is all about ideas. In his *Rhetoric*, he described the three modes of persuasion in public affairs that have become known as *ethos*, *pathos*, and *logos*:

> Of the modes of persuasion furnished by the spoken word there are three kinds. The first kind depends on the personal character of the speaker [*ethos*]; the second on putting the audience into a certain frame of mind [*pathos*]; the third on the proof, or apparent proof, provided by the words of the speech itself [*logos*]. Persuasion is achieved by the speaker's personal character when the speech is so spoken as to make us think him more credible ... Secondly, persuasion may come through the hearers, when the speech stirs their emotions ... Thirdly, persuasion is effected through the speech itself when we have proved a truth or an apparent truth by means of the persuasive arguments suitable to the case in question.[7]

In today's campaign vocabulary, ethos means character, or "credibility." Candidates go to great lengths to establish their own credibility while undermining that of their opponents. Think of the Conservatives' negative ad campaigns against Stéphane Dion ("not a leader") and Michael Ignatieff ("He didn't come back for you"). The logos of policy means very little if the ethos is not compelling, as Dion and Ignatieff found out.

There is nothing irrational in a representative democracy in putting so much stress on ethos. Government is a vast and complicated subject in which most people have only marginal interest and to which they pay only marginal attention, except when something in government affects them directly. Citizens busy with their daily lives

can hardly be expected to answer all governmental questions themselves by debating the merits of policy. What they can do is to debate
who should be trusted to govern. Government is all about authority,
giving those in authority to right to issue commands with the expect-
ation of being obeyed. Ethos confers legitimacy upon authority by
showing that the governor is worthy of trust.

Pathos is the emotion aroused in the campaign by any and all
means, including speeches, advertising, and photo ops. In the period
in which I have worked on or observed Canadian campaigns, fear
has been the most important emotion, followed at some distance
by anger or loathing. The Liberals portrayed Reform leader Preston
Manning (1993, 1997) and Canadian Alliance leader Stockwell Day
(2000) as scary extremists and religious zealots. Then they went after
Stephen Harper (2004) for his frightening "hidden agenda." Out-
rage over dishonesty in government was a major factor in defeating the Liberals in 2006, after the Adscam details came out. Then
the Conservatives went back to fear, raising doubts about Stéphane
Dion's competence (2008) and Michael Ignatieff's commitment to
Canada (2011). The Progressive Conservatives managed to hold on
in Alberta in 2012 and defeat the new Wildrose Party by portraying
it as a frightening bunch of religious extremists, while Wildrose tried
to evoke loathing with allegations of the PCs' corruption. Perhaps I
am jaundiced by the experience of the past twenty years, but I have
come to see fear as the most powerful political emotion in a country like Canada, whose aging population and high standard of living
means that many people have a lot to lose. Canada really hasn't had
a federal election inspired by hope since Pierre Trudeau campaigned
on the theme of the Just Society in 1968, and that mood lasted precisely for one campaign.

To some, it may seem irrational that emotion plays such a large
role in campaigning. Plato's doctrine that reason is the highest fac-
ulty of the soul and should control the passions continues to exercise a powerful influence upon our thinking about right and wrong.
Yet it is not the only philosophically respectable view of morality.
Thinkers of the Scottish Enlightenment, such as Adam Smith in *The
Theory of the Moral Sentiments*, defended the primacy of the emotions. David Hume provocatively wrote that "Reason is, and ought

to be, the slave of the passions."[8] According to some contemporary authorities in evolutionary psychology, morality consists of evolved and genetically based emotions that contribute to survival and propagation in our intensely social species.[9] Psychologist Jonathan Haidt adopted that position in his recent and widely acclaimed *The Righteous Mind.*[10] My point here is not to take sides in these difficult debates but simply to point out that distinguished philosophers and scientists have seen emotion as essential to human decision-making, not as something to be quelled and controlled by abstract reason.

Logos in campaigns refers primarily to policy proposals made by the candidates and parties. The format of campaign platforms has fluctuated somewhat over the years, but the success of the Reform Party's Blue Book and the Liberal Party's Red Book in the 1993 campaign marked a return to the traditional practice of parties publishing a highly detailed campaign platform filled with specific proposals phrased as commitments: "A Party X government will ..." No matter how definite they sound, such platforms are best viewed as an indication of direction, not a set of absolute commitments. No party ever implements its entire platform, and on a few points it may end up doing the opposite of what it promised. More commonly, it will try to fulfill a promise, but often not exactly as worded in the platform. Voters have to keep in mind a number of facts about political promises:

- Conditions change, sometimes quite quickly and unexpectedly. Thus a promise to balance the budget may run into the reality of an economic recession that lowers governmental revenues while increasing outlays such as employment insurance benefits.
- Opposition parties in particular have limited information on which to base their policies, because they do not have access to a full range of government briefings. Thus the Conservatives in the 2005–06 campaign promised to build three new icebreakers for the Arctic, only to find after being elected that the Canadian Forces wanted to spend money on desert warfare in Afghanistan, not polar icebreakers.[11]
- No one has a monopoly on wisdom. It is the height of folly for politicians to insist on fulfilling a campaign promise even after the

consultation involved in the legislative process reveals flaws and shortcomings. The House of Commons and Senate were created to deliberate politicians' promises, not just rubber stamp them.

As I said earlier, policies as enunciated in a campaign are politicians' props. They illustrate what a candidate and party would like to accomplish, which helps voters to decide where to direct their support. But an election of candidates is not a referendum on policy. Professors, journalists, and other observers are wrong to constantly criticize election campaigns for focusing more on personalities and the "horse race" than on policy. A campaign is in fact a horse race, and the most important and exciting question is who will win it.

It is unfortunate that the pejorative sense of rhetoric ("insincere or grandiloquent language," according to my dictionary) has become so common, because rhetoric is an essential part of our heritage from Greece and Rome. It belongs together with science, mathematics, philosophy, law, history, and literature in the intellectual foundations of Western civilization. The Greeks invented the study of rhetoric, and the Romans adopted it, because government in both cultures, at least before the age of empire, was based on consent. Free men – citizens – had the right to participate in popular assemblies that elected officials, passed laws, and acted as juries in lawsuits and prosecutions. Rhetoric was the art by which free men engaged in mutual persuasion. Rhetoric in the Western tradition is based on concepts of personal responsibility, individual freedom, and equality before the law.

Other forms of speech are used in different situations. A subject addressing a superior resorts to pleas or prayers for merciful consideration. It is not a case of persuading an equal as to what is the right course of action, but of evoking an act of grace from someone in authority. And a superior speaking to a subordinate utters commands, not arguments. The Bible is full of marvellous examples of prayers and commands, but it contains little rhetoric in the Greek sense. Moses did not come down from Mount Sinai bearing the Ten Talking Points, but the Ten Commandments. Jesus said to Peter and Andrew, "Follow me, and I will make you fishers of men."[12] He didn't ask for their support; he spoke in the imperative mode. He didn't argue with them, he revealed the Truth to them in parables and miracles.

Rhetoric, in contrast, is the speech of free men who do not know what the Truth is. We have to debate possible courses of action and make a decision by voting, because none among us knows for sure what is to be done. Rhetoric is a confession of humility. No one has possession of the complete truth, and no one has an a priori right to command others. Government must be based on consent, which implies persuasion. Rhetoric is constitutional democracy in action, and political campaigns are a special moment in that action – the point when legislators are chosen for a limited period of time, at the end of which they must undergo another challenge to their right to rule.

CLASSICAL CAMPAIGNING

"Cato, Plato, Cicero, they all make me sickero." This line from a drinking song in Sigmund Romberg's operetta *The Student Prince* was written in 1924, when study of Greek and Latin was still an important part of formal education. Probably the line isn't funny to today's students, because they are not exposed to the classics, and yet the most important aspects of modern government – the rule of law, constitutionalism, elections, democracy, and campaigning – originated in the ancient world. Rome, in particular, had a highly developed culture of political campaigning because, from the fall of the Tarquin monarchs (509 BCE) to Octavian's declaration of the Principate (29 BCE), the executive officers elected by citizens actually ran the republic. There were no political parties in the modern sense, but there certainly was a lot of political campaigning (*petitio*) over a period of almost five hundred years.

The Romans also produced the world's first campaign manual, *Commentariolum Petitionis* (A short guide to electioneering).[13] It took the form of advice to the famous orator Marcus Tullius Cicero from his younger brother Quintus Tullius Cicero, as the elder Cicero prepared to seek the office of consul in 63 BCE. Quintus may indeed have written the tract, or it may have been composed by someone else as a literary exercise, but scholars agree that it faithfully represents the campaigning practices of the late Roman republic. (For convenience, I refer to the author as Quintus and his better-known elder brother as Cicero.)

A prominent lawyer and rhetorician, Cicero had already held the lower offices of *quaestor* and *praetor*. Winning the highest office – consul – would cap his political career and give him and his descendants a permanent position in the Senate. He would have to be elected by the Council of the Centuries (*comitia centuriata*), an assembly of all citizens divided into 193 "centuries," originally groups of a hundred men. Each century cast one indivisible vote, determined by the majority of the men voting within it. To become one of the two consuls to be elected for the year 63, Cicero would have to be approved by an absolute majority of the 193 centuries. So far, it sounds a bit like becoming prime minister of Canada by winning a majority of seats, but there was another twist. Every citizen belonged to a century, but there were disproportionately more centuries composed of wealthy men. If they voted together, they could control a majority of centuries and thus the outcome of elections.

A modern observer is immediately struck by how the deck was stacked in favour of the wealthy. Beyond that, the biggest difference from modern political practice was the absence of mass media. The Romans were literate, of course, but the printing press had not been invented, let alone newspapers, radio, and television. Communication, therefore, meant one-to-one personal contact, as well as public speaking – oratory – of which Cicero was an acknowledged master. But in other respects, Quintus's campaign manual has quite a contemporary feel to it, showing that the essentials of campaigning are permanent, even if the technology of communication changes over time. Quintus did not have the modern vocabulary of politics, but one can recognize modern campaign practices in his advice to Cicero.

Message Discipline and Ballot Question

Quintus writes, "Almost every day as you go down into the Forum, you must bear this in mind: 'I am a *novus homo*. I am seeking the consulship. This is Rome.'" A *novus homo* ("new man," or "outsider") was someone without ancestors who belonged to the Senate.

It was uncommon, though not unheard of, for a *novus homo* to be elected consul; the last case before Cicero's campaign had happened thirty years before. Thus, according to Quintus, Cicero had to present himself always as the sort of outsider who could become consul. He would have to demonstrate "great skill and tact," for Rome was "a city ... where much trickery, deceit, and vice of every kind is to be found, where we will have to put up with the arrogance and insolence, the spite and pride, the hatred and interference of many men." To use Aristotle's term, the campaign would be about *ethos*, character. Cicero would have to show that he was the kind of man who could handle such a challenge, in spite of being a *novus homo*. He would have to turn his quality of being an outsider into an asset, to show himself to be the new leader who could tackle old problems.

Winning Coalition

Quintus enumerates the key support groups that Cicero has to pull together in order to win:

- The *publicani*. These were businessmen who specialized in carrying out public contracts, especially to raise taxes in conquered provinces. They were the richest of the equestrians (see below).
- The *equites*. Equestrians were a distinct class in Roman society to which Cicero himself belonged. Unlike the "patricians" ("men with fathers," i.e., hereditary aristocracy), the equestrians were defined by their wealth, which originally had to be sufficient for them to equip themselves as cavalrymen (*equites*; the Latin word for horse is *equus*) in time of war. In Cicero's time, the equestrian class was far wealthier than that; they were the business community of their day.
- The *nobiles*. These "nobles" were the political class, men whose fathers or grandfathers had been consuls, and hence members of the Senate. Cicero was not yet a *nobilis*, but he would become one by being elected consul. He had to cultivate the *nobiles* to perfect his coalition of the elites who feared that demagoguery combined with plebeian turbulence would destroy the republic.

- *Liberti.* Many freed slaves lived in Rome, and some had become wealthy businessmen. They could be cultivated along with the *publicani, equites,* and *nobiles.*
- Several *collegia,* organizations such as clubs and guilds. The special-interest groups of the day, they were politically valuable because their organizations could be used for campaigning.
- Many *municipia,* local governments outside of Rome. Citizenship had been extended throughout the Italian peninsula, so there were votes to be had beyond the walls of Rome.
- *Amici.* The Latin word *amicus* is usually translated as "friend," but in this context it means something closer to "ally" – anyone who had a personal connection with Cicero, such as legal clients, admirers of his oratory, and men of influence whom he should try to cultivate. Remember that the campaign was essentially an exercise in face-to-face politics, so Cicero could not win just by presenting an abstract image. He had to have his friends working for him, expanding his range of contacts: "See that every single person whom you hold bound to you by some tie has his personal role well defined and specified."

Branding

Quintus advises Cicero to persuade his supporters "that politically we have always been in sympathy with the *optimates* and have never in the least been supporters of the *populares.* The *optimates* (the "best") were politicians who wanted to preserve the status quo, particularly the influence of the Senate, while the *populares* ("populists") were politicians who wanted to use the assembly to legislate on behalf of the ordinary people (*populus*). The Roman republic was riven with class warfare, and Cicero was advised to take sides with the senatorial elite, while explaining away any populist-sounding speeches he had made in the past.

Opposition Research and Negative Campaigning

Quintus points out that Cicero has only two serious opponents, Antonius and Catiline, and both are "murderers since childhood, both are wanton and both are impecunious." He goes on to give a long list of their crimes and perversities and concludes with this pithy advice to Cicero: "See that your competitors are smeared with an evil reputation – which fits their characters – for crime, vice, or bribery." In our day, a candidate might use the fruits of such opposition research to run negative ads against an opponent, but that technology did not exist for Cicero. Instead he delivered a scorching speech against them in the Senate, enumerating their crimes and depravities and accusing them of threatening the republic.

Field Organization and Tour

Quintus advises Cicero to "discover men in every area; get to know them, visit them, strengthen their loyalty, make sure that in their own vicinity they are campaigning for you." Since there were now Roman citizens outside of Rome, they could not be forgotten.

Tactics

Quintus is a font of good advice on how to win over supporters. Here are just a few examples:

- *Entourage:* "I believe it is most important for you always to be surrounded by people ... As far as possible, descend to the Forum at fixed times; a large daily gathering escorting you to the Forum is a source of great esteem and honour." If Quintus were alive today, he would know how to fill a room and stage a photo op.
- *Flattery:* It's a bad thing in normal life but "indispensable for a true candidate, whose expression, countenance, and language are to be adapted and accommodated to the particular wishes and moods of whomever he meets." Enough said.
- *Promises:* You will not like this, says Quintus, because you are a disciple of Plato, but you will have to promise to help people even when you know you can't. "All men naturally prefer you to lie to them than to refuse them your aid ... to make a promise is not definite; it allows postponement, and affects only a few people. A refusal alienates people immediately, and in greater numbers." In

other words, make the promise now and worry about fulfilling it later.

- *Policy:* Avoid taking positions, while practising calculated ambiguity. "You must take very good care in your campaign that men have high hopes and a good impression of your program: however, in your canvassing, you should not adopt a definite policy." Let the senatorial class think you will defend them, make the equestrians think you want peace, and let the common people believe you are not hostile to them because you have sometimes made populist speeches in court.

Edifying? No. Realistic? Yes. If Quintus could be born again into our modern world, he could make a good living as a political consultant and professional campaign manager. He would quickly master our new technologies of communication and use them within his framework of message discipline, coalition-building, brand management, and negative campaigning.

Cicero's campaign was a great success; he was elected consul with the support of every century. While he held office, he suppressed a revolt by his defeated opponent Catiline, and he subsequently remained a major political figure. But it was beyond the power of Cicero or anyone else to save the Roman constitution. He eventually got on the wrong side in the endless factional struggles of the late Republic, and he and Quintus were both murdered on the order of Mark Antony in 43 BCE. Cicero's political career was glorious, but like many political careers, it ended badly. Ask Joe Clark, John Turner, Brian Mulroney, Jean Chrétien, and Paul Martin – to mention some recent Canadian prime ministers whose political exit was less than glorious. But I doubt that Cicero, wherever he may be now, regrets anything. He was, for a while, the Alpha – the greatest leader in the greatest state the world had ever seen.

2

Playing by the Rules

Campaigns don't happen in the abstract. Each campaign takes place in a specific context that gives it a unique flavour. Among the contextual factors, probably the most important are the rules under which the campaign is conducted, at least in polities such as Canada where the law is generally observed.

Of supreme importance is the constitutional framework, specifically whether government is conducted under a presidential or a parliamentary system. We can use the United States and Canada as polar opposite examples of these two constitutional arrangements. In the United States, the president is elected separately from senators and congressmen because the Presidency and Congress are separate institutions in which incumbents serve fixed terms of office. The president cannot dissolve Congress and order a new election, and the members of Congress cannot defeat the president and force a new election. Therefore, all candidates run for office as individuals, with their own campaign managers, fundraisers, pollsters, advertisers, and volunteer workers. The Democratic and Republican National Committees provide loose coordination and sometimes financial assistance, but the chief reality is that of individual campaigns. Canadians visiting the United States at election time will immediately notice that signage identifies the candidate but seldom mentions party affiliation. The same is true of the state and local contests held at the same time as the federal elections, leading to what seems to Canadians to be a confusing welter of individuals running on their own without any overall coherence.

In Canada, on the other hand, the executive and legislative branches of government are virtually fused through the practice of cabinet government. Heads of the government can ask for an election if they are unhappy with the elected House of Commons, as Stephen Harper did in 2008, and members of Parliament can also force an election by defeating the government on an issue of confidence, as happened to Paul Martin in 2005 and Stephen Harper in 2011. The confidence convention, which is intrinsic to responsible government, has led political parties to evolve in the direction of cohesion and discipline to ward off the danger of untimely defeats in the House. When a parliamentary party contests an election, it runs as a team. Legally, all candidates are individuals with their own campaign team, but in practice they are expected to support the party platform drawn up by the leader's advisers. Local candidates mostly repeat talking points furnished by the national campaign. They are urged to spend their time door-knocking and meeting voters in person, not generating new policy positions. They are, for all practical purposes, a regionalized sales force for a national firm.

In one sense, political campaigns in Canada and the United States look much the same. Campaigns in both countries feature paid advertising, rallies, door-knocking, direct mail, voter identification and "getting out the vote" (GOTV) exercises, and extensive travel by candidates and leaders. But they are quite different in organizational terms, because in an American election there is no all-embracing national campaign. Also, the multiplicity of positions to be filled by separate elections in the United States pushes fundraising requirements at least a full order of magnitude higher than what is required in Canada. Canadians can only shake their heads in awe at the amounts that are raised and spent on politics in the United States. The difference is not so much one of national character as of incentives that flow from differing constitutional frameworks.

After the constitution, the most important influence on campaigning is the electoral system. Here Canada and the United States are on common ground in sharing the single-member-plurality (SMP) procedure, also called first-past-the-post. Under SMP, the nation, state, or province is divided into geographical districts, each of which elects one representative ("single member"). The criterion for winning is not to obtain a mathematical majority of votes cast but only to get more votes than any other candidate (a "plurality").

SMP tends to promote a winner-take-all mentality because there is no second prize. You either win or lose; you get elected or you don't. Parties that finish higher in the popular vote tend to get a bonus in terms of seats (the Canadian Conservatives won 39.6 per cent of the popular vote in 2011 but 53.9 per cent of the seats – 166 out of 308), thus increasing the pressure to finish first. In a system of proportional representation, as practised in many European countries, a party may cater to a particular electoral niche; it may be a party of labour, or farmers, or businessmen, or Christians. Its electoral strategy may be to cultivate that niche and get approximately the same vote share in every election, even if that is only 10 per cent. With a 10 per cent vote share translating into 10 per cent of seats, that relatively small party may become an important partner in a governing coalition (countries with proportional representation almost always have coalition governments). Hence parties can pursue ideological purity during the campaign and later negotiate the compromises necessary to build a coalition government.

But under SMP, a 10 per cent vote share is too small to be viable, unless it is highly concentrated regionally. Hence SMP encourages parties not to cultivate narrow niches but to build broader electoral coalitions capable of forming a government. That, in turn, has major consequences for campaigning. Parties under SMP cannot run narrowly focused campaigns catering to small, stable support groups. Given the great rewards for winning and the equally great penalties for losing, parties must appeal to many groups simultaneously. The campaign platform loses coherence because it has to appeal to so many groups at the same time, but that is the price of acquiring the breadth of support necessary to win under SMP.

The logic of SMP also tends to encourage negative campaigning. With such a great premium on winning, it can be rational for parties to go all out against their major opponents. (Of course, other factors are also involved. Electoral law in Great Britain does not allow North American style TV advertising, so there is also no negative advertising.) Proportional representation, in contrast, creates incentives for parties to restrain their attacks, at least against parties with whom there is some likelihood of wanting to form a governing coalition after the election. All-out negative campaign assaults against potential partners might create ill will that would make subsequent cooperation more difficult.

CASE STUDY: PROGRESSIVE CONSERVATIVE LEADERSHIP SELECTION IN ALBERTA

The study of decision rules is hard-core political science but sometimes essential to understand real-world politics. The Alberta Progressive Conservative (PC) leadership selection from 1992 through 2011 is an instance where this is the case.[1]

Under the system first used in 1992, PC members could vote for the leader using a run-off system, with the second ballot containing the top three finishers from the first ballot. The winner was then chosen by alternative ballot, which allowed voters to rank the three finalists in order of preference. Having three finalists was originally meant to placate rural members, who were afraid that Calgary and Edmonton candidates would always dominate if there were only two names on the final ballot. An absolute majority was required for victory, so if none of the final three candidates got 50 per cent+1 on the first count of the second ballot, votes cast for the third-place finisher were transferred to one of the other two, depending on the expression of second preferences. If no second preference had been expressed, the ballot was discarded at that point.

Are you confused? You should be. This was one of the most complex voting systems ever devised by human ingenuity. Both the two-stage run-off and the alternative ballot are commonly used around the world, and indeed both are used in various Canadian jurisdictions for nominating candidates and selecting party leaders – but Alberta, as far as I know, stood alone in combining the two.

Another unique feature of the rules was the ease of obtaining party memberships, which could be purchased for $5 right up to the close of voting at 7 PM on both the first and second ballots. Contrary to practice elsewhere, one could buy a membership in the two weeks between the first and second ballots. Many voters pay little attention until after the first ballot. They wait to see who the finalists are, then decide whom to support. In most parties in most jurisdictions, the prevailing view is that the leader should be chosen by members who have some lasting and genuine attachment to the party. The Alberta PC process, in contrast, was more like an American open primary, where anyone can participate in choosing candidates for any party. There was, indeed, a certain rationale to it. Since the PCs have won every election and been in power continuously since 1971, choosing the PC leader has amounted to choosing the premier. Hence the logic of making it easy for all Albertans to vote for PC leader, if they were interested. Choosing the PC leader was the really important decision, the general election an anticlimax.

Complex decision-making processes create many strategic options. In the case of the Alberta PC leadership election, there were five main strategic avenues, the first being an imperative for all serious candidates, the others representing various ways of triumphing on the second ballot. I present them as alternatives, though they are not mutually exclusive.

OPTION 1: Recruit enough supporters to finish among the top three on the first ballot. If you succeed in this, you have a chance to win, even if you are far behind in second or third place. If you don't do this, it's over. In practice, this requires mainly a combination of selling new memberships and finding support among existing members, though, as Alison Redford showed in 2011, subtle strategic manoeuvres may also be helpful.

OPTION 2: Sell a lot of new memberships between the first and second ballots, which is when many people start to focus on the contest.

OPTION 3: Get the support of the candidates who failed to make it to the second ballot. This task often can be done by promises to make them cabinet ministers or appoint them to other jobs.

OPTION 4: Make an alliance with one of the others in the top three, so that if no one gets an absolute majority on the first count and your ally finishes third, you can benefit from the transfer of that candidate's support (assuming his or her supporters have given you their second-choice support). This deal cannot be a secret one. It has to have a public dimension so that the supporters of your ally are cued to give you their second preference on the second ballot.

OPTION 5: Recruit supporters from outside the party, who may not even intend to vote PC in the general election but who may wish to support the candidate who from their point is least bad.

Three leadership elections with three different winners took place under these rules: in 1992, Ralph Klein; in 2006, Ed Stelmach; in 2011, Alison Redford. Each race showcased a different strategic path to victory.

In 1992, Nancy Betkowski finished atop the first ballot with 16,393 votes, while Ralph Klein finished second, just one vote behind. The third place finisher, Rick Orman, had 7,649 votes, but he decided not to contest the second ballot and recommended to his followers that they support Betkowski. Five of the six candidates who did not make the cut also threw their support to Betkowski. Survey research subsequently found that a little more than half of those who had supported Orman or one of the other failed candidates did in fact vote for Betkowski on the second ballot,[2] so how did Klein manage to win? By bringing in a large number of people, mostly Reform-leaning, who had not voted on the first ballot but were dismayed by Betkowski's left-leaning positions.[3] On the second ballot, Klein's total was 46,245, compared to 31,722 for Betkowski. He thus won easily, and Betkowski subsequently left the PCs, changed her name to MacBeth when she remarried, became leader of the Liberal Party of Alberta, and lost a rematch with Ralph Klein in the provincial election of 2001.

The story was very different in 2006, when Ed Stelmach won. Trailing far behind Red Tory Jim Dinning and Blue Tory Ted Morton, party loyalist Stelmach placed third on the first ballot. By offering jobs to those who had been knocked out of the race, he gathered additional support while Dinning and Morton went full-bore negative against each other. Equally important, Stelmach stayed outside the polarization between the two front-runners, thus becoming the preferred second choice for both camps. Second choices ultimately pushed him over the top, as no one won an absolute majority of first preferences on the second ballot. In this race, the ability to muster support as a compromise candidate between two perceived extremes seems to have been crucial to victory. The three leading candidates also tried to bring in targeted supporters from outside the party, and their efforts showed in the voting results. Morton did best in constituencies where Wildrose was strong, Dinning in ridings where the Liberal vote was relatively high, and Stelmach in areas with lots of Ukrainian voters.[4]

In the next PC leadership race in 2011, all candidates had clearly studied the 2006 experience. Throughout a seven-month leadership campaign leading up to the first ballot, they stayed close together ideologically and mostly avoided personal attacks on each other. Former hard-rock conservative Ted Morton repositioned himself as a moderate, while alleged Red Tory Gary Mar broke the mould by calling for greater private involvement in health care. Clearly all candidates were trying to reach across the spectrum. Once the players came to understand the rules, they had a highly centripetal effect, driving everyone toward the centre in a quest for second preferences.

When the first ballot was counted, the top three were Gary Mar, 24,195; Alison Redford, 11,129; and Doug Horner, 8,635. The biggest surprise was that Redford rather than Morton had made it to the final three. However, many of Morton's 2006 supporters had decamped to the Wildrose Party, while the Redford team had pulled off an astute move shortly before the first ballot. They turned in their membership sales early and then made the membership list available for a public poll of members' preferences. The results, showing Redford far behind Mar but still in second place with 20 per cent, demonstrated that she was a serious contender and encouraged her supporters to take the trouble to turn out for her.[5]

Nonetheless, Mar had opened up a big lead on the first ballot by getting 41 per cent of the vote; and when all three eliminated candidates threw their support to Mar, his victory seemed to be guaranteed. How then did Redford, who had only 19 per cent on the first ballot, manage to win? The short answer is that she made another astute strategic move by announcing that Doug Horner was her second choice. Horner stopped just short of openly reciprocating: "I think it's pretty obvious where you would find my second ballot."[6] Thus was born a de facto alliance of Beta and Gamma against Alpha. Redford also took advantage of the loose membership rules to encourage new supporters to join the party when she promised to dedicate an additional $107 million to the education budget to decrease average class size. The implication that more teachers would be hired was surely not lost on the ever-vigilant Alberta Teachers Association.

Gary Mar was still leading after the first count of the second ballot, but much more narrowly; crucially, he did not get an absolute majority. Horner, who finished third, had to drop out; and 46 per cent of his support went to Redford on the second count, against only 14 per cent to Mar, while 40 per cent of his supporters had indicated no second choice. It was second-choice support from Horner that pushed Redford over the top on the second count.[7] (Not surprisingly, she made him minister of finance and president of the Treasury Board after she herself became premier, thus cementing the alliance between the new Alpha and her Beta.)

To summarize: three races under same rules, three different paths to victory – second-round membership sales, support from failed candidates, a tacit alliance of two of the top three. Such a complicated set of rules does not dictate a single winning strategy; it leaves plenty of room for innovation and creativity. But out of an infinite number of possible strategies, only a few are likely to be successful within this configuration of rules.

Also, in the three leadership races, the winners and other relatively successful candidates had one thing in common: they all took advantage of the party's permeability under these rules to bring in large numbers of outsiders who had little interest in becoming long-term PC members but who supported a particular candidate. In 1992, Ralph Klein moved ahead between the first and second ballots by recruiting large numbers of new members who were really federal Reform supporters but who saw Klein as a better option than Betkowski for premier of Alberta. In 2006, each of the three main candidates sold heavily to outside groups: Ted Morton to Wildrose supporters, Jim Dinning to urban Liberals, and Ed Stelmach to Ukrainians in northern Alberta.[8] In 2011, Gary Mar recruited Chinese voters, while Alison Redford appealed to teachers and other unionized public-sector workers. Throughout these years, the provincial PC party remained a relatively small organization in terms of active members, so swamping it with outsiders became the centre-piece of all winning strategies in leadership races.

Winning by bringing in outside support meant that in each of the three cases the winner was not the candidate supported by most of the PC caucus and party officials. In 1992, Betkowski was the insiders' favourite, but Klein won. In 2006, Stelmach triumphed over party favourite Dinning. In 2011, Mar had the support of caucus and party officials, yet Redford emerged victorious. Interestingly, both Klein and Stelmach were ultimately forced to resign by internal resistance from the party. Klein was a huge success politically, leading the PCs to four majority governments in a row, yet he resigned in 2006 after receiving a lukewarm endorsement in a leadership review. Stelmach won a big electoral victory in 2008, yet was never deeply loved within the party. He resigned in early 2011, when Finance Minister Ted Morton quit after disagreeing with Stelmach over the pending budget.

Redford came into the leader's job with less internal support than either Klein or Stelmach. PC members showed their displeasure by revising the complex leadership selection rules. At a party convention in November 2012, delegates voted to reduce from three to two the number of names on the second ballot, thereby obviating the need for using the alternative vote.[9] Would Redford have won under that rule? She finished second on the first ballot, so she would have gone on to the second round; but with only two names on that ballot, she would not have been able to conduct the graceful pas de deux with Doug Horner that delivered victory to her.

It will be interesting to see if in the future the PCs decide to tighten up their loose qualifications for voting, thereby reducing the role of outsiders in making the final choice. If former finance minister and leadership candidate Ted Morton is to be believed, it may already be too late to undo the damage caused to the PC Party by its leadership rules. Morton has argued that the victories won by Stelmach and Redford with the help of public-sector unionists drove many traditional PC supporters over to the more conservative Wildrose Party, thus splitting the PC electoral coalition and creating a new menace on the right.[10] As in politics generally, the choice of electoral rules can be fraught with unintended consequences.

WHAT DOES IT MEAN TO WIN?

SMP promotes a focus on winning races within individual electoral districts because there can be only one representative of a district at any one time. However, there are many consolation prizes even in the winner-focused world of SMP. A candidate who loses but does relatively well may be laying the groundwork for victory in the next election, based on greater name recognition among voters and a larger database of identified supporters. Also, losing candidates often receive patronage appointments as a reward for their service: senator, judge, ambassador or consul in some desirable foreign city; chief of staff or policy adviser in the office of the leader; cabinet minister or chair of a legislative committee. Even if none of these rewards (which usually go to higher-profile candidates) are available, losing candidates can tell themselves they helped their party by waging an unsuccessful but solid campaign. That's not only consoling, it's true. In our parliamentary system, which puts so much emphasis on team play, it is important even in the most hopeless local contest to campaign well enough to avoid bad stories in the media. And it's important just for those campaigns to exist, even when the candidate is completely out of the running. A party that cannot field a candidate in every riding will come under heavy criticism for not being truly national.

Leadership races also have many consolation prizes. There can be only one winner, but winning leaders usually appoint all or most of their opponents to important jobs after the race is over – cabinet minister if the party is in power, senior critic positions if it is in opposition. Running for leader, even if there seems to be little chance of victory, is a time-honoured way of getting onto the front bench. A striking recent example of such self-promotion is Martha Hall Findlay, who ran for Liberal leader in 2006 even though she had never been elected to any public office (she ran unsuccessfully for Parliament in 2004 against Belinda Stronach, when Stronach was still a Conservative). Winner Stéphane Dion could not make Hall Findlay a critic because she did not have a seat in Parliament, so he appointed her chair of the Liberal Party platform committee. Later he appointed her the Liberal candidate in Toronto Willowdale, at that time a safe riding for the party, and she got elected to the House of Commons in 2008, where she was a prominent Liberal voice until defeated in 2011. Clearly her seemingly hopeless leadership bid in 2006 fast-tracked her rise in the Liberal Party. She ran again for the Liberal leadership in 2013 and was considered one of the more serious of the nine candidates, though Justin Trudeau finished far ahead of everyone else.

The concept of victory becomes even more nuanced when we aggregate district results across the entire system. In fact, there are multiple systemic levels of "winning" and "losing," so that it is not uncommon for several or even all parties in an election to claim victory or bemoan defeat. Consider the following scenarios:

- *Majority government*, as won by the Liberals in 2000 and the Conservatives in 2011. This is clearly the highest goal of campaigning and an unalloyed victory.
- *Minority government*, as won by the Liberals in 2004 and the Conservatives in 2006 and 2008. This doesn't confer as much power as a majority, because the government may not be able to get all its legislation passed and its tenure will be uncertain, but it is certainly better than being excluded from government. A minority government can craft budgets, make order-in-council appointments, carry on diplomatic relations with other countries, and exercise power in a myriad of other ways.
- *Bringing the government down from a majority to a minority*, as the Conservatives did to the Liberals in 2004. This was a "loss" for the Conservatives, because they did not get to form the next government, but it was also a "win" for them because it seriously weakened the Liberals and set up the Conservative victory in 2006.
- *Becoming the official opposition*, as the NDP achieved for the first time federally in 2011 and Wildrose did in 2012 in Alberta. Obtaining the bigger budget and other perks that go along with official opposition status (more questions in Question Period, a bigger budget for research and communications, chairing certain legislative committees) is a huge advantage. Ask the federal Liberals, who failed to hold official opposition status in 2011, and the

Alberta Liberals, who suffered the same fate in 2012, how they feel about no longer being the official opposition.

- *Becoming an officially recognized party* (twelve seats in the House of Commons), which the federal Progressive Conservatives attained in 2000 (with the underground support of the Liberals, who tanked their own candidate in Calgary Centre to give PC Leader Joe Clark an easy ride to the twelfth seat). An official party gets supplementary salaries for the leader and other House officers, money to set up a leader's office and research branch, seats on House committees, and the right to ask questions in Question Period. Being a recognized party gave the PCs the leverage to enter into a more or less equal merger with the Canadian Alliance in 2003 rather than simply being taken over.
- *Gaining even one seat*, which can be a victory, as demonstrated by the Greens in 2011 when their leader Elizabeth May won the Saanich–Gulf Islands seat in British Columbia. As an MP, May gets free travel tickets, money for staff, and mailing privileges. Her presence in the House will also probably guarantee her a spot in the next leaders' debate, a privilege she did not receive in 2011. For the Greens, who are essentially a single-issue advocacy group posing as a political party, having even one seat in the House of Commons is an advantage that other interest groups would love to have.

These multiple levels of victory are all important, but they don't change the basic logic of campaigning under SMP. A party runs to win as many seats as possible, taking whatever level of victory it can get. Contrary to what happens under proportional representation, a party would never run to maintain its vote share, hoping to find coalition partners afterwards.

OTHER RULES

Every country has its own set of rules for the conduct of elections, and these rules often have a major impact on the way campaigns are fought. Here are a few examples:

Electoral law in Japan prohibits campaigners from trying to visit people's homes during the election. Thus door-knocking, the mainstay of local campaigning in North America, is unknown in Japan. It doesn't fit with the Japanese sense of privacy, and also perhaps raises memories of the time when a knock on the door could be a dreaded event, under the fascists who governed Japan from the 1920s through World War II. Rather than door-knocking, Japanese campaigning emphasizes large public meetings.

Voting is mandatory in Australia, which means that parties do not have to engage in voter ID and GOTV to get their supporters to the polls. Voters are almost certain to turn out because they face a fine if they do not. Parties, therefore, invest more in persuasion during the campaign. In comparison to Canadian parties, Australian parties produce a lot more high-quality (glossy paper, lavish illustrations) pamphlets, which they mail to voters.

At the other extreme, voting is not mandatory in the United States, and turnout tends to be low by world standards. But certain unique features in the American system help parties greatly with their direct voter contact (DVC) efforts. Most states hold primaries in which voters register as Republicans or Democrats. And most states release electronic lists of these registrations, as well as lists of people who actually turn out to vote. With a few keystrokes, party workers can download and cross-tabulate these precious databases to produce the Holy Grail of DVC: a list of party supporters who care enough to vote. In Canada, it takes years of voter ID telephone calls and direct mail to build a similar database of supporters, and even then it probably won't contain good data about whether identified supporters actually vote. Given this head start, American parties have been able to afford much greater investments in micro-targeting, renting consumer data and building behavioural profiles to identify likely supporters.[11] Canadian parties are, and will probably remain, far behind in this endeavour. (American data privacy laws are also more permissive.)

In North America, the largest share of the budget for national, state, and provincial elections is spent on paid television advertising, using commercial models. The airways are dominated for weeks by fifteen- and thirty-second spots trumpeting the virtues of candidates and slamming their opponents. In Great Britain, by contrast, paid television advertising is illegal during national campaigns. Instead,

TV networks are required to make time available for party election broadcasts. The PEBS, as they are known, are several minutes long; they are more like little speeches than advertising of the usual commercial type. British parties would almost certainly use American-style advertising if they could – it works for selling everything else, so why not for influencing votes? The law, however, prevents them from doing so.

The common thread in all these cases is that the law prohibits (or occasionally facilitates) a certain form of communication. Parties use as many forms of communication as possible to reach their targets, but if the law outlaws a specific means of communication, parties will shift their efforts towards legal means. And, of course, if the law makes a certain form of communication easier and cheaper, parties will use more of it. The decision calculus is straight out of Economics 101. So regulations of this type change the details of campaigning by causing some forms of communications not to be used and others to be used more heavily, but they don't change the basic nature of campaigning. It is still coalition formation in order to put a candidate or leader in the Alpha position. And so many communications channels are available in the modern world that prohibiting use of one or another hardly prevents a campaign team from getting out its message.

Another type of regulation is a cap on total campaign spending. First introduced into Canadian electoral practice in 1974, the cap has been increased each election to allow for inflation. In 2011, it was about $21 million for a national campaign if the party was running a candidate in every riding.[12] The purpose of such regulation is to provide the proverbial level playing field, so that better-endowed parties cannot simply spend their way to victory. But levelling is easier said than done when parties differ greatly in their fundraising capacity.

The efficacy of the spending cap is limited because it applies only in the so-called writ period, after the governor general has issued the writs for the election. Before the writ period, there is no limit at all on how much can be spent, or for what purposes. The federal Conservatives, whose fundraising capacity in that period was much greater than that of the other parties – in fact, greater than that of all the other parties put together – spent heavily on negative ads targeting the Liberal Party leaders long before the 2008 and 2011 elections. The Conservatives, in my opinion, won both elections before the writ was dropped. They didn't run particularly inspiring writ-period campaigns in either year, but they did so much damage to their main opponent before the election even started that the Liberals could never recover.

In this instance, regulation seems to have had perverse consequences. Designed to level the financial playing field during the campaign, the law allowed the Conservatives to use their financial advantage to devastating effect outside the nominal election period, when their opponents couldn't afford to fight back. Additional Conservative spending within the 2008 and 2011 writ period probably would have had less effect, because during the campaign the Liberals would have had some resources to run countering ads, whereas during the pre-writ period they couldn't afford to reply. Well-meaning regulation may have permanently changed the shape of Canadian election campaigns by extending them into the pre-writ period.

One final example of the importance of rules can be found in the realm of "third-party" advertising – election ads sponsored by entities other than political parties. Such advertising was a major factor in the 1988 federal election, in which corporations and unions spent freely to promote or attack free trade with the United States. Then in 2000, Parliament put strict limits on how much "third parties" can spend on such advertising, so that it no longer figures prominently in federal politics. Yet it has remained a major factor in Ontario, where organized labour has spent even more than the main parties on advertising. The unions have not supported a party, but they have run negative ads attacking the Progressive Conservatives, thereby giving a boost to the PCs' main opponent, which in this period was the Liberals.[13] If the PCs ever win, they will probably change the law, but in the meantime they will continue to face a strong headwind at election time, unless perhaps big business forms its own advertising network in an attempt to balance organized labour.

In Alberta, permissive legislation allowed organized labour to run an expensive negative ad campaign against Ed Stelmach's PCs in the 2008 election. A union front known as "Albertans for Change" paid for ads indicting Stelmach for having "no plan."[14] After the Tories won, they changed the law to prohibit this sort of third-party advertising, but the unions were active again in 2012. This time they used extensive telephone trees, email blast-outs, and autodial messages urging supporters and their families not to vote for Wildrose. Third-party campaigning seems here to stay, but the specific form it takes will depend on legislated election rules.

Examples could be multiplied endlessly, but the main point should be clear by now. All campaigning takes place within a specific context of constitutional law, legislation, and regulation. The rules define the game. Democratic campaigning is always about persuasion through rhetoric, but there is no such thing as a universal winning strategy. Strategy will always be relative to the constitutional arrangement of offices; to legislation that permits, limits, or forbids certain forms of persuasion; and to whatever a specific party or candidate would consider a "victory" within that milieu.

3

Strategy I: Positioning

Campaigning is the use of rhetorical persuasion to build an electoral coalition. Persuasion involves messaging from a sender to recipients. As explained earlier, *logos,* rational argument, is an important part of persuasion. Political argument does indeed have an important rational aspect, but its sender is addressing millions of people simultaneously, most of whom do not follow public affairs closely or systematically. Thus, communications of this type cannot avoid relying on shorthand expressions as a form of condensed rationality. The most important of these is the "left-right" spectrum, which captures the underlying features of many policy arguments.

This chapter draws on approaches to political science known as game theory and rational choice. Readers who have not had any formal training in these fields may find the presentation in the first half of the chapter somewhat technical. But the difficulty does not last; the second half of the chapter presents the results of the analysis in nontechnical, practical language that can be applied directly to campaign strategy. Please slog through a few models with me, dear reader!

SPATIAL MODELS OF POLITICS

A spectrum of possibilities can be conceived of as one or more dimensions in an intellectual space, a mental world. One way of understanding a mental world is to map it onto a so-called spatial model, which can be a one-dimensional line, a two-dimensional surface, a three-dimensional space, or a multi-dimensional hyper-

Left	Centre	Right
NDP	Liberals	Conservatives

Figure 3.1
Linear model of Canadian political parties

space. I begin this discussion with one- and two-dimensional models, because anything more than that is difficult to depict on the printed page and hard to understand intuitively. I will then say a little about multi-dimensional models.

The simplest and most widely used spatial model is the left-right spectrum or dimension. Parties, candidates, ideologies, platforms, and so on are said to be more or less conservative or liberal, where conservative is symbolized by "right" and liberal by "left." Ideally, we would like to measure such positions in the sense of putting a cardinal number on them, such as an IQ score; but we can construct a usable dimension as long as we can order the positions (points) in relation to each other, even without being able to measure them in cardinal terms. Figure 3.1 shows how most political observers would order the three main Canadian political parties: the Conservatives, Liberals, and New Democrats. The length of the line segments doesn't show how far the parties are from one another. The positioning on the line simply shows their ordinal relationship.

This linear model makes intuitive sense, because on a wide variety of specific issues, the three parties have assumed positions that can be ordered in the same way, even though the meaning of the underlying dimension may be somewhat different, depending on the issue area. In economic matters, which are usually the most salient to Canadian voters, "left" connotes government intervention, regulation, public ownership, and redistribution to promote equality of result. "Right" connotes free markets, enforcement of private property rights, and equality of opportunity rather than equality of result.

Spatial models were first developed in economics to analyze locational decisions made by firms. They helped explain puzzles such as why two or more gas stations are often found at the same intersection. The economist Anthony Downs made the pioneering applications of spatial models to politics when he used them to represent the locational decisions made by political parties when they take positions in order to compete against each other in elections.[1] His first and simplest model was a straight line similar to that shown in figure 3.1 Underlying that model are a number of simplifying assumptions about the behaviour of voters and political parties:

- All voters have political positions (ideal points) that can be represented as points in a geometric space.
- Political parties assume point-like positions in an attempt to appeal to voters.
- Voters, as rational actors, vote for the party located closest to their own ideal point. They use the party's location as a guide to what sort of policies it would enact if it became the government, and they naturally want policies as close as possible to their own preferences.
- There is only one significant dimension of political difference in the society, namely, the ideological spectrum of left and right.

It should be obvious that these assumptions do not fully depict the real world. Not all voters have positions that can be described in terms of left and right, which are intellectual terms that have meaning only to those who follow politics in some detail. Many voters pay little attention to politics and, if they do, may be more attracted to personalities and party labels than to policies. They may cast their ballots for all kinds of reasons other than the policy positions assumed by parties, such as family tradition or respect for honesty and competence. Parties, for their part, generally cannot communicate a position with point-like clarity; like anxious squid, they are apt to emit a baffling, ink-like cloud of statements. And, while the left-right dimension seems to be present in most countries most of the time, politics can often be multi-dimensional, involving conflicts over issues such as language, ethnicity, and religion that cut across the standard right-left dimension. But assumptions do not have to apply perfectly in order to be useful. If they apply fairly well to a considerable fraction of voters, they can generate a model with some degree of explanatory and predictive power.

THE MEDIAN VOTER THEOREM

Downs's best-known result is his application of the median voter theorem to the competition of political parties. The median voter is the one whose ideal point is positioned in the middle of all points along the relevant dimension of competition; that is, there are just as many voters to the left of that voter as to the right. It can be shown that, in any voting system where members are free to vote according to their true preferences, and where those preferences can be laid out along a single dimension, the winning position is that of the median voter.[2]

Rather than give a formal proof, let me illustrate how this works. Imagine a committee of fifteen members, in which everyone can vote freely. If everyone votes, the minimum winning coalition is eight. The median voter, call her M, is the one who has seven voters to her left and seven to her right. If the members of the committee are rational, they prefer to ally with other members whose ideal points are closer to rather than further from their own. They do not hop over others to make coalitions. Thus M will be included in any winning coalition of eight, so the other members have to defer to her wishes in order to bring her onside.

The median voter theorem is a powerful and highly general explanation of why democratic processes tend to produce results reflecting the views of those in the centre of the preference distribution. Voters further to the left and to the right tend to be chronically dissatisfied with the results of democracy. I should know: I have free-market preferences that are more extreme than those of most Canadians (and most voters in most countries), so I am perpetually disappointed by governments, even by governments that I support. It has taken me decades to come to terms with this situation. On the other hand, if I were the median voter, the system would work effortlessly to let my views triumph. I console myself by remembering that I'm lucky in other ways, such as in living in Alberta, where the taxes are low and the mountains are high.

To apply the median voter theorem to electoral politics, we must take account of the existence of political parties. In his simplest model, Anthony Downs, who is American, did this by assuming that there were only two political parties competing for power, and that the duopoly did not have to worry about new parties getting into the competition because barriers to entry were high. This is quite a reasonable approximation of American politics, where Republicans and Democrats rule the roost and other parties only occasionally make a difference. Barriers to entry are indeed extraordinarily high in the American federal system, particularly for election of the president. Each of the fifty states has its own set of rules for electing delegates to the Electoral College, which legally chooses the president, and a party wanting to put up a candidate for president has to get on the ballot in fifty different states. It's an organizational challenge that only the strongest parties can meet. Some new parties have succeeded in getting on the ballot, but no new party has managed to elect a president since the Republicans first won a victory for Abraham Lincoln in 1860.

Another major barrier to entry, also applicable in Canada, is the single-member-plurality (SMP) electoral system, which tends to reward larger parties and punish smaller ones. Smaller parties, such as the Greens, can win seats only if they manage to concentrate their votes in a certain area, thus managing to win a particular seat, as Elizabeth May did in Saanich–Gulf Islands in the federal election of 2011. But while barriers to entry are high in Canada, they are not as high as in the United States, and that is one reason why new parties have been more viable here. The Canadian party system since 1921 has usually been "two-party-plus" rather than strictly two-party. That is, there have been only two parties, usually the Conservatives and Liberals, with a realistic chance of winning government, but other parties such as Social Credit, the CCF, and NDP have been able to elect MPs and have a presence in the House of Commons. Indeed, the NDP may have replaced the Liberals as one of the two major parties in 2011, although the jury is still out on that.

If there are only two parties, as Downs assumed, they will tend to position themselves as close as possible to the median voter, because the goal is to get 50 per cent+1 of the votes, and that goal can only be achieved by forming a coalition that includes the median voter. Parties have to settle near the median to have any chance of building a winning coalition that includes the median voter plus all voters to

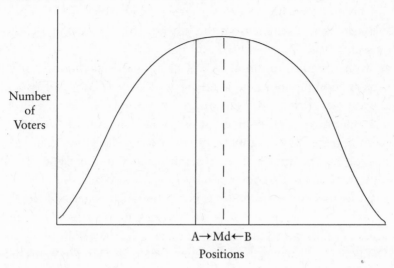

Figure 3.2
Simplest model of two-party competition

one side or the other (see figure 3.2). Hence no party will ever want to position itself elsewhere than at the median, because to do so allows the other party to cut it off from a majority of voters.

Although Downs's first model is admittedly simplistic, it correctly predicts the competition between two large centrist parties that has generally characterized politics in the five "Anglo-Saxon" democracies (Britain, Canada, Australia, the United States, and New Zealand, up to the introduction of proportional representation in New Zealand in 1996). All these countries have had electoral systems that restrict competition to two large parties (or coalitions of parties in Australia),[3] and those two parties or coalitions have tended to converge on similar positions. To cite some Canadian examples, the Liberal opposition of the 1980s and early 1990s heavily criticized the main initiatives taken by Brian Mulroney's Conservative government, such as free trade with the United States, the Goods and Services Tax, a low target rate of inflation, and privatization of Crown corporations; yet the subsequent Liberal government of Jean Chrétien did not depart from any of these policies and even pushed some of them further. More recently, many commentators have remarked on how Stephen Harper's Conservatives in power don't seem that different from the Liberals in power. Similarly, the NDP seems to be moving to the centre. It dropped the word "socialism" from its constitution at its 2013 national convention,[4] and it has been adopting more moderate positions on a number of issues. For example, in the realm of foreign and military affairs, the NDP, which once advocated pulling out of NATO, voted on 14 July 2011 to continue the Libya bombing mission for another three months – a mission in which the only discernible Canadian interest seems to have been to maintain cooperation with our NATO allies.

Even if the Downsian model is not entirely accurate, it is clearly a useful first approximation. Also, it is not hard to build greater degrees of realism into the model. For example, the ideological position taken by a party is more like a line segment than a point. That is, it cannot be perfectly precise, and, in a world of imperfect information, having a broader position may allow one to overlap with a competing party and thus attract some of its support. Moreover, party leaders do not have perfect freedom to position the party wherever they wish in order to attract votes; they also have to pay special attention to the views of the people who volunteer time and money to keep the party going. These volunteers and donors tend to be more extreme, in one direction or another, than the median voter. It is the fact that they are off centre, so to speak, that creates an incentive for them to volunteer time and money to modify the "natural" equilibrium at the position of the median voter. Volunteers and donors, therefore, tend to pull their parties away from the centre, and leaders must balance that pull against the imperatives of vote maximization.[5] Adding all of this to the simplest model gives a more realistic one in which two parties compete with overlapping but discernibly different positions (see figure 3.3).[6]

THIRD PARTIES

If we relax the constraint that there can be only two political parties, is there a strategy by which a third party can enter the system and even displace one member of the duopoly? One possibility comes from a model developed by Steven J. Brams for American

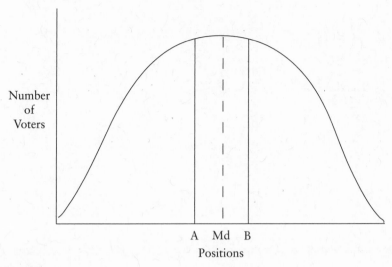

A   Md   B
Positions

Figure 3.3
Refined model of two-party competition

presidential primaries and extended by Réjean Landry to the case
of party competition in a parliamentary system. Assume that a new
party C is trying to break into a system dominated by old parties A
and B. One obvious move would be for C to position itself just to the
right of B (to the left of A would amount to the same thing).[7] If such
a move were possible, C would be closer than B to most right-wing
voters and should attract their support, thus finishing ahead of B.
The number of members that C would elect would depend (in a first-
past-the-post voting system like Canada's) upon the geographical
concentration of the conservative voters for whom it was contesting
with B. If such voters were evenly dispersed across many constituencies, it is possible that C's challenge would do nothing but produce
a landslide for A, whose left-wing support would be unaffected. But
whether or not C can realistically elect many members the first time,
the model suggests that it should be able to outflank and eventually
finish ahead of B, thus positioning itself to enter the duopoly in the
future (see figure 3.4).[8] I call this model "Invasion from the Margin."
In its simplest form, it is, of course, patently unrealistic. It predicts
wave after wave of successful invasions from both left and right,

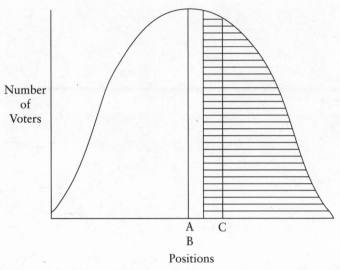

Figure 3.4
Brams/Landry model of third-party entry

leading to a virtual kaleidoscope of parties. In fact, politics does not look like that anywhere in the world. The tendency is always for a small number of parties to assume long-term dominance.

In addition to SMP voting, two other factors impeding Invasion from the Margin are inertia and imperfect information. Like any purveyor of goods and services, an established political party has a huge advantage in reputation, credibility, and name recognition over a new competitor. To have any hope of success, the recent entrant must differentiate itself from the established party. To do so requires assuming a position not too close to the duopoly – for if C is only slightly different from B, why would voters who are used to B take the risk of supporting C, about whom they know very little? But taking a position far out toward the tail of the opinion distribution in order to promote clear differentiation carries its own risks. The ends of the spectrum harbour extremists whose active support can be counterproductive for winning elections: communists and anarchists on the left, racists and fascists on the right. Thus, a new party playing Invasion from the Margin must find a position far enough away from its main competitor to differentiate itself, but it must also draw an effective line beyond itself so that it does not get discredited by extremists.

Once the new party finds its more extreme position, how should its established competitor respond? One option is for the established party to move outwards toward the new party. Since the established party is by hypothesis operating in the region of the opinion distribution where voters are most numerous, it needs to take only a relatively small step away from the centre to win back a substantial number of voters who might be attracted to the new party. According to the logic of the spatial model, voters lying to the right of the midpoint of line segment BC in figure 3.4 should vote for C, while voters lying to the left of the midpoint should vote for B. A move by B to the right also shifts the midpoint of BC to the right, thus transferring some voters from C back to B. For this reason, Downs, who was aware of the idea of Invasion from the Margin, dismissed it as unworkable. In his opinion, it would not enable a new party to break into the system, though it might succeed in moving the position of an existing party away from the centre, at least for a time.[9]

Downs's rejection of Invasion from the Margin may be valid for American politics, where the barriers to new-party entry are extraordinarily high, but it is untenable as a general proposition. There are two major modern examples of its success in Canada. First is the CCF/NDP, which established itself in Canadian politics in the 1930s by outflanking the Liberals on the left. As the model predicts, it had problems with extremists on the far left, but it eventually managed to drive out most of the communists and fellow-travellers. It vaulted over the barrier of SMP voting by relying upon the votes concentrated in the working-class neighbourhoods of major cities (Vancouver, Winnipeg, Toronto), manufacturing centres (Windsor, Hamilton, Oshawa), and unionized natural-resource extraction sites (mining, forest products). Over time it displaced the Liberals as a governing party in Saskatchewan and Manitoba and drove the British Columbia Liberals into a merger with former Social Credit and Reform supporters. At the federal level, the NDP seemed stalled for many years, but in 2011 it won 103 seats and became the official opposition, relegating the Liberals to third place.

The Reform Party also engineered a successful invasion from the margin, but from the right. Its hastily organized campaign yielded no seats in 1988, but in 1993 Reform won 52 seats, while the Progressive Conservatives won only two. The PCs rebounded slightly in 1997 and 2000 but never managed to push the Reformers back. They finally merged in 2003 with Reform, by then renamed the Canadian Alliance, to form the Conservative Party of Canada. When Reformer Stephen Harper won the resulting leadership race, it was as if the old Conservative Party had been resurrected, but now under the new management of more conservative Westerners.

The two cases histories are different in detail, but they both illustrate how it is possible for Invasion from the Margin to work in a parliamentary system with SMP voting. The recipe for success is for the new, more extreme party to find a regional base, cut deeply into its nearest rival's traditional base of core voters, and eventually take it over by merger or drive it down to a point where it is no longer relevant or even disappears. All this can take years or decades, in contrast to the instantaneous results of frictionless linear models. But the real world is sticky, not frictionless. It can take a long time for a new party to build a reputation and overcome the inertial advantage of its older rival.

One caveat, however, is in order. A party that has been challenged from the margin may be able to preserve its dominance by moving away from the challenger, if its opponent on the other side is weak. That is essentially what the Alberta Progressive Conservatives did in 2012. Challenged on the right by Wildrose, they moved to the left, into territory traditionally occupied by the Liberals. Demoralized by factional in-fighting, bereft of money, and led by a leader who seemed not to understand what was happening, the Liberals could not defend their turf. Their vote share fell from 26 per cent in 2008 to 10 per cent in 2012. Large numbers of Liberals voted PC, and the PCs were re-elected in spite of losing half their previous supporters to Wildrose.

CAMPAIGN IMPLICATIONS

This simple analysis has several powerful implications for political campaigning. The first is quite straightforward and unambiguous in its recommendation to a would-be governing party: *An established party that is running for government should campaign from the centre, as long as it does not face a serious threat from further left (for a liberal party) or further right (for a conservative party).*

The classic example of violating this rule was Barry Goldwater's presidential campaign in 1964, when he deliberately moved away from the centre and suffered one of the worst defeats in American history. In Canada, Stephen Harper's positioning of the Conservative Party illustrates the positive consequences of moving toward the centre when conditions allow. After the 2003 merger, the Conservatives faced no challenge on the right. Hence Harper could afford to moderate his previous reputation for dogmatic conservatism and move the Conservative Party toward what he would once have derided as the mushy middle. The party's vote share grew in every election from 2004 through 2011 as its image became more centrist.

The second rule applies to new parties trying to break into the system: *A would-be new party should adopt a more extreme position, either on the left or right, and target its nearest competitor for destruction.*

Successful examples include the CCF/NDP and Reform, as discussed above. Another case, on which it is too early to pass final judgment, is the Wildrose Party. Under Danielle Smith's leadership it assumed a position further right than the Progressive Conservatives. In the 2012 Alberta election, Wildrose won 34 per cent of the popular vote and 17 seats, becoming the official opposition. In effect, Wildrose succeeded in detaching about half of the previous PC support by offering a more full-blooded conservative alternative; but as just mentioned, it was handicapped by the weakness of the Alberta Liberals, which allowed Premier Redford to re-position the PCs further left.

Invasion from the Margin is more likely to succeed than Invasion from the Centre. A spectacular case in point is Mel Hurtig's well-funded but now forgotten National Party, which failed in trying to squeeze itself between the Liberals and the NDP in the 1993 election. The same fate befell the nascent Alberta Party, which tried to squeeze between the Progressive Conservatives and Liberals in the 2012 Alberta provincial election.

The closest thing to a successful Invasion from the Centre in recent Canadian politics was the rise of Mario Dumont's Action Démocratique du Québec, which took advantage of polarization between the Parti Québécois and the Liberal Party of Quebec on the dimension of national unity. Dumont managed to find a niche for his party with a rather vague position that could be caricatured as "separation if necessary but not necessarily separation." However, it is also significant that his party never won more than a few seats until it decided to play Invasion from the Margin on the economic dimension in the 2007 election, outflanking the Liberals on the right by offering a more free-market platform. In 2007, the ADQ won forty-one seats and became the official opposition to a Liberal minority government. The ADQ's subsequent rapid decline was due more to personnel failures in a suddenly expanded party than to any failure of positioning.

Although the evidence suggests that Invasion from the Margin can work for a new pary, it works in a paradoxical way. It allows a new party to assume a more extreme position as a way of displacing a more centrist competitor, but that new party is itself on a journey to the centre taking years or decades. The extremism of the early years is bound to yield to the moderation of success, if indeed the entry strategy leads to any significant degree of real-world success. The median voter theorem still applies, but over a long period of time rather than instantaneously. In a one-dimensional voting game, the position of the median voter is always the equilibrium, the natural resting place. Its attractive power leads all parties to it sooner or later, even if they deviate initially for strategic reasons of party competition.

The third implication, which applies to established parties faced with a challenge from the margin, is more ambiguous. It is actually a pair of different implications, depending on the larger political configuration: *An established party faced with a serious challenge from the margin should move outwards to meet that challenge if it is blocked by a strong competitor on its other flank.*

At any time, there are always many fringe parties, both on the left and the right. Most are too extreme, or are not well enough organized and funded, to pose a threat to anyone except themselves. The

Conservatives do not need to worry about Christian Heritage, nor the New Democrats about the Marxist-Leninist Party of Canada. But party leaders must be able to recognize a serious threat when it arises.

Reform posed such a threat to the Progressive Conservatives in 1993, though not in 1988. The PCs had rightly ignored Reform in 1988, but that strategy proved disastrous in 1993. In that election, Preston Manning's "Zero in Three" approach to balancing the budget gained a great deal of support on the right side of the spectrum among voters who were worried about Canada's seemingly endless federal deficit spending. But PC leader Kim Campbell did not put anything on the table to compete with Manning, and indeed spent much more energy defending spending on social programs than on explaining how she would balance the budget. She acted as if she wanted to compete with the Liberals to the left of her rather than with Reform to the right. But the Liberals in 1993 had recovered from their earlier defeats and were now a powerful, well-organized force that could hold their ground against Campbell's leftward *démarche*.

In the event, Reform swept the West and split the PC vote in Ontario so badly that the PCs could not elect a single member in their historic heartland. If Campbell had, so to speak, ridden out to confront Reform directly, addressing the concerns of those more conservative voters who had historically always supported her party, the PCs might have lost the 1993 election to the Liberals anyway, but they might have strangled Reform in its infancy and thus survived to fight again. As it was, the 1993 defeat put the PCs on a downward path ending in the 2003 merger with the Canadian Alliance.

I am not trying to bash Kim Campbell. At the beginning of the 1993 campaign, Reform was polling about 10 per cent, while the Liberals and Progressive Conservatives were virtually tied in the low to mid 30s. At that point in time, it may have been reasonable to regard Reform as a nuisance that could be ignored while the big parties played their traditional game of fighting over the median voter. But Reform grew so much during the campaign that it polled 19 per cent on election day, and at that level it was a lethal threat to the PCs. Campbell, I suppose, can be faulted for not having been agile enough to have changed strategy during the campaign; but anyone who has ever been involved in practical campaigning knows how hard that is to do, particularly where policy is involved. Changes to the platform during the campaign look like panicky opportunism and often do more harm than good. In truth, Campbell failed to foresee the future – not an uncommon human failing.

The Liberals, over many years, had more success in beating back the CCF/NDP. Their main strategy was to let the further left party run interference for new ideas and then adopt them as their own after their popularity had been proved. The list is long, including baby bonuses, old-age pensions, public health care insurance, creation of Petro-Canada, and opposition to NAFTA in 1988. Adopting CCF/NDP policies allowed the Liberals to paint their rivals on the left as "Liberals in a hurry"[10] – good people with good ideas, but not practical enough to be entrusted with government. The NDP breakthrough in 2011 suggests that the Liberal strategy may ultimately have failed, but it worked well for them for almost eighty years – an eternity in politics.

A fourth implication: *An established party faced with a serious challenge from the margin can move toward the centre, away from the challenge, if it is not blocked by a strong competitor on its other flank.*

Movement to the centre builds on the phenomenon known as strategic voting. In such cases, voters opt to vote for their second choice rather than their first in order to prevent a victory by their third or fourth choices. Imagine parties A, B, and C arrayed in that order from left to right on a single dimension. If voters are rational, the supporters of party A will have the preference ordering A > B > C. That is, if they cannot have A, they would rather have B than C because B is closer to their ideal point. If the supporters of A thought that A had little chance to win and C really had a strong chance to win, it would be rational for them to vote strategically for their second choice, B, in order to prevent a victory by C. The same reasoning would apply to rational supporters of C, whose preference ordering would be C > B > A. If they thought C couldn't win and A had a strong chance, they should vote for B in an attempt to forestall their worst outcome. The reasoning is less clear-cut but still applicable to supporters of B, whose preference ordering might be either B > C > A or B > A > C. Supporters of B might still vote strategically for their second choice in order to prevent a victory by their third choice.

Canadian history records many instances of voters behaving in precisely this way. Most supporters of the further-right Reform Party of British Columbia switched to voting Liberal in 2001 after the 1997 elections results had made it clear that the NDP would otherwise keep on winning. Clearly the preference ordering of BC Reformers was Reform > Liberal > NDP, and they wanted to prevent another victory by their third choice. An example on the other side of the political spectrum took place in the federal election of 2004, when a certain number of NDP supporters, particularly in Ontario, switched to the Liberals toward the end of the campaign in order to prevent a victory by Stephen Harper's Conservative Party of Canada.[11] In both these cases, as in strategic voting generally, fear is the dominant motive – fear of getting stuck with one's least preferred option. Of course, the centrist parties play on this fear. BC Liberals told Reformers in 2001 that the NDP was sure to win unless they (Reformers) switched to the Liberals, and the federal Liberals told NDPers in 2004 that only the Liberals could win and thus prevent Stephen Harper from enacting his dreaded hidden agenda.

Playing on fear to encourage strategic voting is a common feature of campaigning, but in some cases it can become part of a larger strategy of repositioning. A clear-cut example of that is the Progressive Conservative victory in the Alberta election of 2012. Alison Redford, who became PC leader and therefore provincial premier in fall 2011, had begun her career working for Joe Clark and was known as a Red Tory. As leader, she was now confronted with the defection en masse of the further-right portion of the PC voting coalition. She could have tried to regain that conservative ground, but, sensing Liberal weakness to her left, she chose instead to poach voters from that side. As detailed in the final section of this book, she emphasized how "frightening" Wildrose was and aligned herself with causes dear to the left (public education and medicare). She even ran ads stressing that hers was a new party ("Not your father's PC Party"). Her strategy would not have worked if the Alberta Liberals

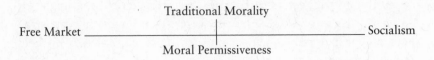

Figure 3.5
Cross-cutting dimensions of political cleavage

had been as strong and united as the federal Liberals were in 1993, when Kim Campbell tried something similar. But the Alberta Liberals were already in woeful shape, with an empty treasury and open factional fighting that had led the previous leader, David Swann, to resign, to be replaced by PC defector Raj Sharman.

MULTI-DIMENSIONAL POLITICS: THE REVENGE OF THE MATRIX

It is time to make things more complicated. The analysis up to this point has assumed that there is only one relevant dimension of difference along which political conflict takes place. We have used the left-right dimension because that seems omnipresent in modern societies, but it could be anything. The main point is that we have assumed only one dimension, and if that assumption is met, the position of the median voter is the equilibrium of the voting game, though in the real world that may take years or decades to achieve.

The left-right dimension, however, can be deconstructed into components that may line up in a perpendicular rather than parallel fashion to each other. For example, it is common to speak of both economic and social conservatism and liberalism. Many conservatives who support free markets and property rights (they believe in economic freedom) are also pro-life and against gay marriage (they believe in the restraints of traditional sexual morality). And there are many liberals who support government intervention and redistribution (they believe in government control over the economy) who are also pro-choice and in favour of gay marriage (they oppose government control over sexual behaviour).

The apparent paradoxes can be better understood by depicting economic and sexual freedom as two distinct and cross-cutting

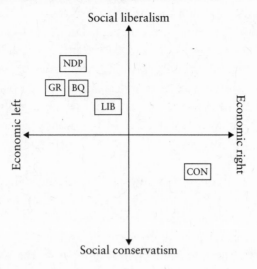

Figure 3.6
Two-dimensional location of Canadian political parties

dimensions, as illustrated in figure 3.5.[12] In this world, each person's ideal point is located not on a line but in a two-dimensional space. This may not seem like a big change, but it has huge implications, because according to the McKelvey Chaos Theorem, there is no equilibrium in a voting game of more than one dimension.[13] Any position can be trumped by another position that will attract a bigger coalition of supporters. Thus the clarity of political competition in a one-dimensional world gets very foggy in a matrix of two dimensions or more.

A common dimension of political contestation, almost as widespread as the left-right dimension, is ethno-religious-linguistic conflict. This divergence usually comes down to issues of community identity. What should the primary language and/or religion be? Who should be in the polity (separatism, as in Quebec and Scotland), who should be out of it (expulsion of minorities, as in Uganda), and who deserves special treatment (affirmative action, preferential policies)? It is very common around the world for politics to become polarized along some dimension of conflict over communal identity. In such cases, given that the left-right dimension is ubiquitous, politics becomes two-dimensional.

The second dimension in Canadian history consisted originally of conflict over religion and language but is now overlaid with debates about the future of Quebec – that is, whether it belongs inside or outside of Canada. Whatever the issues of the day, Canadian politics always threatens to degenerate into a polarizing communal conflict – English versus French – which could threaten the existence of Canada as a state. Canadian political parties, therefore, have to take up positions in a two-dimensional space, as shown in figure 3.6.

The absence of equilibrium in two-dimensional competition leads to instability in political party competition. One aspect of that instability is the emergence and persistence of new parties outside the Liberal-Conservative duopoly, such as the Progressives, CCF/NDP, Social Credit, and Reform, mostly based in the West; and the Ralliement des Créditistes and the Bloc Québécois, based in Quebec. These are only the most significant federal examples; for a more complete though not exhaustive list of new federal and provincial parties, see table 3.1.[14]

Another aspect of instability is the sudden decline in fortunes of an existing party – often, but not always, accompanied by the rise of a new party. Recent examples are the replacement of the Liberals by the Progressive Conservatives as the leading federal party in Quebec in 1984; the reduction of the Progressive Conservatives to two seats in 1993, as Reform and the BQ took over much of their previous support; and the reduction of the BQ to four seats in 2011, when the NDP won fifty-nine seats in Quebec. To be sure, these sharp swings can be explained by the interaction of a multi-party system with SMP voting; but the deeper question is, why does Canada have so many political parties despite the tendency of SMP to promote a two-party system? The answer lies in the two-dimensional character of Canadian politics, which tends to fragment voter blocs through cross-cutting cleavages. Reformers were Progressive Conservatives who could not abide Brian Mulroney's favouritism towards Quebec. BQ voters were Quebec nationalists temporarily brought under the PC banner by promises of constitutional change, which Mulroney ultimately could not deliver. Most were neither Conservative by tradition nor conservative by philosophical inclination.

Table 3.1
New political parties in Western Canada and Quebec

Western Canada

Provincial Rights Party (P)	1905
Non-Partisan League (P)	1916
Progressives (including United Farmers parties) (F+P)	1919
Co-operative Commonwealth Federation (F+P)	1932
Social Credit (F+P)	1935
Social Credit Party of British Columbia (P)	1952
Western Canada Concept (F+P)	1980
Western Canada Federation (F+P)	1980
Confederation of Regions (F+P)	1983
Reform Party of Canada (F)	1987
Reform Party of British Columbia (P)	1989
National Party (F)	1992
Progressive Democratic Alliance of British Columbia (P)	1993
Saskatchewan Party (P)	1997
British Columbia Unity Party (P)	2001
Alberta Alliance (P)	2002
Wildrose Alliance Party (P)	2008

Quebec

Parti National (P)	1885
Nationalist League (as political party) (F)	1911
Action Libérale Nationale (P)	1934
Union Nationale (P)	1935
Union des Electeurs (F+P)	1939
Bloc Populaire Canadien (F+P)	1942
Ralliement des Créditistes (F)	1957
Parti Québécois (P)	1968
Ralliement Créditiste du Québec (P)	1970
Equality Party (P)	1989
Bloc Québécois (F)	1990
Action Démocratique du Québec (P)	1994
Québec Solidaire (P)	2006
Coalition Avenir Québec (P)	2011

The political scientist who has offered the deepest analysis of multi-dimensional politics is William Riker. Although ideological conflict is ubiquitous in democratic politics, in principle the number of potential issue dimensions is unlimited, says Riker.[15] He argues that political entrepreneurs on the margins are constantly trying to raise new issues, seeking dimensions of cleavage that will pry apart existing coalitions. He sees a "natural selection" of issues in which most such attempts fail but an occasional one succeeds in bringing about a major realignment.[16] He has even introduced a new term, *heresthetic*, to describe the process. *Heresthetic* is related to "heresy," derived from the Greek verb meaning "to divide." A heresthetic manoeuvre is a new way to divide political supporters, for example, Preston Manning and Lucien Bouchard telling Western and Quebec voters to focus on their regional grievances rather than the national promises of the PCs. Politicians, according to Riker, use rhetoric to persuade voters to support them but heresthetic to define the dimension along which voters should situate their concerns.[17]

CAMPAIGNING IN HYPERSPACE

All of this has important implications for political campaigning in Canada. An early step in all campaigns is for the campaign strategists to define the "ballot question," which encapsulates the most important issue for the party. The wording of the ballot question is usually not revealed as such to the public, but it guides all the party's communications during the campaign. One of the things that a ballot question attempts to do is to lay out the dimension along which debate will take place. Political dimensions have no independent existence. They are mental realities that exist only in the consciousness of voters. The first step toward winning the battle for office is to define the dimension along which voters will position the alternatives in their minds.

The Conservative ballot question in 2011 was obviously something like "Whom do you trust to maintain Canada's prosperity in these difficult times?" In Riker's terms, this was a heresthetic manoeuvre, its purpose to guide voters to think along the economic left-right dimension. If that move was successful, Conservative rhetoric would then try to make voters agree with Conservative economic policies by pointing to alleged past and future benefits. But such agreement wouldn't matter very much unless the voter had already taken the prior step of deciding that economic issues were the most important ones to think about.

The BQ, in contrast, came out of the gate in 2011 with quite a different ballot question: "Whom do you trust to stop Harper from winning a majority of seats?" To the extent that the question was supposed to encourage voters to think about the Conservatives' alleged antipathy to "Quebec values," it was a refined way of getting voters to think in polarized Quebec-Canada terms. That framing may have worked to deter Quebec voters from supporting the Conservatives, but it may also have been too subtle. In the end, more voters in Quebec decided they trusted the NDP than the BQ to "stop Harper."

Because of the absence of equilibrium, maxims about campaigning in political hyperspace cannot be as categorical as about campaigning in a one-dimensional world, where everything revolves around occupying the position of the median voter, either now or in the long run. I can, however, offer two generalizations that should be helpful much of the time. The first is directed to large parties: *A major party hoping to form government should try to create a single dominant dimension of conflict in voters' minds and occupy the position of the median voter along that dimension.*

Normally that dimension would be the left-right one, but it might be an ethno-linguistic dimension amidst a crisis of national unity. Whatever the case, it is helpful to a large party to fight along a single overriding dimension, which allows voters to be attracted into a large pool, whether extending to the left or right of the median, that can furnish enough seats to form a government. This technique amounts to framing the vote decision by getting one's ballot question accepted in people's minds, in a way that helps a large party.

The advice to smaller parties would be the reverse: *A minor party fighting for space should try to establish in voters' minds a new dimension of conflict that cuts across whatever dimension has been established by its main competitor.*

Establishing a new dimension of difference in voters' minds opens the possibility of breaking up a major party's coalition and winning some of those voters for the minor party. Fragmentation of the electorate will usually help a minor party. The entry of the BQ into federal politics furnishes a classic illustration. By the time of the 1993 election, Brian Mulroney's constitutional policy lay in ruins; the Meech Lake Accord and the Charlottetown Accord had both failed. If the Conservatives were going to prevail that year under

Kim Campbell, it had to be on their economic record, including successful privatization of several Crown corporations, tax reform (GST), and North American free trade (NAFTA). Yet Lucien Bouchard told Quebec voters that what mattered most was the Conservatives' failure to satisfy Quebec's demands for self-determination. The *beau risque* of seeking constitutional reform had failed, and now it was time to push for independence. The two parties struggled to establish a dimension of difference in Quebec, and the BQ was more successful in getting its dimension accepted.

Earlier we saw how Preston Manning sought to break into the political system by positioning Reform to the right of the Progressive Conservatives and going after their core voters, who were inevitably to the right of the median voter position that Mulroney had tried to occupy. But Manning, a natural practitioner of heresthetic, also tried to find at least one new dimension of difference to break up the Mulroney coalition that had been so powerful in Western Canada. He experimented with three different formulas: the West against the rest, the rural hinterland against rural Canada, and the ROC against Quebec. The first dimension was particularly important in getting Reform off the ground, for a new party needs a regional base to succeed under SMP. The third probably did the most to propel Reform from fringe party (less than 10 per cent vote share) to serious party status (almost 20 per cent vote share). Many Canadians outside Quebec were outraged by the Mulroney government's attempt to push through the Meech Lake and Charlottetown accords, and Reform was the only party to oppose those attempts.

A more recent example concerns the plight of the Liberal Party of Canada after the 2011 election. Now reduced to a third party, the Liberals seem to occupy the centre space between the Conservatives to the right and the NDP to the left. Some prominent Liberals have tried to capitalize on this position by trumpeting the virtues of being in the centre. But, as Antonia Maioni, a political scientist at McGill, told the Liberal caucus in summer 2011, it is also possible to seek political recovery by opening up some new dimension of difference that cuts across the standard light-right dimension on which the Conservatives and NDP are ensconced: "Move away from the middle of the road. For years, Liberals have fed off the notion of moderation and centrism, of being neither here nor there. But the middle of the road can be a dangerous place – especially if you don't know where you're going. The Liberal Party's challenge is to reimagine the political spectrum as a multidimensional space, not just a flat line where they struggle to hold an imaginary middle position."[18]

The existence of multiple dimensions of conflict is what makes campaigning, and indeed politics, so interesting and challenging. If there were only a single dimension of conflict, campaigning would be a mechanical business of positioning oneself near the median voter, enlivened only by invasions from the margin by new parties that would also move towards the median voter after displacing older parties. As the equilibrium position, the median voter is the "Strange Attractor" of one-dimensional politics.

But there is no equilibrium, no Strange Attractor, in the multidimensional real world. Political entrepreneurs can try out new dimensions in their never-ending struggle to position themselves in voters' minds. New issues can thus emerge from obscurity into the spotlight of political competition. National unity, language, race, gender, the environment – none of these fits neatly into the standard left-right dimension of government intervention and redistribution versus free markets and property rights. Yet all can become influential in the political hyperspace of multi-dimensional competition.

4

Strategy II: Triage and Concentration

Eine Operation ohne Schwerpunkt is wie ein Mann ohne Charakter. [An operation without *Schwerpunkt* is like a man without character.]

Field Marshal Paul von Hindenburg[1]

In an ideal world, campaign planners would go logically and systematically through all the steps of the process to define and build a winning coalition of voters, using each step as a platform for the next. In the real world, however, time is often in short supply, and campaign planners are sometimes inexperienced and distracted with other tasks. For example, the Conservatives had only two months between 20 March 2004, when Stephen Harper won the leadership of the party, and 23 May, when the governor general issued the writs for the election.[2] In circumstances like that, the execution of essential steps in the planning process is rushed, and phases get telescoped into each other or carried out simultaneously or out of sequence. But even if the real world is messier than the ideal, there is still value in looking at an ideal process for developing campaign strategy.[3]

The central principle of campaign strategy is that, in a world of scarce resources and legislated spending limits, it is necessary to focus spending where it will do the most good. Competitive elections are won or lost at the margin, in battleground ridings and among swing voters. Effective strategy means relying on a clear-headed process of triage to determine which ridings and demographic groups can be considered safe in the coming election, which are hopeless (for the time being), and which are on the cusp but can be tilted in your direction with the application of extra effort. The concept is somewhat like *Schwerpunkt* (centre of gravity, or focal point) in the classic work *On War* by Carl von Clausewitz.[4] The similarity is not surprising, for the political competition between parties is a domesticated version of warfare, and political and military campaigns have many things in common.

Whatever party leaders may say in public about their objectives, it is crucial for campaign planners to design strategy around realistic objectives. There can and should be contingency plans if things start to look much better ("roll the dice") or worse ("save the furniture") than expected, but the main plan should be based on a sober assessment of what is realistically possible. The rest of this chapter focuses on parties that have a credible chance of forming the next government and therefore will try to win a majority of seats if possible, and at least a plurality.

In terms drawn from game theory, the goal is to build a Minimum Winning Coalition (MWC).[5] Politicians often speak as if they would like to get everyone's vote, but in fact that would be counterproductive. Voters are attracted into an electoral coalition by persuasion, which includes promises of rewards. The more supporters you have, the more open hands you will face if you do win power, and the more difficulty you will have satisfying the expectations of your coalition members for favourable policies, patronage appointments, and symbolic gratification. Larger-than-necessary winning coalitions have often proved unstable in Canadian politics. For example, Diefenbaker's Conservative coalition won a sweeping victory in 1958, as did Mulroney's coalition in 1984; however, both proved exceptionally fragile because the leaders in power could not satisfy demands from their Quebec supporters without alienating supporters elsewhere.

In contemporary Canadian federal politics, the MWC for winning a majority government is about 40 per cent of vote share. In an uncertain world, some cushion is required, so a party will aim a little above that – but that's the range where a majority government becomes possible. In 2008, the Conservatives came close with 38 per cent of popular vote but did not secure a majority of seats. They did succeed in winning a majority of seats in 2011, with a 39.6 per cent vote share. Of course, the size of the MWC is not a constant; it depends on the configuration of parties at any point in time.

If Canada were to revert to strict two-party competition, the MWC would rise to something slightly above 50 per cent.

DEFINING A GEOGRAPHIC COALITION

Winning a Canadian federal or provincial election means winning more seats than your rivals do. For strategic purposes, you should therefore begin by performing a triage of seats into the categories of

- seats that are safe for your party;
- battleground ridings that could go either way (this will include seats you now hold but fear you could lose as well as seats you don't hold but think you might win); and
- seats that are hopeless for your party (in this election, although maybe not forever).

In the first attempt at an analysis, you can use what I call the "Rule of Ten." Canadian experience suggests that a strong local campaign backed up by a vigorous Direct Voter Contact (DVC) program can increase a party's vote share by as much as 10 percentage points over the results of the last election. That is, if a party got 30 per cent of the popular vote last time in a riding, it might be able to raise that to 40 per cent by going all out and pouring in resources to win. It is thus logical to designate as battleground ridings those in which the margin of victory or defeat (MOV or MOD) for your party was 10 points or less in the preceding election. If you lost by 10 points or less last time, you have a shot at winning this time; if you won by 10 points or less, you have to be afraid of losing.

The Rule of Ten is a rule of thumb for making a practical decision about classifying ridings. In fact, increasing your vote share by 10 percentage points through DVC is a long shot. But if you can afford to follow the Rule of Ten, you will identify almost all the ridings where the outcome is uncertain. If restricted resources force you to follow, let's say, a Rule of Five, you will have to neglect some ridings where you might have a chance to steal from opponents as well as some where your own party's hold on the seat is not totally secure. The more comprehensive strategy is better if you can afford it.

This is, however, just the first step in triage, because it doesn't take sufficient account of candidacy factors. Canadian research suggests that, independently of the resources devoted to the struggle, the candidate can also make a difference of 10 percentage points, maybe even more.[6] Incumbency is almost always an advantage, unless the incumbent has become notorious for corruption, incompetence, or erratic behaviour. There are also "star candidates" who may be well known to the public from previous careers in business, media, arts and entertainment, or public service. Thus, after making the first analysis of ridings based on past results, one should take a second look at ridings where candidates may make a difference. This is a case-by-case process with several factors involved, but we can consider a couple of examples to show how it might work. Let's say that in the last election an NDP challenger knocked off a Liberal incumbent by a margin of 5 percentage points. Normally that would be considered a battleground riding because of the Rule of Ten, but let's suppose that the new NDP incumbent has acquired a good reputation, the former Liberal incumbent has disappeared from the scene, and the Liberals have now nominated an unimpressive candidate no one has ever heard of. If resources are short, the campaign planner might tell the NDP incumbent that he's on his own and not to expect any special help from the national party. On the other hand, if the former Liberal incumbent has stayed politically active and is running again in an effort to win the riding back, the NDP will almost certainly designate this as a battleground riding and pour in extra resources to help its new incumbent get re-elected.

Concentration of resources on battleground ridings is the essential strategic principle. Close elections are won or lost at the margin. The party must focus its efforts on ridings where the outcome is in doubt. This is not always easy to do, because almost all candidates running for a major party believe they have a chance to win and so demand as much help as they can get from the national party. But a party that fritters away its resources on hopeless contests, or spends all its money too early before it is clear where the marginal seats are located, will not win the election.

Concentration of resources can mean many different things, including some or all of the following:

- Transferring extra money from the national party to the targeted riding (remembering that local campaigns have their own spending limits that have to be observed)
- Offering organizational assistance, either by sending in experienced campaigners or by giving advice from the national war room
- Tilting the media buy so that advertising is heavier in targeted ridings. Media markets do not correspond perfectly with riding boundaries, but targeted ridings often come in clusters (e.g., the working-class areas of Toronto for the NDP) that fit into a single media market. Similarly, safe seats are often found in clusters, such as the province of Alberta for the Conservatives or, before 2011, the west Island of Montreal for the Liberals. The Conservatives would have been silly to spend more than the minimum on advertising in Alberta, and likewise for the Liberals in anglophone Montreal.
- Scheduling one or more visits from the so-called leader's tour during the writ period of the campaign. In practice, this strategy is often backed up by visits from other popular figures in the party – the so-called secondary or surrogate tour. Visits can attract local media attention and galvanize local party workers. However, they must be managed carefully, because they can also be a distraction for the candidate and workers at times when they should be out door-knocking rather than entertaining visitors.
- Arranging a program of Direct Voter Contact. I am speaking here of an organized and expensive program of identifying supporters, persuading the undecided one at a time, and getting out the vote (GOTV) at the end of the campaign. In theory and occasionally in practice, this can be done by the local campaign through a combination of direct mail, telephone calls, and door-to-door visits. Normally, however, the national campaign will have to maintain the database while organizing and paying for the telephone calls and direct mail. There is just too much to be done in too short a period of time for most local campaigns to manage it properly. A good DVC program is the single most effective weapon available to the national campaign to assist local campaigns in battleground ridings.

Table 4.1
Triage

Geographic coalition	Demographic coalition
Safe seats	Core supporters
Battleground ridings	Swing voters
Hopeless ridings	Confirmed opponents

To summarize, a geographic MWC is built by triaging ridings into safe, battleground, and hopeless categories. Candidates in safe seats (usually incumbents) will be expected to win their own ridings without special help from the national campaign. Candidates in hopeless ridings will be encouraged to do their best, and a few will actually win, since triage and prediction can never be totally accurate. All candidates in these two categories will get the standard package, including a platform, templates for advertising and signage, and the party's training program, while special assistance will be reserved for where it can do the most good – in the battleground ridings.

DEFINING A DEMOGRAPHIC COALITION

Just as a geographic MWC has to be defined in order to target organizational efforts, especially DVC, a demographic MWC has to be defined in order to guide policy formation and advertising. The basic principle of triage applies, as shown in table 4.1.

But if the general idea is the same, the method by which the triage is performed is different. Geographic triage is carried out by analyzing past results at the riding level, overlaid with assessments of incumbency and candidate strength. Demographic triage is carried out with quantitative survey research, supplemented by qualitative research (focus groups), especially to highlight the perceptions and views of swing voters.

Political parties poll regularly but also usually commission a large baseline poll to prepare for an anticipated election. Such a poll must be carried out early enough that its results can influence the composition of the platform and the advertising creative work. Six months ahead of the election is about right, though it is not always easy to achieve that kind of precision in the real world. Having fixed election dates, as in Ontario and British Columbia, makes scheduling easier; but federal fixed-election-date legislation has been disregarded in the context of minority government, so it cannot always be depended upon. The sample size should be large, at least 2,500 and preferably more, because conclusions are needed about relatively small groups within the population – for example, not just about women in general but about, say, married women in the suburbs of Toronto.

Triage is achieved by combining results from a number of different questions, such as the following:

- Which party did you vote for in the last election?
- If an election were held today, which party would you vote for?
- How committed are you to this choice? Very committed, committed, or not very committed?
- Which party would be your second choice?
- If undecided, are you leaning toward a particular party?
- Is there any party that you would never vote for?

The results can be added up in different ways, but in general we can say that Liberal core supporters would be those who voted Liberal in the last election (if they were eligible to vote), who would vote Liberal if the election were held today, and who say they are committed or very committed to their choice. Committed opponents would be the mirror image; that is, they voted for another party in the last election, they would vote for another party if the election were held today; they are very committed or committed to their choice; they do not have the Liberals as a second choice; and indeed, they say they would never vote Liberal.

In between the extremes of core voters lie the persuadable target voters, who are actually of the most interest to campaign strategists. These voters might fall into various subgroups, including the following:

- Those who voted Liberal last time but now say they support another party. The Liberal campaign will want to know why they have defected and what is necessary to get them back.

- Those who say they would vote Liberal today but are only weakly committed to their choice. Why are they wavering, and how can their support be solidified?
- Those who are undecided but say they are leaning Liberal. What would cause them to make up their mind in the Liberal direction?
- Those who are supporting another party but have the Liberals as their second choice. What would make them switch to Liberal?
- Those who do not indicate any degree of Liberal support as such but who have a favourable view of the Liberal leader.

The combination of core supporters and persuadable target voters is known as the party's "universe" of support. The universe is essentially the demographic realm within which a party is realistically justified in expending short-term resources to win votes. Voters outside the universe can still be approached, but they will require a long-term strategy that goes well beyond a single campaign. For example, the Conservative Party has since early 2005 deliberately tried to get more support from visible-minority voters. The effort has involved three campaign platforms and several policy innovations while in government, plus innumerable outreach efforts by party leaders and staff.[7] These efforts finally paid off in the 2011 election, when the Conservatives attracted enough ethnic voters to win a large number of seats in the Greater Toronto Area (GTA).[8]

In short, a party will operate mainly within its universe but will probably also have one or more long-term growth initiatives. Within its universe, which constitutes the short-term horizon, a party will need to do two things: (1) keep its core supporters happy so they will not be tempted to go elsewhere; and (2) increase its coalition by bringing on board some of the persuadable target voters. There is an inevitable tension between these two objectives because offers to persuadable voters will probably involve policies that core supporters are not enthusiastic about or perhaps actively dislike. But such ventures are necessary precisely because the swing voters have not yet been attracted by what appeals to core voters. Occasionally a party has so many core supporters that it hardly has to worry about attracting new supporters, but that is a rare luxury in competitive political systems. Normally, if the party hopes to win, its leadership

Table 4.2
The Conservative demographic coalition

Favouring Conservatives	Intermediate	Favouring opponents
Men		Women
Western	Ontario	Quebec and Atlantic
Evangelical Protestant	Mainstream Protestant	Non-religious
	Roman Catholic	
Married	Widowed, divorced	Never-married
Self-employed	Employed	Unemployed
	Private-sector union	Public-sector union
Rural	Suburban	Urban
Middle-aged	Seniors	Youth

will have no choice but to try to balance the expectations of core supporters against the demands of persuadable target voters.

Having defined its universe, the party's researchers must also establish its demographic contours. What are the characteristics of core supporters, swing voters, and confirmed opponents? Expressed in qualitative rather than precise quantitative terms, table 4.2 provides some sample demographic aspects of the Conservative universe outside Quebec prior to the 2006 election.

The effect of these characteristics tends to be additive. Thus the probability that a middle-aged, married, self-employed, evangelical Protestant man living in a small town in Western Canada is a Conservative core supporter approaches 100 per cent. On the other hand, the probability that a young, unmarried, non-religious woman living in downtown Toronto and working for a public-sector employer is a Conservative approaches 0 per cent. Most people, of course, are not so stereotyped; they have a mixture of characteristics, some of which are statistically associated with voting Conservative, others associated with supporting other parties. But the additive principle is still the key. The closer a person is to the demographic stereotype of Conservative voters, the more accessible that person is likely to be to Conservative appeals. In practice, this means the best way to build a coalition is by moving incrementally outward from core support rather than making big leaps.

Let's give some specific examples. The Conservative Party prior to the 2006 election, like other conservative parties around the world, had a "gender gap." That is, it tended to have more support among men than among women. If it was going to win, it needed to get more votes from women. That meant finding ways to appeal to female voters who were already closest to being Conservative supporters: for example, married, middle-class women in suburbs or small towns, rather than young, unmarried women living in central cities. Or, in terms of religion, the Conservatives were doing very well with evangelical Protestants but not as well with Roman Catholics, historically a Liberal support group. The party needed to get more Catholic votes, which seemed a more realistic possibility than getting more votes from atheists, because Roman Catholics – at least practising Catholics – share values and beliefs with evangelical Protestants.

Going into the 2006 election, therefore, the Conservatives had a research-based strategy of trying to bring more married women and Roman Catholics over to their side, believing that these demographic categories contained many voters who resembled typical Conservative voters in other respects and just needed a little encouragement to make the transition. In addition, the Conservatives also had a long-term strategy of trying to build support among certain ethnic and visible-minority voters. Again the additive principle was central. For example, even if Chinese voters had overwhelmingly supported the Liberal Party for decades, there were many Chinese whose demographic profile resembled that of typical Conservative voters – married, middle-class, middle-aged, self-employed, perhaps even evangelical Protestant, such as adherents of the Christian and Missionary Alliance, which has many Asian members. Such voters would be a logical place for the Conservatives to go prospecting.

Once target and non-target groups are established, strategists even give them nicknames to make them come to life. For example, in the lead-up to the 2005–06 campaign, Conservative strategist Patrick Muttart gave names to many groups of interest, either positive or negative, to the party. "Zoe" was his label for a group among which the Conservatives were unlikely to make much progress – young single women in central cities. He even built a biography for "Zoe" to make her come alive. He depicted her as a recent sociology graduate living with her cat in downtown Toronto, doing yoga and eating vegetarian food. She probably wouldn't vote at all, but if she did, it would be NDP or Liberal rather than Conservative. Such stereotyping helps those planning campaign communications to visualize the people to whom they want to appeal and the types of communication that would reach them.[9]

By itself, the additive principle leads only to intuitions about which demographic subgroups might be open to a party's appeals. These intuitions must be checked through survey research, by discovering how many members of demographic subgroups lean towards your party or have it as their second choice, testing their openness to the party's policies, and looking for breakthrough policies that might bring them on side. Qualitative research is also useful. Once quantitative analysis has isolated demographic targets, members can be recruited to join discussion groups, where they can talk about their perceptions of the party, their hesitations about supporting it, and their aspirations for what government can accomplish. It is, for example, crucial to learn whether members of a target group are hesitant because they don't like the leader or don't like the policies. If the leader is seen as stiff and unapproachable, he can be dressed in a sweater and open-necked shirt when the ads are being filmed. If the policies are wrong, the draft platform can be changed. Or maybe both need to be done.

In any case, it is essential to base decisions on research about what is likely to work with target voter groups. Research is particularly important because those who work for the party are loyalists, whose views may be typical of the core supporters who keep the party going year in and year out, but not of the target voters whose support must be acquired to build a winning coalition. Party strategists cannot afford to trust their own intuitions, because they themselves are not typical of the people they are trying to attract. Wildrose made a mistake of this type (discussed in detail in chapter 9) in constructing its platform for the 2012 Alberta election.

THE STRATEGY OF PERSUASION

Defining geographic and demographic coalitions is the essential prerequisite for developing communications strategy for the campaign.

A campaign is an organized effort to persuade people to join your coalition, and communication is the means by which persuasion takes place. But for communication to be effective, the intended audience has to be known. You want to speak persuasively to your universe of voters, and more especially to undecided but potential supporters, and most especially to potential supporters in the battleground ridings that must be won to achieve victory in the election.

The platform is the most basic communications instrument. At one time the platform was printed and distributed in large quantities; now it is posted on the party's website. In either case, the platform is read by only a small fraction of voters, but it is crucial because it guides all other communications, including advertising, the leader's speeches, press releases, and responses to attacks.

The platform is conventionally understood as a set of policies that a party's elected representatives will implement if they form the government. This statement seems to imply that policy is the end and the campaign is the means. But that relationship is reversed from the standpoint of the campaign strategist, in whose eyes the platform and all its policies are a means to achieve the end of winning the election.[10] From that perspective, as Anthony Downs has argued, parties don't try to get elected in order to implement their policies; they adopt policies in order to get elected.

As suggested above, the platform has to have some "red meat" items designed to hold the loyalty of core supporters. For example, the 2005–06 Conservative platform contained several promises of across-the-board tax cuts – reduction of the GST from 7 per cent to 6 per cent and then to 5 per cent, lowering of corporate income taxes, and elimination of the capital gains tax under certain circumstances. These policies appealed strongly to Conservative core supporters, who tend to think that taxes – all taxes – are too high and should be lowered. But there were also several highly targeted tax credit or grant policies, of which the Child Care Allowance – $100 per month for each child under six – was the most visible. Others included:

- $1,000 Apprentice Incentive Grant
- Apprenticeship Job Creation Tax Credit
- tools tax deduction

- increase from $1,000 to $2,000 in the pension income tax amount eligible for a federal tax credit
- exemption of the first $10,000 of student scholarship income from taxation
- $500 textbook tax credit
- $500 tax credit to parents for registration fees and memberships for physical fitness activities for their children
- federal tax credit for use of public transit[11]

These platform items were an attempt to reach groups that had been targeted by campaign planners on the basis of research – parents of school and university age children, skilled workers, and retired people – because they were open to voting Conservative but needed a little more inducement.

Targeting groups of voters is essential to building a winning coalition, but it can look like a crass appeal to self-interest. Hence the platform, and the party's whole communicative posture during the campaign, must also sound themes that appeal more broadly to voters' sense of the public interest. Here are three examples:

- Barack Obama made "change" the theme of his 2008 campaign for the presidency. "Change" was in fact a code word for several different things: electing the first black president in American history, replacing a Republican with a Democratic administration, transcending the highly polarized atmosphere that had marked American politics since the Clinton years of the 1990s, and perhaps many other things that voters might read into such an amorphous concept. As a result, the Obama team put on the most exciting campaign in American politics since that of John F. Kennedy in 1960.
- In 2005–06, the Conservatives made integrity in government a major theme because the Liberals were stuck with the blame for the Quebec sponsorship scandal. The Conservatives proposed an "Accountability Act" as the first of their "Five Priorities" during the campaign. There were many other policies in the Conservative platform, but they kept ringing the changes on accountability because that seemed to capture the mood of the electorate.

- By the late 1970s there was a widespread sense in Great Britain that the country was in decline and that the trade unions, some of which were led by communists, were running wild. The Conservatives, led by Margaret Thatcher, thus turned the 1979 election into a veritable crusade against socialism. Thatcher previewed this theme almost as soon as she became leader, saying in 1976: "I call the Conservative Party now to a crusade ... I appeal to all those men and women of goodwill who do not want a Marxist future for themselves or their children or their children's children."[12]

Failure to sound a convincing overarching theme can make even the most carefully constructed platform difficult to sell. In 2004, the Canadian Conservatives had a detailed platform with lots of appeals to targeted groups, but the overall thematics were rather mushy. What exactly did the campaign slogan "Demand Better" mean? Stephen Harper did not repeat this mistake, as he emphasized accountability in the 2005–06 campaign, leadership in 2008, and fear of a Liberal-NDP-BQ coalition in 2011.

A useful tool in establishing the major theme of a campaign is the so-called SWOT analysis. A term also often used in the business world, SWOT is an acronym standing for Strengths, Weaknesses, Opportunities, and Threats.[13] Typically a group of strategists, numbering anywhere from five to twenty, will spend half a day reviewing the situation, not just from their own perspective but from the viewpoint of their major opponent. Table 4.3 offers a fraction of what a SWOT analysis might have shown prior to the 2008 election campaign.

I don't know if the Conservative strategists actually carried out this SWOT analysis, but they acted as if they had. They used their financial advantage to run negative ads attacking Stéphane Dion's competence as well as his "Green Shift" policies, and positive ads of Stephen Harper looking casual in a blue sweater and speaking in friendly, reassuring tones. They also pre-empted the threat of an economic downturn by calling an early election, although that required Harper to ignore his own fixed-election-date legislation. The Liberals, on the other hand, seemed less strategic. Dion emphasized the Green Shift, even though lots of polling data showed that voters

Table 4.3
Hypothetical SWOT analysis for the 2008 general election

STRENGTHS	
Conservatives	*Liberals*
Leader respected for competence	Best-established party brand
Lots of money for pre-writ ads	
WEAKNESSES	
Conservatives	*Liberals*
Leader widely mistrusted	Leader widely seen as incompetent
	No money for pre-writ ads
OPPORTUNITIES	
Conservatives	*Liberals*
Spend money on negative ads against	Somehow heighten mistrust of
Liberal leader	Conservative leader
THREATS	
Conservatives	*Liberals*
Economic downturn could cause voters	Leader's preoccupation with
to turn against government	environmental policy could backfire

were turning against it, and he didn't come up with anything compelling to take advantage of Harper's potential personality weaknesses. The Liberals almost got lucky when the economic downturn became manifest in the last two weeks of the campaign, but by then the Conservatives had done so much damage to Dion's image, and he had associated himself so totally with environmental themes, that he could not make himself seem a plausible leader for an economic emergency.

THE MECHANICS OF PERSUASION

Once the platform and thematics are in place and some version of a SWOT analysis has been conducted, the strategist must consider the mechanics of "getting the message out." The national campaign will conduct the "air war" in the media while leaving the "ground war" of personal contact to the local campaigns, with the important exception of the DVC campaign in targeted ridings. The media campaign will have two branches: advertising, which has to be paid for, and news coverage, which is earned primarily through the leader's tour.

Paid advertising may or may not be the most important part of a campaign – that will depend on circumstances – but it is usually the most expensive. A fully funded national campaign ($21 million in 2011) may well spend about 60 per cent of its budget on advertising. Creation and production of the ads may cost $1 million or even more, while the rest will go to the media buy. The media buy is so large because television, the most effective form of political advertising, is so expensive. National campaigns rely largely on television, with sometimes a little radio and/or full-page newspaper advertising. Viral marketing on the Internet is becoming more and more important but tends to complement and reinforce television advertising rather than replace it. Outdoor advertising – signs and billboards – is generally left to the local campaigns.

The media buy, which may make up as much as half the entire campaign budget, should be driven by the geographic and demographic coalitional analysis. Geographically, it is vital to make the media buy heavier where there are targeted ridings. Some aspects of this are easy to achieve; for example, the Conservatives and Liberals both spend little on advertising in Alberta, the Conservatives because they hope to win every seat, and the Liberals because they don't expect to win any. But it is harder to focus the media buy when target ridings are scattered. Particularly in remote rural ridings, radio can be a cost-effective tool because the reach of a radio station may correspond more or less with the boundaries of a targeted riding.

Demographically, the objective is to place ads on the shows ("properties," as they are called in the business) that are watched by the sorts of viewers the campaign is trying to reach. News and public affairs programs are important in that the people who watch them are likely to vote, and so advertising there does not waste money on people who aren't interested. Beyond that, professional media buyers have access to exhaustive statistics on the demographics of television audiences. Some of the science is pretty obvious. To reach male voters, choose hockey, golf, fishing, and other sports shows (except figure skating); to reach female voters, go to the "soaps" (for stay-at-home moms) or dramas about personal relationships. But media buyers can go far beyond the obvious by breaking down the demographics of media properties by all the usual variables, including gender, age, income, marital status, and place of residence.

The advertising creative process should also be driven by the coalitional analysis. Ads designed to reach a young, hip audience (good for selling cell phones but a questionable expense in politics, since young people are less likely to vote) would be different from ads designed to reach Mom and Pop relaxing at home after an exhausting day of work and coping with children. Most of the people who do advertising creative are young, hip urbanites, but their job is to understand their clients' needs, and that is where the research comes in. If the creative team knows the demographics of the target groups the party is trying to bring into its coalition, they should be able to reach that audience.

Earned media is garnered largely through the organized madness of the leader's tour, in which the party rents a combination of planes and buses to haul the leader, staff, and media people around the country for the length of the campaign. The leader might bring along twenty to thirty staff members, and there might be a similar number of print journalists, columnists, and electronic reporters with their microphones and camera crews. Media companies now pay more than $10,000 a week for each seat on the leader's tour, so they expect it to generate headline stories for their newspapers or broadcasts.

If the leader's tour is going to be effective, it must be meticulously planned, and the planning must be driven by an understanding of the party's coalition and target voters. The principle of triage applies to choosing geographic destinations. While the campaign will want to touch down in all major media markets of the country at least once, it will want to spend most of its time in battleground ridings, not in safe or hopeless seats. Thus the Conservatives will probably stop only once in Calgary, even though it is Prime Minister Harper's home city. Reporters accompanying the tour will interpret it as a sign of weakness if the tour starts to visit ridings previously thought to be party strongholds and will start filing unflattering stories about the tour. Nonetheless, it may be necessary to "save the furniture" in the late stages of the campaign if the polls are unpromising. Correspondingly, if the party seems to have captured a wave, it may send the leader to ridings previously thought unwinnable. But in spite of these potential variations, the best course is usually to concentrate on the battle-ground ridings designated as such when the campaign was planned.

It is not enough to visit the right places. The tour must also dramatize its messages in ways calculated to reach target demographic groups. It has to generate the right pictorial opportunities ("photo ops") for television coverage and print-media illustrations. For example, when Stephen Harper announced tax credits for children's sports programs in 2005, he staged the announcement in a dojo where kids were taking karate lessons. Perhaps he shouldn't have worn a suit, but he has a weight problem and looks better in boxy business attire than in casual clothes. In any case, the setting and the resulting visuals were arresting enough to get on front pages of newspapers and to be played in TV news broadcasts, thus attracting the attention of the parents everywhere in Canada who were the target of what was really quite a small-scale policy.

Enormous effort goes into planning the leader's tour. It is no small feat to schedule the correct ridings and then find locations for announcements and photo ops that will fit both the geographic location and the demographics of the target groups. You wouldn't announce Wheat Board policy in Toronto, because you want to be surrounded by farmers and tractors, and you wouldn't announce immigration policy in rural Saskatchewan, because you want to be surrounded by visible minorities when you make your statement. All this is perfectly obvious and yet not always easy to achieve when you have to combine it with the demands of keeping to schedule, maintaining security, and satisfying local party organizers who want the leader at a rally.

STICKING TO THE SCRIPT

Campaigns are dynamic in nature, so there must be some flexibility in the plan to adjust to changing circumstances. An issue may unexpectedly arise, causing the leader's tour to change its itinerary to address it in an appropriate location. Opponents may come up with hard-hitting negative ads requiring response ads to blunt their effectiveness. Revelations about something the leader said or did years ago may divert the campaign from getting out its own message. To cope with such contingencies, the campaign must have a process for crisis management, allowing the war room managers to discuss things with the leader and key advisers who are on the tour.

But while flexibility and crisis management are important, it is usually best to stay as close as possible to the script. If the campaign is properly planned, it is based on months of thinking and hundreds of thousands of dollars of research. What are the odds of coming up with a better plan on the spur of the moment under great pressure during the heat of a campaign? Let me give a couple of examples from personal experience with Conservative campaigns.

- In 2004, Conservative polling numbers soared after Stephen Harper performed well in the English leaders' debate, and we decided to go for broke, hoping that talk of winning a majority government would create a bandwagon effect. But instead of a self-fulfilling prophecy, we produced a self-induced train wreck. Voters began to look more carefully at Harper once we started talking about winning a majority of seats, and an unfortunate press release caused the whole bubble to burst. The lesson? We weren't working from a plan to win a majority of seats, so we shouldn't have suddenly started to talk about it late in the campaign.
- The Conservatives were doing everything right in the first three weeks of the 2005 campaign, rolling out new policy every day, and the media were saying that our campaign was the best. Yet our polling numbers, measured in terms of the ballot question ("If the election were held today, which party would you vote for?") barely moved. Many of us in the war room, including me, started to get nervous, worrying that we needed to do something – anything – else. But campaign manager Doug Finley stood fast, saying, "Stick to the plan." He was right. We were making progress as voters were becoming aware of our positions, which eventually led to a change in voting intentions.

LANGUAGE AND COMMUNICATION

Although pictures and graphics are important, language is the main means of political communication – posing special problems in countries such as Canada, where more than one language is spoken. The problem would be relatively easy to solve if the issue were simply one of translation. To the extent it could be afforded, the campaign would hire people to translate ads, pamphlets, signs, and other campaign materials into whatever languages were thought necessary to supplement English.

That is essentially what the federal Conservatives did in 2004, when they were faced with running a national campaign only two months after Stephen Harper won the leadership of the newly constituted Conservative Party of Canada. As I describe in my book *Harper's Team*, Harper's campaigners at that time, especially at the senior level, consisted almost entirely of employees and contractors from English Canada. All campaign materials, from the platform through the tour script to advertising and signage, were developed in English. We then had them translated into French because we knew we had to campaign in Quebec. Partway through the campaign, we also started getting requests from British Columbia ridings for materials in Mandarin, Cantonese, and Punjabi, to which we responded as best we could in the little time available.

Translation into the languages of immigrant groups is not problematic as long as you have confidence in the translators. Within these groups, older members and some recent arrivals may face language barriers, but they are basically participating in the same system and considering the same issues as other Canadians. Giving them a pamphlet in Korean or Tamil is a convenience to help them participate more effectively, but it does not mean they constitute another political culture.

The situation is quite different, however, in Quebec, where the French language is spoken by millions of people in dense geographical contiguity. Francophones in Quebec do have a different political culture; they have different values from other Canadians and place importance on different issues. Indeed, the whole political configuration was different in 2004, because the BQ was the Conservatives' main opponent in Quebec rather than the Liberals, who were the Conservatives' main opponent in all the other provinces. Thus, Conservative ads which pilloried Liberal fiscal irresponsibility worked reasonably well in English; but the French translations, if they had any effect, probably drove voters to the BQ, because in Quebec that party was, for most voters, the best way to defeat the Liberal candidate in their riding. The 2004 Conservative campaign was only superficially bilingual, and it's not surprising that the party did not win any seats in Quebec that year.

The moral of the story is that campaigning in more than one language is not just a matter of translation. *You have to develop an indigenous campaign in that language.* To do so means having an entire team – candidates, strategists, writers, pollsters, and advertisers – operating in that language and familiar with the cultural milieu. The Conservatives did much better in 2005–06, when they put such a team together. Specific issues with resonance in Quebec were selected for emphasis, even to extent of having a distinct Quebec platform. Quebec advertising was designed to focus on the BQ, which of course had no relevance in other provinces.[14] The result of having an indigenous campaign was victory in ten ridings in Quebec in 2006, as compared to none in 2004.

But there's still another complication. Although French and English in Canada represent two political cultures with different values, issues, and personalities, they are not "watertight compartments." National media companies operate in both languages, so news travels across the linguistic divide, sometimes upsetting the most carefully crafted platform. In the 2008 election, the Conservatives hoped to expand the Quebec beachhead they had built in 2006. They seemed to be on their way, polling about 30 per cent of the vote in the early stages of the campaign, when they blindsided themselves with the notorious "culture cuts." These small reductions in expenditure to certain cultural programs played well outside of Quebec but not in *la belle province.* The BQ jumped on the issue, and Conservative support went into a sharp slide, leading the party to win only ten seats instead of the hoped-for twenty or thirty. The Conservatives' Quebec campaign was fully indigenized, but it was undone by external developments in their English-language campaign.[15]

The bilingual challenge in Canadian campaigning is not so much a problem to be solved as an issue to be managed. A party that hopes to govern will have to put on a full-scale campaign in Quebec as well as across Canada, and the Quebec campaign has to be indigenized to have any chance of success. Yet one cannot prevent repercussions across the divide. The NDP will have to live with this in the 2015 campaign, now that they have more seats in Quebec than in all the other provinces put together. The NDP has taken several positions that are very popular among francophones in Quebec, most notably insistence on 50 per cent+1 as the decision threshold in a referendum on sovereignty, but those positions are toxic elsewhere. There is no good English translation for that stance! In the last analysis, language is vital for political communication, but politics is even more important.

PART II

The Changing Reality
of Campaigning

5

The Technology of Persuasion

In the most basic sense, political campaigning is always the same. It always involves the use of persuasion to build a group of supporters in pursuit of some specific objective, such as electing a candidate to office, getting control of the legislative assembly, or passing a law by means of a referendum. Persuasion through rhetoric is a constant factor, but how persuasion is carried out depends crucially on the means of transportation and communication available at the time. The general rule seems to be that new means of transportation gradually replace former ones, whereas new means of communication are added onto, but don't replace, the older ones. Over time, transportation has become more efficient, allowing candidates, and especially leaders, to appear before voters over ever-widening geographical distances. Communication as well has become more efficient, allowing candidates to address larger audiences, but it is also more complex, requiring candidates to reach voters through multiple channels. Starting in the late eighteenth century, when democratic procedures began to emerge, let us look first at transportation, then communication.

BEING THERE

By the late eighteenth century, officials were being elected to office in Great Britain, Canada, the United States, and France. There were no party leaders in the modern sense of the term, and even if there had been, it would have been out of the question for the leader to tour an entire province or nation, as now happens. Transportation at that time meant walking, riding on horseback or being pulled in a horse-drawn carriage, or travelling in a boat propelled by oars, animal power (canal barges), or sail. All were extremely slow by modern standards. Elections thus had to be local affairs, with candidates going by carriage to address public meetings in some of the major locations in their districts.

The harnessing of steam power began to revolutionize transportation, starting with steamboats in the 1810s and railways in the 1820s. Prominent party figures, especially leaders of the legislative caucuses, could now travel more widely, attending rallies in major cities outside their own constituencies. In vast countries such as Canada and the United States, however, it took a long time before truly national campaigns became possible. Steamboats could only reach a limited number of places, and it took decades to build a national network of rail lines. Wilfrid Laurier in 1917 was the first Canadian party leader to visit the western provinces by train during a national election.[1]

Rail dominated long-distance travel in North America from the mid-nineteenth to the mid-twentieth century, giving rise to the so-called whistle-stop campaign. Once almost every town was on a rail line, politicians could travel from town to town, giving a short speech at every stop. In the United States, Harry Truman's successful campaign in 1948 included a lot of whistle-stopping. Even today, presidential candidates will sometimes incorporate a train segment into their campaign plans, because it attracts a lot of media attention and furnishes colourful photo opportunities. But the railway has long since been replaced by the airplane as the mainstay of long-distance travel in political campaigning. In Canada, John Diefenbaker still depended on railway whistle-stopping as late as the 1965 election,[2] but from 1968 onwards the airplane has been the main form of long-distance travel, as in the United States.

The most important effect of these developments in transportation has been to help nationalize campaigns. A leader of a major Canadian party will usually visit all ten provinces and perhaps one or more of the three territories during a national campaign, in an effort to be seen and heard everywhere. The leader's national presence makes it virtually impossible for a local candidate to run on a platform that differs significantly from the national platform. If there are differences, the leader is sure to be asked about them when he touches down near the local candidate's riding. Hence the party will do everything it can to make sure that all candidates are "singing from the same song sheet."

Since 1968, Canadian national parties have become quite similar in the way they make the leader's tour the centerpiece of their national campaigns. There are minor differences from time to time and from party to party, but the leader's tour has become standardized. For the duration of the writ-period campaign, each party leases a jet as well as a number of buses. The jet is used to hop around the country, while the buses are used for local transportation, sometimes resembling the old whistle-stop campaign if they tour a stretch of rural countryside. "Message events" are used to roll out parts of the platform, while mass rallies galvanize local workers and voters.

From a communications point of view, the most interesting thing about the national leader's tour is that it carries the national media with it. Major print and electronic media buy seats on the tour so they can send reporters, columnists, and videographers to cover the party leader. Media people don't usually spend an entire campaign with one party; it is more common for them to travel several days, or perhaps a week, with one party, then shift to another. This pattern is less the case with provincial leaders' tours, where the media often drive out to meet the tour at its stopping places rather than travel with it.

Parties like the leader's tour because it gives them a degree of control over the media. Campaign personnel choose the destinations and the venues, and they know which reporters they'll be dealing with. They appoint a wagon master and baggage handlers to deal with reporters' physical needs, and spinners to work on their minds. The media, in turn, buy into the leader's tour because it guarantees them stories. A reporter travelling with the tour will be able to file at least one news story a day, and perhaps some updates and "thumb sucking" analytical pieces.

These are good reasons for the leader's tour to exist in its present form, but it must also be said that the whole thing is highly artificial –

the leader and an entourage of twenty-five to thirty staffers, flying around the country with twenty-five to thirty reporters and cameramen, each side trying to manipulate the other. The party, in its desire to control its news coverage, constructs highly artificial message events in which the leader reads a prepared speech, poses for photo ops, and answers a few questions. The "people" in attendance will be screened for reliability as well for being representative of the demographic groups the party is trying to reach that day – seniors if pensions are at issue, parents with young children for announcing a sports camp tax credit, new Canadians as a backdrop for immigration policy, and so on. Reporters are given a news release and backgrounder to guide them toward writing the kind of story the party would like to see.

It is all meant to give the media what (the party thinks) they need, yet the media naturally grow restive at so much force-feeding. In the past ten years, cell phones, email, the Internet, and social media have allowed journalists to break out of the cocoon the party tries to spin around them on the leader's tour. Rather than focusing on the leader and listening to what handlers are telling them, reporters on the tour now spend much of their time reading stories online and taking calls from other parties suggesting ways they can embarrass the leader and party with whom they are on tour. The more that parties try to induce coverage by controlling reporters' environment on tour, the more reporters try to find their own information and develop their own critical perspectives.

It is not surprising, therefore, that parties and media are both dissatisfied with the contemporary Canadian leader's tour. Campaign managers are beginning to think they are spending a lot of money to generate negative rather than positive stories, while the media complain about having to pay so much for canned information and contrived photo ops. Marjory LeBreton, who was part of Conservative leader's tours for almost fifty years, has speculated that maybe that institution, in the form that we know it, has reached the end of the road.

"I had the privilege of travelling with John Diefenbaker during the fall of 1965," she recalls. "The 1965 Diefenbaker national tour travelled the country almost exclusively by train – the last time in Canada that the train was used for this purpose. I mention this only to suggest that I may have travelled on the last national campaign tour to use designated charter aircraft to transport the leader, the accompanying staff and media to the various regions of the country."[3]

Electronic communications have now become so pervasive that the leader's physical presence around the country may no longer be necessary. "Technology can deliver a story/message from anywhere at any time – is there a more efficient and less costly way to report the news using all of the new age technologies?" asks LeBreton.[4] Given the tight discipline prevailing in Stephen Harper's entourage, LeBreton would probably not have made her statements unless Harper was dissatisfied with his 2011 leader's tour and open to new ideas.

Perhaps we are heading towards a new version of the "front-porch" campaigns conducted by James A. Garfield in 1880, Benjamin Harrison in 1888, William McKinley in 1896, and Warren Harding in 1920. In these campaigns, the candidate stayed at home, meeting voters and giving speeches on his own "front porch."[5] Warren Kinsella describes how Mark Hanna, McKinley's campaign manager in 1896, made it work:

Hanna sought, and received, the assistance of Republican railway moguls, obtaining passes for the curious to travel, free of charge, to William McKinley's front porch in Canton, Ohio. One million people made these "pilgrimages," as they were called, and McKinley made more than three hundred speeches from his front steps. Hanna meticulously orchestrated every pilgrimage – ensuring the media were present to record the encounters, asking Mrs. McKinley to serve lemonade to the crowds, and even carefully scrutinizing the remarks of those who were to introduce the Republican candidate so that the campaign's key themes (the gold standard, high tariffs, high wages, and prosperity) were emphasized.[6]

In the 2015 campaign, will we see Stephen Harper greeting voters in the back yard of his Calgary home, while his wife, Laureen, and their children, Ben and Rachel, serve lemonade to the crowd? Probably not. But many of the photo ops and message events on which all parties' leader's tours now depend could be staged as easily at home as on the road, and then everyone could go home and sleep in their own bed at night. It probably won't come to that, but the leader's tour as we now know it cries out for major revisions.

IN THE BEGINNING WAS THE WORD

Through the eighteenth and well into the nineteenth century, few countries held elections for public office; even in those that did, few people could vote, since the franchise was limited to adult male property owners and often restricted by race and religion. There was no secret ballot; voting took place by show of hands or some other mechanism. Travel was difficult. Given all these circumstance, political campaigning mainly took the form of candidates delivering speeches before live audiences gathered in a pub or on the village common. The speech was the main vehicle of *logos,* while the absence of the secret ballot meant that much persuasion took the form of bribery and intimidation.

Politicians' oratory held pride of place, right down to the rise of electronic media in the twentieth century. Politicians were accustomed to speak for hours at a time, both in Parliament and on the campaign trail. Crowds listening to these long campaign speeches could be enormous, counted in the thousands or even tens of thousands assembled in city squares or military drill halls. In the hard-fought campaign of 1911, Liberal leader Wilfrid Laurier spoke to an estimated 120,000 people in the province of Quebec alone.[7] Although the Liberals were defeated in that campaign, Laurier certainly lived up to the appellation "the silver-tongued Laurier" that he had earned by speaking on behalf of Louis Riel in the House of Commons in 1886.[8]

Print was also a factor in these early days. Newspapers had emerged in continental Europe in the seventeenth century and became part of life for educated people in the English-speaking world in the eighteenth. The same printers who published newspapers also produced posters, handbills, and pamphlets to advertise political meetings, and they also printed politicians' speeches and public letters for distribution to potential voters.

Over the course of the nineteenth century, representative government became more democratic in the modern sense. Many more people (all of them men until the enfranchisement of women in 1893 in New Zealand) received the right to vote as the property franchise was relaxed and finally abolished. As a result, political candidates had to reach larger audiences. When candidates had been elected by a few hundred people, they could address them all face to face, but that became harder and eventually impossible as numbers grew. Introduction of the secret ballot also made the electoral process less personal, by rendering bribery and intimidation less useful as political weapons. Threats and rewards lose their effectiveness if you can't know for sure how people will vote in the privacy of the ballot box.

Newspapers helped accommodate these new needs. The nineteenth century press was politicized in a way that we can hardly imagine today. Newspapers were generally owned by close supporters of politicians, often by politicians themselves. There was little attempt at objective reporting. Newspapers printed the speeches of politicians they supported, reported their doings, and carried editorials endorsing them. Today, newspapers may take sides on their editorial pages, but even the most partisan, such as the *National Post* and the *Toronto Star,* make an effort to report the news objectively. By contrast, objective reporting in the nineteenth century had to emerge out of the clash of partisan newspapers; it certainly could not be found within the pages of any single paper.

Newspapers were unchallenged as the dominant communications medium until the 1920s, when radio became commercially viable. Politicians quickly learned how to exploit the new medium. They learned to give speeches that could be interesting even if the viewer could not see the speaker, and to communicate in less bombastic ways, as in President Roosevelt's "Fireside Chats." Electronic media took another giant step forward when television became commercially available in the 1950s. Parties experimented with campaign ads in that decade, but TV really came into its own as a political medium in the 1960s, with the Nixon–Kennedy debates in 1960 and the first truly effective negative ad in 1964 – the Democrats' "Daisy" ad, implying that Barry Goldwater was a reckless nuclear warmonger. In Canada, Pierre Trudeau's 1968 campaign was a landmark. Trudeau was far more telegenic than Lester Pearson and John Diefenbaker, who had dominated politics in the decade before him.

Television is still recognized as the most powerful medium for reaching voters, but it is increasingly challenged by the Internet, which has made remarkable progress in the last twenty years. Voters now get political information from websites, blogs, and social media as well as newspapers, radio, and television. And, of course, the older media have converged with the Internet, so that anyone can now go online to read a newspaper, listen to radio, watch television, or find books and magazine articles about politics. Yet there is a relationship of symbiosis rather than replacement between the Internet and older media. The Internet furnishes a powerful new means of delivering content, but it has not driven older media out of business. Content that is professionally developed and edited for newspapers, radio, and television still dominates the Internet, at the same time as amateur outlets have elbowed their way in.

This pattern illustrates a general truth about communications technology that differentiates it from transportation. Railroads replaced horse-drawn carriages for long-distance travel in general, and political campaigning in particular, and now airplanes and buses have almost entirely replaced railroads for the same purposes, at least in North America. But no communications technology has fallen into complete obsolescence in the past three centuries. Political candidates continue to give speeches to live audiences, even as those speeches are also broadcast over radio and television and live-streamed on the Internet. Campaigns still print posters and billboards and distribute pamphlets, while candidates also have blogs, Facebook pages, and Twitter accounts. Campaigners still care about coverage in newspapers, even as they also worry about radio and television.

Technology has made transportation more efficient, but it has made communications more complex and therefore more expensive. Campaigns today must seek to deploy all channels of communication simultaneously and symbiotically. Consider advertising: A state-of-the-art campaign will prepare an ad for television, with a sound-track version that can also be used for radio. It will also place the ad on YouTube and place a hotlink to the YouTube version on Facebook and Twitter, requesting supporters to help the ad "go viral" by forwarding the link to their friends. The ad may also refer viewers to a dedicated website where they can get more information in the form of archived newspaper articles, TV clips, and book and magazine excerpts.

Or take the oldest form of political communication, the candidate's speech. The candidate will give that speech live to influence the people in the room, but even as he is speaking, his campaign team will be Tweeting about it to a wider audience. The campaign will also videotape it for posting on its website and YouTube, so that others can watch it or perhaps download it as a podcast. The campaign will distribute a press release based on the speech, and perhaps the text of the speech itself, to facilitate accurate reporting in print media. Beyond that, the speech will have been written with certain highlights that can easily be excerpted for playing on radio and television news. The ability to "give good clip" is essential if the candidate is going to reach out beyond the people in the room.

And don't forget the symbiosis with paid advertising. While the campaign records its candidates' speeches to get raw material for advertising, other candidates will do the same for opposition research. It is now very simple for a campaign to send its workers equipped with cell phones to other parties' rallies to record speeches and find segments that can be used in attack ads. And all the ads, both positive and negative, may be run in paid rotation on TV and radio, posted on websites, and distributed electronically through email and social media.

Technological progress has had a paradoxical effect on political communications. New technologies have democratized the process, opening doors for new, usually much younger, amateur practitioners who have grown up with the new media and understand how to use them. But because the old media never seem to disappear, innovation always brings more complexity, and hence a need for more professionalism to manage all the symbiotic effects. As technology multiplies the number of communications channels, they all have to be deployed strategically to solidify the coalition that the campaign is seeking to build.

WINNING THROUGH INNOVATION

The American political consultant Dick Morris has written that being the first to make effective use of a new communications technology can deliver political victory: "Every decade or two – since at least the turn of the twentieth century – a new communications tool has emerged and revolutionized the relationship between voters and candidates. And the politician who was astute and adventurous enough to seize it has usually been able to ride it into power." But the key to that success, Morris emphasizes, "is not just to use the medium, but to understand it – to grasp its 'message,' and the inescapable impression the media conveys, almost regardless of what is actually being said."[9]

Morris is more on the Republican than the Democratic side (though he did work for Bill Clinton), but his three main examples are all Democratic presidents: Franklin Roosevelt, John F. Kennedy, and Lyndon Johnson. Roosevelt saw radio's potential for intimate communication, which he exploited in his "Fireside Chats" with American voters. Kennedy won the 1960 presidential debates with Richard Nixon because he understood the visual requirements better than Nixon, who tended to think of TV as "radio with pictures." In fact, those who listened to the debates on radio thought that Nixon had won, but TV viewers were more impressed by Kennedy's appearance and demeanour. Lyndon Johnson, far from telegenic himself, grasped the potential of TV for negative advertising and demolished Barry Goldwater with the famous "Daisy" ad.

Canadian parallels exist. In 1935, William Aberhart's exploitation of radio made an important contribution to the sweeping victory of his Social Credit League in the Alberta provincial election. Aberhart had previously learned to use the new medium to extend his reach as an evangelical preacher. He not only gave sermons on the radio but presented interesting material such as radio plays. His classic "Branding Irons of the Antichrist," starring himself and Ernest Manning, deserves to be better known.[10] He also used radio to bring people into the Calgary Prophetic Bible Institute's religious education program, which he ran through the mails – the equivalent of driving listeners to a website, in today's terms. When he embraced

Social Credit in the depths of the Great Depression, Aberhart continued his pioneering use of radio. He presented radio plays such as the famous *Man from Mars* series, and he used radio to recruit members of his Social Credit discussion groups.

In 1968, Pierre Trudeau became the first national politician in Canada to really make television work for him. He was young and handsome, in a somewhat unconventional way. His wealth, bilingualism, education, world travel, and sense of style gave him an iconic presence on camera. He spoke coolly and laconically, in contrast to the bombastic rhetoric of John Diefenbaker, which had roused voters of earlier generations. Even without speaking, he could produce electrifying visual footage, as when he refused to leave the reviewers' balcony when a Montreal parade turned into a riot.[11] Trudeau was truly a new man for a new electronic age.

More recently, Barack Obama has become the canonical example of using new communications technology to win power. It takes an effort now to recall how far behind Hillary Clinton he was when he started. Clinton had seemingly overwhelming advantages in experience, reputation, connections, fundraising capacity, and the support of major Democratic players, starting with her husband. But, assisted by Facebook board member Marc Andreessen, the Obama campaign deployed Facebook, Twitter, YouTube, and many other portals to recruit donors, volunteers, and voters.[12] There was an "open source" feel to the early Obama campaign. Volunteers used social media to organize themselves into local work groups – organizing meetings, making phone calls, raising money, choosing delegates in those states with a caucus system, getting out the vote in those states with primaries. That fit perfectly with the Obama image of youth, change, and a vaguely messianic vision of populist transformation. Consider the slogans: "We are the ones we have been waiting for,"[13] "He is 'the one'" (said Oprah Winfrey, echoing the *Matrix* movies),[14] and "Yes, we can."[15]

The closest Canadian parallel thus far to Obama's success with social media is the victory of Naheed Nenshi in the 2010 Calgary mayoralty race.[16] Four months before the October vote, Nenshi was standing at about 1 per cent in the polls.[17] Hardly anyone gave him a chance against his more experienced and better-known opponents.

But like Obama, Nenshi used social media to raise money and create a volunteer support base, as well as popularize his knowledge of urban issues. Toward the end, once that base had been created, the Nenshi campaign had the resources to use the older tools of politics, such as door-knocking, television advertising, and phone banks.

It is significant that the Calgary mayoralty race, like most such races in Canada, was non-partisan. Nenshi was running as an individual, not a member of a party. Obama was also running as an individual when he sought the Democratic presidential nomination. Even as the Democratic candidate for president, he was an individual (actually, a two-person team, with vice-presidential candidate Joe Biden). Republicans and Independents could vote for Obama-Biden while also voting for Republican candidates for senator and congressman, if they wished.

The individualism of non-partisan municipal races and of the American separation of powers system is, I think, a better fit with "open source" social media than the rigid discipline of Canadian political parties. Canadian parties have, of course, adopted the Internet and social media. Parties and candidates have websites, blogs, Facebook pages, and Twitter accounts; they put their ads up on YouTube. But it almost all amounts to carefully edited top-down communication. Candidates state their positions, announce when and where they will be speaking, and encourage donors to give money and volunteer to join the campaign. Open-source communication – self-organization at the local level – simply doesn't fit well with the Canadian model of disciplined parties. Volunteers working and speaking independently would soon become an embarrassment to the party because they would speak in the vernacular rather than the scripted language of the official campaign. Opposition parties and the media would pounce on their "gaffes," and the campaign would have to disown them or bring them under control.

Yaroslav Baran concludes that social media have not had a transformative influence on federal politics in Canada.[18] To be sure, the new media have taken their place alongside all the old media in the arsenal of political communications. They have drastically speeded up the pace of communication, as Tweets have largely replaced formal press conferences. Sometimes an indiscreet Tweet or Facebook picture posting provides short-lived entertainment, but social media haven't changed Canadian campaigning in any fundamental way. Canadian campaigns remain highly disciplined and controlled from the centre. They are not any more open, democratic, or surprising because ads are posted on YouTube or candidates Tweet while they are travelling to their next rally.

If any Canadian political figure on the horizon will be able to make more creative use of social media, it should be Justin Trudeau. His youth makes him part of the demographic group most open to social media. He is handsome and has a famous name, and there is something charismatic about his personality that tends to draw people, even though he doesn't have much to say in conventional terms. Now that he is Liberal leader, it will be interesting to see whether his team can make social media work as well for him as it did for Obama. This could become the kind of game-changer that Dick Morris has written about, because no other current party leader has the right characteristics to take hold of social media.

Morris's hypothesis about winning power through exploitation of new communications technology hasn't yet come true in Canada with respect to social media, but there is a less obvious application in the interrelated complex of powerful personal computers, database software, high-speed printers, and predictive diallers. Together, these innovations, which go back to the late 1970s and early 1980s, facilitate voter contact through direct mail and telephone calling. Door-knocking can also be part of the mix if the results are fed into the same database. In modern campaign jargon, the whole complex is referred to as direct voter contact (DVC). The main applications of DVC are grassroots fundraising (harvesting small contributions from large numbers of donors) and voter identification coupled with get out the vote (GOTV) operations (identifying your supporters and encouraging them to vote).

These applications of information technology are certainly not new. Canadian parties have been using them since the 1980s. But (as I explain in more detail in chapter 6) the Conservative Party of Canada has worked out a more efficient integration of the various technologies to produce a grassroots fundraising system that, while small by American standards, is uniquely productive in the Canadian context. Ever since 2005, the Conservatives have been raising two to three times as much each year as their main rival, the Liberals, and indeed more than all the other parties put together.

They have used this financial advantage to fund a permanent campaign model whose most obvious and effective feature has been sustained negative advertising directed against the Liberal leader during the pre-writ period. They did this against Stéphane Dion starting in 2007 for the run-up to the 2008 election; against Michael Ignatieff starting in 2009 for the run-up to the 2011 election, and against Justin Trudeau, beginning on the day after he was chosen Liberal leader. The 2008 and 2011 elections were in a sense over before they started, because the Liberal leaders' polling numbers had been driven down to such depressed levels. If the Liberals had had the money to respond in kind, they might have neutralized the effect of the Conservative ads, but they did not. Hence it is reasonable to argue that the Conservative financial advantage, based on effective integration of database technologies, was decisive in propelling them towards majority government.

So Morris's hypothesis does apply to contemporary Canadian politics: the Conservatives have achieved supremacy by exploiting a new technology – except that in this case the technology was not very new. What the Conservatives achieved was more effective integration of several DVC approaches that were already decades old. Like other Canadian parties, the Conservatives have also been trying to tap the fundraising potential of the Internet and social media, but so far without any dramatic breakthroughs. Morris could be proved right again in the future if the Liberals under Justin Trudeau find a way to adapt the Internet and social media to the requirements of the Canadian disciplined-party system. This is the new frontier of Canadian politics waiting to be crossed.

6

The Importance of Money

Money isn't everything in campaigning. Campaigns endowed with more resources sometimes lose, as demonstrated by the failure of the Charlottetown Accord to receive ratification in the referendum of 1992. The pro-Accord campaign had the services of Conservative, Liberal, and NDP strategists, as well as ten times as much money as the ragtag forces opposing the Accord – mainly the Reform Party plus an ad hoc coalition of (mostly) Trudeauvian Liberals. Yet the Accord lost badly in the actual voting.

But in spite of such exceptional cases, money is both important and useful. No campaign manager would ever wish to have less rather than more money. So it's important to study the fiscal framework of modern Canadian elections, and the effect that it has had on campaign practices.

The modern era of Canadian political party financing began in 1974, when Parliament passed a series of amendments to the Canada Elections Act. Those reforms established spending limits on national and local election expenses, generous tax credits for political contributions, stronger disclosure provisions, and reimbursement for a portion of election spending by parties and candidates who met certain qualifications. For the first time, Canadian political parties became substantially supported by taxpayer funds, both directly (through campaign rebates) and indirectly (through tax credits to contributors).[1]

CHRÉTIEN'S 2003 REFORMS

In 2003, with little public consultation or input from opposition parties, the Liberal government introduced and Parliament approved Bill C-24, An Act to Amend the Canada Elections Act and the Income Tax Act (Political Financing). The new law radically altered the sources of income for political parties in Canada by

- banning corporate and union contributions to national political parties;
- limiting corporate and union contributions to candidates and local party associations to $1,000 a year;
- imposing limits on individual contributions ($5,000 year, adjusted for inflation);
- making the schedule of tax credits more generous in an effort to encourage individual giving; and
- increasing campaign rebates from 22.5 per cent to 50 per cent of national campaign expenditures (60 per cent for the transitional year 2004).[2]

The new law also introduced a generous system of publicly funded quarterly allowances to help replace the revenue lost from eliminating corporate, union, and high-end individual contributions. The annual value of the quarterly allowances paid directly to the national parties would equal the total number of votes received by a qualifying party in the previous election multiplied by $1.75, adjusted annually for inflation.[3]

Only two years after Bill C-24's changes took effect, the newly elected minority Conservative government made further changes by introducing the Accountability Act, which banned corporate or union contributions to all party entities and candidates and decreased the individual contribution limit to $1,000. It maintained the quarterly allowances, however, even though the Conservatives had opposed the allowance system when it was established.[4]

As table 6.1 shows, during the years from 2000 through 2003 before the passage of Bill C-24, the Liberal Party was by far the most successful among federal parties at raising money from corporations,

Table 6.1
Total contributions from corporations, associations, and trade unions (2007 dollars)[1]

	2000	2001	2002	2003	2000–03
Liberal	13,101,019.00	6,691,023.00	5,448,848.00	11,339,963.00	36,580,853.00
Canadian Alliance	7,686,049.00	873,989.00	1,121,519.00	1,530,311.00	11,211,868.00
PC	2,843,576.00	1,478,274.00	1,076,865.00	1,168,986.00	6,567,701.00
NDP	3,225,986.00	1,511,464.00	1,121,680.00	5,308,675.00	11,167,805.00
BQ	595,785.00	70,605.00	105,450.00	87,509.00	859,349.00
Green	0.00	1,075.00	1,600.00	63,300.00	65,975.00
Total	32,042,458.79	12,063,123.34	9,830,127.92	21,165,886.61	72,135,329.61

Source: Elections Canada.

1 Tom Flanagan and David Coletto, "Replacing Allowances for Canada's National Political Parties?" SPP Briefing Papers (University of Calgary), vol. 3, no. 1 (January 2010), 3. All conversions for inflation in this table were calculated using the Bank of Canada's inflation calculator (www.bankofcanada.ca/en/inflation_calc.htm).

trade unions, and associations, and thus was the most likely to suffer relative disadvantage from the effects of Bill C-24, even though the bill was introduced by a Liberal government.

Had individual contributions been limited to $5,000 in those years, table 6.2 shows that the Liberal Party would have lost about $640,000, or 3 per cent of its income from individual donors, while the Progressive Conservative Party would have lost about $490,000, or 4.2 per cent of its revenue from individual contributions. The Canadian Alliance, which raised considerably more money from individual contributions than did other parties, would have lost 2.1 per cent of its revenue from individual donors. Overall, these amounts are very small compared with what the parties lost under the other provisions of C-24, which deprived them of donations from corporations, unions, and other organizations.[5]

When we compare the amount parties would have lost over the last four years of the old system with the amount they received in quarterly allowances in the following four years, we see that no party was negatively affected, while some became significantly better off. Table 6.3 indicates that, between 2004 and 2007, Canada's five main parties received more than $114 million in allowances.[6] In other words, the quarterly allowances alone represented an increase of almost $40 million, or 54 per cent, in revenue for

Table 6.2
Amount of individual contributions lost if limit was $5,000 (2007 dollars)

	2000	2001	2002	2003	Total revenue lost with $5,000 limit (2000–03)	% Lost
Liberal	139,052.28	92,306.30	102,700.95	313,559.41	647,618.95	3.08%
Cdn. Alliance	564,508.11	12,329.62	27,280.29	18,352.78	622,470.79	2.10%
PC	221,981.87	108,131.75	101,882.98	17,430.06	490,518.32	4.21%
NDP	48,432.43	27,820.02	142,974.65	73,605.13	292,832.24	1.43%
BQ	480.73	–	–	–	480.73	0.02%
Green	0.00	–	–	17,986.66	17,986.66	3.62%
Total	974,455.42	240,587.69	374,838.87	440,934.04	2,071,907.69	2.40%

Source: Elections Canada

Table 6.3
Quarterly allowances paid to political parties, 2004–07 (2007 dollars)

	2004	2005	2006	2007	2004–07
Liberal	9,774,907.57	9,498,080.45	8,770,143.20	8,517,049.00	36,560,180.22
Conservative	8,461,918.38	7,662,540.97	9,604,289.21	10,218,123.00	35,946,871.57
NDP	3,083,774.59	4,055,184.73	4,717,196.22	4,923,795.00	16,779,950.54
BQ	2,923,325.05	3,203,395.85	3,018,856.63	2,953,218.00	12,098,795.54
Green	523,694.00	1,061,905.00	1,199,287.00	1,262,641.00	4,047,527.00
Total	24,767,619.60	25,481,107.01	27,309,772.26	27,874,826.00	114,447,874.14

Source: Elections Canada

the parties, compared with what they had raised from corporations, unions, and individual contributions over $5,000 in the preceding four years. According to Prime Minister Chrétien's policy adviser, Eddie Goldenberg, Bill C-24 was supposed to be more or less revenue neutral, leaving parties about as well off afterward as they had been before the new law was passed.[7] Obviously, however, the bill's authors overshot the mark in the course of the legislative process.

The relative impact of the quarterly allowances on each party was different, but no party was made worse off in absolute terms as a result of the new legislation. A comparison of the figures in the last column of Tables 6.1 and 6.3 shows that, between 2004 and 2007, the Liberal Party received almost exactly the same amount as it had raised from corporations, unions, and individual contributions in excess of $5,000 in the previous four years (in inflation-adjusted dollars), and so profited very little from the legislative changes. On the other hand, the Bloc Québécois profited greatly: over the four years from 2000 through 2003, the BQ raised less than $1 million from corporations or unions, but in the following four years received more than $12 million in quarterly allowances. This outcome incited vociferous criticism of the program from Canadians who believe that public money should not help support a party dedicated to an independent Quebec.[8]

Be that as it may, the allowance system demonstrably channelled much more money – about 50 per cent more – to Canada's main federal political parties than the parties had to forgo by giving up corporate, union, and high-end personal contributions. Parties had been able to get along with considerably less money prior to 2004. After C-24 took effect, no party was worse off, and most were significantly better off.

REIMBURSEMENT

Another feature of Bill C-24 that substantially increased revenues to political parties was the increase in reimbursement for national campaign expenses from 22.5 per cent to 50 per cent (60 per cent as a transitional measure in the 2004 election year). This meant that a party could pay for its national campaign with 50-cent dollars.

And the amounts of money involved were substantial: the campaign spending limit in 2004 was about $18 million and was increased in every election after that until it surpassed $21 million in 2011. The Conservatives, to take an example, thus received about $40 million (in 2011) dollars for these four elections over an eight-year period. This sum amounted to about half the money the Conservatives received in quarterly allowances over the same period. The calculation would be different for each party, but the effect was the same: a very considerable increase in disposable income on top of the effect of the quarterly allowances. Once again, C-24 poured a lot more money into the system.

It is not surprising, therefore, that Canada had four federal elections in eight years. Ever since the passage of C-24, parties have not had to worry about amassing a war chest to fight elections. As long as their financial status was sound enough to secure a line of credit, they could borrow enough to pay for the national campaign, knowing that they would get half of that back through the rebate and that the quarterly allowances would soon take care of campaign debts. The rebates and subsidies, working in tandem, played a major role in launching Canada into the period of "permanent campaign" described in the next chapter. Minority government by itself would not have led to four elections in eight years if the parties had not been able to afford so much campaigning. They did it "because they could."

PARTY FUNDRAISING

Parties, of course, continued fundraising after C-24. However, they could no longer ask corporations and unions for donations, and they could not take more than $5,000 a year from individuals for the national party (reduced to $1,000 a year after 2006). The new game, in other words, was grassroots fundraising, and the Conservatives were much better at it than the other parties. Table 6.4 shows fundraising totals for the national parties for the years from 2004 through 2012, the last year for which complete Elections Canada data are available.

After 2004, the Conservatives raised more money in most years from individual contributions than did all the other parties put

Table 6. 4
Political party contributions, 2004–12 ($ millions, not adjusted for inflation)*

	Cons.	Lib.	NDP	BQ	Green
2004	10.91	4.72	5.19	.86	.35
2005	17.85	8.34	5.12	.73	.41
2006	18.64	9.06	3.97	.53	.83
2007	16.98	4.47	3.96	.43	.97
2008	21.18	5.81	5.41	.71	1.62
2009	17.70	9.06	4.01	.62	1.12
2010	17.42	6.40	4.36	.64	1.29
2011	22.74	10.11	7.43	.79	1.71
2012	17.25	8.37	7.68	.43	1.70

* Data for 2012 are the sum of the four quarterly returns; revised annual returns were
not available at the time of writing, except for the BQ.

together, and, except in 2009 and 2012, more than twice as much
as their chief rival, the Liberals. No wonder the Conservatives were
the most eager participants in the period of "permanent campaign,"
particularly in the very expensive pre-writ advertising described in
the next chapter. They were rolling in money.

Why were the Conservatives so much better than their rivals at
grassroots fundraising? The short answer is that necessity is the
mother of invention. The Conservative Party of Canada was formed
by merging the Canadian Alliance (originally the Reform Party) with
the Progressive Conservatives. Reform, because of its populist politics and libertarian economics, had never attracted much corporate
support, and the corporations cut way back on the Progressive Conservatives when they ceased to be a serious contender to win power
after 1993. By the time of the 2003 merger, therefore, both parties
had been surviving for ten years or more largely on grassroots fundraising and had become quite good at it. After the merger, synergy,
plus some further innovations, made them even better. Let's take a
closer look at the history.

The roots of the Conservative success story go back to the electoral
reforms of 1974, which introduced tax credits for federal political
contributions. John Laschinger, then executive director of the Progressive Conservative Party, moved quickly to capitalize on the new
legislation by developing a mass direct-mail program. He learned the

trade from an American direct-mail consultant, Bob Odell. Laschinger started prospecting, and by 1984, when the PCs came to power, they had 80,000 names in their donor database. This new financial capacity was at least part of the explanation for the PCs' success in winning the elections of 1979, 1984, and 1988.[9] Of course, in those days of virtually unregulated corporate donations, the PCs were also taking in large amounts of money from big business. After PC fundraising became a casualty of the 1993 electoral disaster, the party's national office retained control over its donor database. As corporate giving declined dramatically, direct mail had to keep the party going. Direct mail was not as productive as before, but the party continued to maintain a large database with extensive backlists.

The new Reform Party of Canada, most of whose supporters had previously voted for the Progressive Conservatives, expanded the Tory direct-mail program. From the beginning, the Reform Party's founders had the good sense to keep all membership and donor information in a single, centrally controlled database. Corporations showed little interest in supporting Reform, so it was the party's "sustainer letters" that kept it going. During the 1990s, Reform also started using a professional call centre to supplement direct mail with "phon-a-thons" (sic) – twice-yearly telephone blitzes. Although it tried hard to break into the game of corporate fundraising, Reform never had much success at that level, so it was not really well funded. However, its emphasis on membership renewal and modest donations built up a large and highly productive donor database.

When the Canadian Alliance was formed in 2000, it had one extraordinary year of corporate support, but that quickly faded when the new party failed to live up to expectations. For all practical purposes, then, Canadian Alliance fundraising was the same as Reform's – not much corporate giving but lots of direct mail and telephone solicitation. However, several things happened in 2000–03 that laid the groundwork for future growth and development.

First was the introduction of modern methods of voter identification. While some candidates developed databases of supporters, Reform and the Alliance had never had an effective system of voter identification at the national level. There had been an Alberta call centre in the 2000 election, but as a result of a nasty internal squabble, no legacy data were kept for the next election. But the first Harper leadership campaign (2001–02) emphasized voter ID. Volunteer call centres in Calgary and Ottawa used a stripped-down predictive-dialler system to call repeatedly through the entire Reform backlist, first to identify supporters, second to persuade leaners, and third to get out the vote. Parallel to this, direct mail was used with the same list for fundraising.[10] Later on, fusion of the two approaches would produce remarkable synergies.

In the fall of 2002, the Alliance decided to develop a new data-base that would include membership and donor data as well as voter ID data. The same software developers who had produced Track Right for the Ontario PCs developed a somewhat similar database for the Alliance – the Constituency Information Management System, known as CIMS. The Alliance had the same experience with this as everyone has with IT projects – delays, cost overruns, tech-ies on top rather than on tap, goal displacement, and mission creep. Harper, who was never very enthusiastic about it, used to call it "the Conservative Party's own gun registry." Fortunately he allowed development to proceed.

The other important thing that happened in these months was linking up with the Responsive Marketing Group (RMG), a Toronto-based calling company that had at various times done voter ID and/or fundraising for the federal PCs, the Ontario PCs, and other provincial conservative parties. After RMG president Michael Davis made a presentation in spring 2003 and was hired by the Alliance, fund-raising efforts started to grow in volume and sophistication.

The October 2003 announcement of the merger between the Canadian Alliance and the Progressive Conservatives led to the second Harper leadership campaign. The challenge of voter ID was greater than in the first Harper campaign, for merger of the Alliance and PC databases had produced a list of over 300,000 current and past members. The task was too big for volunteer call centres, so the Harper campaign engaged RMG to do it. Davis promised, and he was as good as his word, to make voter ID pay for itself. In the event, RMG raised half a million dollars for the leadership campaign by asking for contributions from those who identified themselves over the phone as Harper supporters. This was the first large-scale demonstration that voter ID and fundraising could be linked, though it was limited to a leadership race and additional steps would have to be taken before making the leap to the much larger arena of a national election.

The Conservative Party had a very comprehensive and expensive voter ID program for sixty-six targeted ridings as part of its 2004 campaign. The general model – not adhered to perfectly in all cases – was for a so-called "Blue" riding to contribute $20,000 of its own money, matched by $40,000 or more of national campaign money, to pay for intensive telephone voter ID and GOTV in the riding. Not only did the effort help win far more close races than the Alliance or PCs had ever been able to do but it left a legacy in CIMS of hundreds of thousands of identified supporters to be added to the names of hundreds of thousands of present and past party members. These large lists were supplemented by riding-level door-knocking data, which were also entered into CIMS. Adding all these sources together, by the end of the 2004 campaign CIMS held some degree of information – sometimes sketchy, sometimes quite complete – on almost a million and a half past and present Conservative supporters.

The stage was now set for Michael Davis's third big idea – a massive "reconfirmation" exercise. Beginning in the fall of 2004, RMG called through the supporter database, inviting non-members to join and make a donation. Again, enough people responded positively to pay for the whole project.

The Conservative Party has been following the same model ever since: spend heavily on Voter ID and GOTV in targeted ridings during election campaigns, combine that with door-knocking data and membership sales from nomination races, then fundraise from the list of identified voters using direct mail, email, and telephone solicitation. At this point CIMS must contain data on millions of Canadians who have exhibited some degree of support for the Conservative Party. With steady work, that can yield the more than 100,000 donors who fund the Conservative Party each year.

It is almost, but not quite, a perpetual motion machine. The reason it cannot sustain itself forever is that everything depends on the popularity of the leader and the party's message. As long as the party's leader and message are popular with the "grassroots" – in this case Conservative Party members and voters – the money will come in. As Senator Irving Gerstein, chairman of the Conservative Fund, likes to say, "Message equals Momentum equals Money." But if the grassroots lose confidence, the money can dry up overnight. In other words, mastering the mechanics of databases, direct mail, call centres, and the Internet is necessary but not sufficient for successful grassroots fundraising. But at least for now, Stephen Harper and his message of incremental conservative change are very popular among Conservative members and voters, and the system is working reliably.

The other point that needs to be emphasized is the high cost of the Conservative system. All that telephone contact and direct mail does not come cheap. In 2010, for example, the party spent $7.2 million to raise $17.4 million, so the net income from donations was only about $10 million.[11] That moderates, but does not contradict, the impression that the Conservatives have a huge fundraising lead over the other parties. Also, the telephone contact and direct mail, expensive though they are, have the side benefits of keeping the party in touch with supporters and continually updating its database, thus facilitating the Voter ID and GOTV efforts that are a key part of Conservative campaign doctrine.

Successful grassroots fundraising played a key role in bringing the Conservatives to majority government status. Because of the rebate and subsidy system, all parties were able to run fully funded national campaigns, but only the Conservatives had the money to pay for expensive pre-writ television advertising. As detailed in the next chapter, they spent millions before the 2008 and 2011 elections, driving voters' estimation of Liberal leaders Stéphane Dion and Michael Ignatieff so low that the Liberals were virtually out of contention before the writ was ever dropped. Conservative fundraising changed the model of federal campaigning, perhaps for a long time to come. Pre-writ advertising has always existed to some degree, but for the Conservatives it became the key to success.

THE HARPER REFORMS, 2011

When Parliament convened after the 2011 election, the new Conservative majority government announced that it would legislate an end to the quarterly allowances. The allowances would be continued through the 2011–12 fiscal year, after which they would be phased out in three steps, following the Conservatives' platform commitment. That means that parties will receive 75 per cent of the present amount in 2012–13, 50 per cent in 2013–14, 25 per cent in 2014–15, and nothing thereafter. Thus, between the 2011 election and the next election, currently expected for October 2015, each party will receive the full subsidy for one year, plus 150 per cent of its current annual subsidy over the following three years, as compared to 400 per cent if the fiscal regime had not been changed.

That sounds like a big cut, and it is. But it is also true that parties' financial requirements will be smaller, because there will not be another election for four years, whereas in the recent years of minority government, parties were paying for an election campaign every two years. Given this reduced spending requirement, the reduction in federal subsidies will not drive anyone into bankruptcy before the next election. The Liberals will have the toughest challenge – to start spending like a minor party. That won't be easy, after having been a contender for government since Confederation. Yet many other parties, including the NDP, the Canadian Alliance, and the Progressive Conservatives after 1993, have run balanced budgets in straitened circumstances. The Conservatives and NDP, with their much larger phase-out allowances, will easily pay off any 2011 debts and still be in good shape for 2015.

The 2015 election will be decisive for the future of the centre-left in Canada. Unless the Liberals, reinvigorated by Justin Trudeau's leadership, are able to resume their leading position in federal politics, the parties of the centre-left are likely to face serious financial problems. As they try to pay back campaign debts without corporate and union donations, or subsidies from the federal treasury, the Liberals, NDPs, and Greens will confront an unpleasant reality – there may not be enough financial room for three centre-left parties in Canada. The 2011 election showed there is not enough political space, as the NDP surge put a majority Conservative government in office by defeating the Liberals in Ontario. The 2015 election may show that there is not enough financial room, either.

If the Liberals under Justin Trudeau do not win in 2015, the centre-left parties will have to become more realistic about the Conservative nightmare they face – a well-funded, cohesive party of the centre-right, commanding about 40 per cent of the popular vote. In Canada's first-past-the-post electoral system, such a party wins every time against three underfunded, bickering opponents running against each other to determine who will become the official opposition. There may have to be a merger or an electoral coalition, or one or more of these parties may have to go out of business if the centre-left can ever hope to win again.

Maybe Harper has done the Liberals, NDP, and Greens a favour by cutting off their lolly. If he were as Machiavellian as his critics allege, he would have kept the allowances in place, thus encouraging the centre-left parties to remain separate. Ending the allowances is in the self-interest of these parties (or at least of their supporters) in the long term, because it will drive them to cooperate in order to compete with the Conservative juggernaut. The Conservatives should erect a monument to Jean Chrétien for his 2003 party-funding reforms, which took away the Liberals' longstanding advantage in corporate fundraising. The three parties of the centre-left may someday want to erect a monument to Stephen Harper for pushing them to harmonize their efforts.

It is, of course, also possible that the Liberals under Justin Trudeau will return to their former pre-eminence in both public support and fundraising. Trudeau had no trouble raising money in his leadership race, and the Liberals were looking very strong in the polls at the time of revising this book (late 2013). Perhaps the safest way to talk about the future is this: unless Trudeau succeeds in resurrecting the Liberals, the three parties of the centre-left will face a joint financial shortage after 2015.

OTHER OPTIONS?

Is there any chance that a government, whatever its political complexion, might open up new sources of party finance after the 2015 election? Three options would amount to restoring old but now prohibited options: corporate and union donations, high-end individual contributions, and government subsidies. A fourth option, occasionally discussed but never tried in Canada, would be a taxpayer check-off system.

Re-legalizing corporate and union contributions could, in fact, make a big difference, since these were the historical mainstay of Canadian party finance, but this is very unlikely to happen. "Corporate" is a bad word on the left, and "union" is a bad word on the right. Moreover, there is a segment of conservative/libertarian opinion that, following Milton Friedman, also opposes corporate donations because it means allowing corporate executives to make decisions with other people's money.[12] Given all these potential sources of opposition, restoration of corporate and union contributions seems improbable.

In contrast, the limit on individual contributions may well be raised at some point. The present limit of $1,200 ($1,000 adjusted for inflation) is not very much in today's world and could be raised to $2,000 or $2,500 without inflaming public opinion. But the new amount of money raised by increasing the donation limit would probably not be very great. One simulation suggested that the increase in revenue to all parties taken together caused by raising the limit to $5,400 would only be in the range of $2–3 million a year – not enough to make much of a difference to parties deprived of the much greater revenue from corporate and union donations as well as subsidies.[13]

The Conservatives are not about to reinstate the quarterly allowances, but it is possible that a government of the left might do so, whether it was Liberal, NDP, or some combination of the two. There would be some popular outcry, judging from the popular approval that greeted the Conservatives' abolition of the subsidies, but a government with a majority could probably ride out the storm. However, it would also have to control the Senate, whose already strong Conservative majority will be even stronger by 2015; moreover, a leftist government might fall or be replaced before it could reshape the Senate through the power of appointment. Hence I would not look for a quick return of the subsidies.

The leaves the possibility of going in another direction altogether, toward a taxpayer check-off system. In its platform for the 2004 general election, the Conservative Party of Canada, into which the Alliance and PCs had merged, promised to replace the party allowances with such a system: "We will eliminate the current per voter annual subsidy for federal political parties. Instead, we will include a check-off box on taxpayers' T1 forms that will allow Canadians to direct a nominal amount towards the registered political party of their choice. This choice will not affect taxpayers' refunds or amounts owing."[14] However, the 2005, 2008, and 2011 platforms were silent on this issue.

The best-known model for such a system is the taxpayer check-off system used in the United States as part of the public funding of presidential primary and election campaigns. Legislation of this type was first passed in 1966 but was suspended a year later. The current system dates from 1971, though the details have been revised a number of times.[15] In the current form of the American system, tax filers can tick a box to give $3 of their tax liability ($6 for a married couple filing a joint return) to the Presidential Election Campaign Fund. In reality, taxpayers make a decision about the use of public money; ticking the box does not increase their tax liability or reduce any refund. Nor do they make a decision about which candidate or party will receive the donation; all money is divided among presidential candidates according to formula.

The taxpayer check-off seemed viable for a while, but the proportion of taxpayers using the check-off has declined sharply in recent decades. After reaching a high of 28.7 per cent in 1980, it dropped to 7.3 per cent in 2006.[16] With about 134 personal income tax million returns filed in 2006,[17] the presidential check-off generated about $30 million in that year. Barack Obama opted out of public funding in 2008 because he could raise much more money privately, and neither Obama nor Mitt Romney participated in 2012. Congress may well abolish the taxpayer check-off as it grapples with mountainous deficits.[18]

But the failure of the taxpayer check-off to cope with the huge expenses of American presidential politics does not mean this system could not be useful in Canada. Canadian rules might be very different from those of the American model. A Canadian system to replace federal party allowances would have to authorize contributions to parties, not candidates; taxpayers would direct their donations to their chosen party, not to an anonymous fund. Also, a Canadian taxpayer check-off could start off with a higher contribution amount, say $5 or $10, or it could include a variable scale of contributions. Also, it could receive initial publicity as a major reform of the political system to put control over political parties in the hands of taxpayers. Because Canadian political parties, unlike American presidential candidates, are continuing long-term entities, they would probably develop programs to encourage their members and supporters to utilize the taxpayer check-off, thus bringing further encouragement to bear. Canadians might be more willing to participate once they realized that cancellation of the allowances meant it was up to them to decide how parties would be supported, and that ticking the box would not cost them anything out of their own pockets.

It is anyone's guess what a taxpayer check-off system redesigned to fit the Canadian party system might raise. My personal opinion is that it would be worth trying because the costs would be low and the system has several features that might be widely attractive across the political spectrum:

- Contributions would be the result of voters' individual choices, updated every year. They would not reflect the results of a previous election even after public opinion had shifted.
- The individual amounts would be so small that no one could shout "Plutocracy!"
- Parties would have incentives to encourage citizens to make use of the opportunity, thus leading them to maintain closer contact with their supporters.

Given the American experience, a taxpayer check-off system might be a useful initiative, but it would probably not generate enough revenue even to come close to replacing the $30 million a year previously provided by the subsidies. In short, it seems likely that Canadian political parties are going to have to learn to live on short rations, with cooperation or merger on the left being one logical reaction to the shortage of funds.

7

The Permanent Campaign

One of the most interesting developments in Canadian politics in recent years is the rise of the "permanent campaign," in which political parties seem at all times to be as much preoccupied with campaigning as with government and opposition. The most visible aspect of the permanent campaign is the growth of pre-writ advertising, pioneered by the federal Conservatives but also practised by the other parties to the extent that they can afford it. This chapter chronicles the growth of the permanent campaign, particularly of pre-writ advertising, which is its most expensive feature. The context is the minority governments that existed in Canada from 2004 to 2011, as well as the public funding regime introduced in 2004 (Bill C-24), which made much more money available to political parties. Permanent campaigning at the federal level was dialled back somewhat after the Conservatives won a majority government in 2011 and thereafter focused for two years on actually governing, but observers speculate that a shift toward campaign mode seems likely in fall of 2013.[1]

MINORITY GOVERNMENT AND THE PERMANENT CAMPAIGN

Canada has seen an extraordinary amount of campaigning since the beginning of this century, as shown in table 7.1. In fact, campaigning has been even more prevalent than the bare facts of the table indicate, for the minority governments elected in 2004 and afterwards were liable to be defeated at any time. Thus federal parties had to maintain non-stop election readiness from early 2004 onwards,

Table 7.1
Canadian national political campaigns, 2000–11

National Election Campaigns	
Date	Winner
2000	Liberals
2004	Liberals
2005–06	Conservatives
2008	Conservatives
2011	Conservatives

Leadership Campaigns	
2000 (Canadian Alliance)	Stockwell Day
2001–02 (Canadian Alliance)	Stephen Harper
2003 (NDP)	Jack Layton
2003 (Greens)	Jim Harris
2003 (Progressive Conservatives)	Peter MacKay
2003 (Liberals)	Paul Martin
2004 (Conservatives)	Stephen Harper
2004 (Greens)	Jim Harris
2006 (Greens)	Elizabeth May
2006 (Liberals)	Stéphane Dion
2009 (Liberals)	Michael Ignatieff*
2011 (Bloc Québécois)	Daniel Paillé
2012 (NDP)	Thomas Mulcair
2013 (Liberals)	

*Campaign simply ratified choice already made by Liberal caucus and party executive.

when Paul Martin became Liberal prime minister and indicated he would soon be asking for an election.

These years deeply affected Canadian government and political culture. After so many years of continuous campaigning, federal politicians became almost like child soldiers in a war-torn African country: all they knew how to do was to fire their AK-47s. In short, we were living in a period of "permanent campaign," to borrow the phrase first coined in the United States to describe the continuous interweaving of politics and government.[2] The permanent campaign goes far beyond pre-writ advertising to include many other organizational initiatives. I describe some of what the Conservatives did in this regard because I am most familiar with that party, but the implications are general: all parties are bound to imitate at least part of what the Conservatives have done.

Organizational Changes

Perhaps the most important development has been the creation of a permanent position of campaign manager reporting directly to the leader. The older pattern for Canadian parties, when elections happened only every four or five years, was to appoint a campaign committee a year or so before an election was expected. There might also be a separate committee or task force to prepare the platform, as Paul Martin and Chaviva Hošek did with the Liberal Red Book before the 1993 election.

In today's Conservative model, however, everything is centralized. There is no campaign committee. The platform is developed by the leader's policy advisers, who report directly to him. Other aspects of the campaign are prepared under the direction of the manager, who again reports directly to the leader rather than to a separate campaign committee. Fundraising is carried out by direct-mail and telemarketing contractors working with the national director and chairman of the Conservative Fund. Because there is no need to network with corporate and high-end individual donors, there is no semi-independent corps of well-connected fundraisers who might exert an influence on the structure of the campaign.

In this situation of always being prepared for political warfare, message discipline is naturally carried to great lengths. Loose lips sink political ships. Conservative staffers and operatives almost never talk to the press and risk loss of employment if they do. MPs religiously follow official talking points. Even (maybe I should say especially) ministers are carefully controlled through the PMO.

Policy development within the party also had to take second place. The 2005 Montreal convention was all about policy, because it was necessary to have a policy manual for electoral purposes, to deflect opponents' charges that Harper was pursuing a "hidden agenda." But after that, national conventions were repeatedly postponed because of electoral exigencies. When one was finally held three and a half years later in Winnipeg, there was some discussion of policy, to be sure, but it was a secondary feature of the event. Election readiness has largely replaced policy development as the party emphasizes fundraising, campaign training, and building grassroots teams for signage, door-knocking, and phone-banking.

Just as chronic warfare produces a garrison state, permanent campaigning has caused the Conservative Party to merge with the campaign team, producing a garrison party. The party is today, for all intents and purposes, a campaign organization focused on being ready for and winning the next election, whenever it may come.

The Fear Factory

Early in 2007 the Conservatives rented state-of-the-art premises in Ottawa for a "war room," the command and control centre of a national campaign. Dubbed the "fear factory" by a Liberal wag,[3] the war room was quickly leased, furnished, and wired. It included a TV studio so the party could stage its own press conferences. It was kept continually available until the 2008 election was finally called on 7 September. The cost would have been considerable – hundreds of thousands of dollars a year – but it was a great convenience for a campaign manager not to have to scramble for space and furnishings on short notice. As a signal to the other parties that they were in for a fight if they toppled the government, the normally secretive Conservatives granted the media a tour so they could write stories about it.[4] However, the lease on the premises was allowed to expire in late 2012, amid a dispute about back rent.[5]

A Jet for the Leader's Tour

The centerpiece of a campaign for a national party is the so-called leader's tour, in which the leader travels around Canada by a combination of airplane and bus, making announcements and staging events. Having a jet to move the leader, staff, and accompanying media representatives is essential, because Canada is such a big country. The Conservatives, having leased their campaign jet from Air Canada in previous elections, quickly made a deal with Air Canada after the 2006 election to get a jet whenever they might need it. Such deals are expensive – again, hundreds of thousands of dollars a year – but they are necessary for getting a jet on short notice.

Having a campaign airplane in place allowed the Conservatives to play brinksmanship games in Parliament without worrying about being defeated.

In contrast, the Liberals, whether from organizational problems or financial difficulties, did not lock up a jet until the last minute, when Air Inuit leased them a twenty-nine-year-old Boeing 737. (The Conservatives claimed it was 20 per cent less fuel-efficient than their own Airbus A-319.) Moreover, the Liberal jet was not ready until Day 4 of the 2008 campaign,[6] and then suffered a mechanical breakdown that grounded it in Montreal on 16 September.[7] The Liberals may have saved money by not leasing a jet in advance, but they paid a high price in terms of bad publicity directly contrary to the environmental theme of their Green Shift campaign platform.

Direct Voter Contact (DVC)

Conservative campaign doctrine emphasizes voter ID and GOTV (get out the vote) programs in targeted swing ridings. In simplest terms, this strategy means contacting voters by mail, telephone, or doorknocking; asking them about their political concerns and preferences; and recontacting identified supporters at the close of the campaign to encourage them to vote.[8] Ongoing grassroots fundraising helps build a base for writ-period DVC because it builds supporter lists and keeps contact information up to date. Voter ID between elections is now a standard part of Conservative campaign doctrine.

By-Elections

An effective DVC program is particularly useful in by-elections because turnout is always low. Using DVC to get supporters to the polls while others are staying home can lead to striking upset victories. As the appendix discusses at greater length, Conservative by-election successes played a significant role in the party's progress from official opposition in 2004 to majority government in 2011. Each of the five times that the Conservatives took a seat away from another party in these years helped to build momentum and position the party for improvements in the next general election. The

Conservatives did this in four by-elections in the pre-writ period before the 2008 election, winning two new ridings and coming close in two others where they had been given little chance.

They pulled off another coup in the by-elections of 9 November 2009, winning back Bill Casey's Nova Scotia riding and taking a seat away from the Bloc Québécois in rural Quebec. The latter achievement touched off another round of stories about how the Conservatives were back in the game in Quebec and might be able to win enough seats there in the next election to finally earn a majority government. Media commentators, however, have little understanding of how campaigns are actually conducted, and hence tend to over-interpret by-election results as representing broader trends in public opinion. In fact, the Conservative by-election victory in Quebec was due mainly to its aggressive DVC campaign in a race where the BQ no longer had the advantage of incumbency. With a turnout of only 36 per cent, it was possible to win by mobilizing existing supporters rather than winning over a lot of new voters.

The Conservatives struck again in November 2010 when they narrowly elected Julian Fantino in the suburban Toronto riding of Vaughan.[9] Their close victory in this heavily Italian and historically Liberal riding was the harbinger of the Conservatives' success with Toronto-area ethnic voters in the 2011 general election, which provided the additional seats necessary for a majority government. Voter ID and GOTV helped eke out the by-election victory, showing again the importance of keeping the campaign machine tuned up and ready to go.

The point is that every opportunity counts in a period of minority government. The party that keeps its campaign weapons sharp at all times and uses them strategically when the occasion arises is more likely to build an advantage over its opponents than a party that sleepwalks its way through the pre-writ period.

Harper's team never rests. A campaign manager reporting directly to the Conservative leader, not to a committee, is always on the job. Voter ID linked to fundraising goes on 363 days a year (Christmas and Easter excepted). With the cash flow from such aggressive fundraising, the party can afford to spend millions on advertising, even years in advance of the writ, and to train candidates and workers,

especially in the use of the potent DVC program and the CIMS database. Activities funded by the House of Commons can also be channelled to political purposes – travel to targeted ridings and ethnic
communities, mail-outs with a response coupon for voter ID, public
opinion research to find policies that will resonate with target demographic groups. All parties do some of these things some of the time,
but the Conservatives are unique in the scale on which they operate and the degree to which everything is coordinated. They have
produced a campaign equivalent of Colin Powell's doctrine of "overwhelming force," applying all possible resources to the battleground
ridings where the election will be won or lost.

THE GROWTH OF PRE-WRIT ADVERTISING

Advertising is an essential part of any political campaign run by a
major Canadian political party, and it is usually the most expensive. Historically, most of the media buy for advertising was concentrated during the writ period, lasting from five to eight weeks.
Pre-writ advertising also took place, but it was usually confined to
the weeks just before the election was expected to be called, because
conventional wisdom held that advertising carried out too far ahead
of the actual campaign would be forgotten and lose its impact. Thus,
shortly before the 2004 election campaign began, the Liberals put
up an attack website, entitled "Stephen Harper Said," and ran ten
days of TV and newspaper ads to steer voters to the Internet site. The
Conservatives responded as quickly as they could with their own
website about Paul Martin.[10]

We can take this exchange as the beginning of the modern period of pre-writ advertising. Since 2004, however, it has grown enor-
mously in size and scope. The Conservatives have led the way, but
other parties have tried to follow suit, albeit within the constraints
of their more limited financial means.

The first Conservative experiment in pre-writ advertising came in
early 2005, when the party ran print ads in ethnic and rural newspapers opposing gay marriage. The campaign lasted several weeks
and cost about $300,000. The goal was to use the debate over
gay marriage, then in full swing in Parliament, to attract socially

conservative ethnic voters, Roman Catholics, and rural residents in ridings the Conservatives hoped to win in the next election.[11] The Conservatives made considerable progress with all these targeted groups. One cannot ascribe causation to the ads alone, but they were the start of a long-term recruiting process.

The second Conservative experiment with pre-writ ads came at the end of summer 2005, when the party spent about $1 million to run a suite of television ads featuring the leader and other caucus members talking about Conservative policy. These ads had been produced in the spring of 2005 when the Conservatives were trying to trigger an election by defeating Paul Martin's Liberal government in the House of Commons. After spending $.5 million on creating and producing the ads, the party didn't want to waste its investment and so ran the ads in the late summer.[12] It was more a display of determination and financial muscle designed to shore up the base than it was a serious attempt to attract voters; indeed, at that time, no one had any idea that Paul Martin's government would be defeated in November 2005.

Conservative pre-writ advertising increased in scale and became demonstrably more effective with several waves directed against Stéphane Dion, starting almost as soon as he became Liberal leader in December 2006 and continuing right up to the eve of the 2008 election. On 28 January 2007, the Conservatives rolled out three ads ridiculing Dion and paid for them to run on Canadian TV networks when they were broadcasting the Super Bowl. The most effective of the three ads, entitled "What Kind of Leader Is Stéphane Dion?" used footage from the Liberal leadership candidate debates. It showed Michael Ignatieff at his most professorial, saying, "Stéphane, we didn't get it done" (referring to the Liberals' commitment to cut greenhouse gas emissions under the Kyoto Protocol), and Dion replying in high-pitched, heavily accented English, "This is unfair! You don't know what you speak about. Do you think it's easy to make priorities?"[13] Just by letting the Liberals speak, the ad brilliantly showcased the divisions within the party as well as Dion's prickly personality and difficulty in communicating in English.

The ads received a lot of free publicity and repetition in the news media precisely because it was so unusual for a party to purchase paid advertising outside the campaign period. Indeed, amplification in the news media may have had more impact than the paid media buy, as the notion that Dion was "not a leader" worked its way into the standard narrative, becoming a fixture in stories about Dion and the Liberals. Although most people, when asked by pollsters, denied that the ads would influence their vote, they, and the news narrative they helped create, almost certainly contributed to the dismal leadership rankings that Dion quickly started to gather in polls.[14] By early April 2007, only 17 per cent of respondents in a Nanos poll viewed Dion as the best leader, compared to 42 per cent who picked Stephen Harper.[15]

On 29 May 2007, the Conservatives launched another flurry of radio and TV ads targeted at Dion, this time over the Liberal-dominated Senate's holdup of the government's bill to limit senatorial terms to eight years. The theme was "Stéphane Dion is (once again) not a leader."[16] These ads could hardly have depressed Dion's leadership numbers lower than they already were, but they may have helped keep them low.

The third cycle of Conservative ads was a pre-emptive strike against Stéphane Dion's Green Shift, which he was planning to unveil in June 2008. The Tories beat him to the punch with radio and TV ads labelling it "Dion's tax trick" and "Dion's tax on everything."[17] Running all summer, mostly on radio in battleground ridings, the ads contributed to the Green Shift's loss of popularity. When it was unveiled in June, the platform had been supported by a majority of respondents in an Ipsos-Reid poll. When the writ was dropped in September 2008, a majority opposed it.[18]

Ten days before the writ was dropped, the Conservatives launched a new series of six positive ads about Stephen Harper. Apparently designed to rub the sharp edges off the prime minister's personality, they showed him dressed in a blue sweater, talking about sentimental topics such as his family, immigrants, and veterans.[19] The background music was somewhat schmaltzy, but the ads fitted the Conservative campaign strategy of portraying Harper as the safe choice and Dion as risky. They may have contributed to the surge in polling numbers with which the Conservative campaign began; five polls released between 7 and 10 September 2008 showed an average

Conservative lead over the Liberals of 12.8 percentage points.[20] A Harris-Decima poll taken during the first week of the campaign showed that far more people had seen Conservative ads than had seen those of the other parties, a result that certainly owed something to the jump that the Conservatives got on the other parties through their pre-writ campaign.[21]

Conservatives resorted to advertising again in December 2008 to attack the proposal for a Liberal-NDP coalition. One radio spot ran as follows:

> In the last election, Stéphane Dion gave his word. He said his Liberals would never form a coalition with the NDP.
> We cannot have a coalition with a party that has a platform that would be damaging for the economy. Period.
> But now he's cut a deal with the NDP. And he's working with the separatists to make it happen. He even thinks he can take power without asking you, the voter. This is Canada. Power must be earned, not taken.[22]

That the coalition proved to be highly unpopular with voters outside Quebec was not due entirely, or even mainly, to these ads. However, they played their role as part of an all-out media onslaught by the Tories, using all the resources available to them, including speeches in Parliament and public statements by the prime minister. The ads gave the media one more thing to report within this overall game plan.

Shell-shocked by the success of Conservative advertising, a Liberal strategist predicted in 2007 that the Conservatives would again go negative as soon as the Liberals picked a new leader to replace Stéphane Dion: "Within minutes of the new leader winning in Vancouver, the Conservative party will have TV commercials on the air branding the new leader as elitist/weak/a socialist/left-handed/a Leafs fan/or some other equally silly label. The new leader will want to strike back but will be told there is no money for competing ads and that he/she needs to still raise $1-million to pay off the leadership debt."[23]

In fact, however, the Conservatives waited until June 2009 to unleash a barrage of ads against Michael Ignatieff. Their theme, supported by a dedicated website,[24] was "Just Visiting." According to the ads, Ignatieff's thirty-four-year absence showed that he did not really care about Canada. He had come back only to lead the Liberal Party and thus get a quick ticket to 24 Sussex Drive. He was "just in it for himself," in the words of one ad – it was all about Ignatieff's ambitious drive for power and not about the welfare of Canada's people.[25] The campaign was expensive, likely costing at least $4 million.[26]

The ads ran all summer without seeming to hurt Ignatieff, but the notion that he was "just visiting" was working its way into the narrative about him in the news. Then, Ignatieff announced at the beginning of September that he was going to trigger an election at the earliest opportunity, saying to a Liberal caucus meeting, "Mr Harper, your time is up."[27] The move backfired, because it seemed to confirm what the ads said, that Ignatieff cared only about his own advantage and would force an election that most Canadians did not want. At that point, Liberal polling numbers started to fall precipitously, until by October they were ten to fifteen points behind the Conservatives in all polls. In an early November Nanos poll, only 18 per cent of respondents thought that Ignatieff would make the best prime minister – numbers similar to those garnered by Stéphane Dion in spring 2007.[28] The fall was not due to the ads alone, but they had given voters a way to interpret Ignatieff's behaviour and thus helped grease the skids for the Liberals' slide.

Also in fall 2009, the Conservatives for the first time resorted to pre-writ advertising in an attempt to pass legislation. In order to build support for Manitoba MP Candice Hoeppner's private member's bill to abolish the long-gun registry, the party ran radio ads in rural ridings held by the Liberals and NDP. The ads encouraged listeners to call their MP and express support for Hoeppner's bill.[29] MPs always deny that they can be influenced by such tactics, but the bill passed second reading by a much larger margin than anyone anticipated, 164 to 137, as twelve NDP members, eight Liberals, and one independent supported it. The Conservatives repeated some of their advertising and campaign tactics when the bill came up for third reading, but this time the bill failed after Liberal leader Michael Ignatieff required all his caucus members to vote against it.[30] Advertising in support of bills can be useful, but it cannot work miracles if the numbers are just not there.

Finally, renewed pre-writ advertising seems to have been quite important to the Conservative election victory of 2011. In December 2010, Ignatieff announced that the Liberals would not support the Conservatives' next budget, expected for February or March 2011.[31] Whatever good reasons he may have had to make this statement, it gave the Conservatives lots of time to respond. Starting in early January 2011, they rolled out a new suite of anti-Ignatieff attack ads for television and played them in heavy rotation until the government fell in late March. The ads highlighted Ignatieff's supposed ambition for power and willingness to make a coalition with the NDP and BQ. The Liberals, without money to pay for a response, had to absorb this punishment for almost three months.[32] Their polling numbers, which had been not far from the Conservatives in December, fell precipitously once the ads began to work. By the time the writ was dropped, the Conservatives had built up a double-digit lead and Ignatieff's leadership evaluations were down in the same territory as Dion's had been in 2008.[33] The Conservatives had opened up such a big lead in the pre-writ period that they could then get away with playing it safe in a classic front-runner writ-period campaign.

Estimating the effect of political advertising is notoriously difficult because so many things are happening at the same time. But it is fair to say that every time the Conservatives ran a series of ads in the extended pre-writ period between 2005 and 2011, things moved in the desired direction: winning over the support of ethnic, Catholic, and rural voters; driving Stéphane Dion's leadership ratings down and keeping them down; making voters sceptical of the Green Shift; making them feel better about supporting Stephen Harper; encouraging them to dislike Dion's coalition with the NDP; driving down Michael Ignatieff's numbers after he became Liberal leader; helping pass Candice Hoeppner's long-gun registry bill on second (though not on third) reading; and softening up the Liberals in preparation for the 2011 election campaign.

Although no quantitative studies have been done on this point, I believe the ads may have worked their effect as much through news coverage as through the actual media buy. Political advertising often works that way. For example, the famous 1964 "Daisy" ad, in which Lyndon Johnson implied that Barry Goldwater was too reckless to be trusted with his finger on the nuclear trigger, played only once on network TV.[34] That single exposure set off a firestorm of discussion in the media and permanently sealed Goldwater's fate in the 1964 election. Similarly, though not so dramatically, the pre-writ Conservative ads were extensively discussed in the media, and their message worked its way into the day-to-day narrative of news coverage. I would propose as a hypothesis for future testing that the target of pre-writ advertising is as much the media, which can make ads affect public opinion by integrating their message into news coverage, as it is the voter. In this tableau, the size of the media buy may not be critical, although it has to be large enough to convince media observers that the ad campaign is real. The media won't spend much time discussing Internet ads because they understand that such ads can be produced by a teenager at home, but they will pay attention if they believe a party is investing serious resources in an ad campaign.

The success of Conservative pre-writ advertising has led other parties to compete in this realm. In January 2009, as soon as Ignatieff announced he would support the Conservative government's budget, the NDP took out radio ads to condemn him: "He's propping up Stephen Harper. Michael Ignatieff failed his first test as Liberal leader. Jack Layton is the only leader strong enough to stand up to Harper and get us through this economic crisis."[35]

For their part, the Liberals reportedly spent $2 million on TV ads in late summer 2009 to introduce Ignatieff's campaign slogan, "We Can Do Better."[36] The English-language ad, officially known as "Worldview" but widely derided as the "Enchanted Forest" or "Magic Forest," showed Ignatieff in a woodsy setting (actually a Toronto park) explaining how Canada should "think big" and "take on the world."[37] Released in anticipation of a fall election, the ads failed to stop the slide in the polls that the Liberals endured following Ignatieff's 1 September announcement that he would try to force an election as soon as possible.

The Liberals resorted to advertising again in January 2010, as part of their campaign against Harper's prorogation of Parliament. They posted three radio ads on their website entitled "Cover Up,"

"Present," and "Fermeture."[38] Consisting of thirty-second sound tracks plus simple visuals for the Internet, the ads argued that Harper had "shut down Parliament" because he had "something to hide" about the torture of Afghan detainees, climate change, and so on. The messaging and tone were similar in spirit to many past Liberal ads about Harper's alleged "hidden agenda."

When they released the ads on 10 January, the Liberals said they would run radio and print versions in the coming days, but it is unclear how large the media buy was, or indeed if there was any at all. I never heard the ads on radio or saw them in any newspaper. Be that as it may, the Liberals did spark some media commentary just by posting them on their website. The effect can't be measured directly, but Conservative polling numbers were in free fall throughout January 2010, until they had reached a virtual tie with the Liberals by the end of the month – quite a drop from the fifteen-point lead the Conservatives had enjoyed in November 2009.

After a Conservative majority government was elected in 2011, pre-writ advertising continued. The Conservatives released some ads against Bob Rae as interim Liberal leader and against Tom Mulcair after he won the NDP leadership race, but the effort was rather half-hearted. The party spent only $1.4 million on all forms of advertising in 2012.[39] The NDP, however, spent $1.9 million in 2012 trying to define Mulcair as their new leader.[40]

The Conservatives then went full-bore after Justin Trudeau in spring 2013. The day after Trudeau won the Liberal leadership, the Conservatives released three ads mocking him as an inexperienced lightweight, "just in over his head."[41] The ads appeared to be backed by a fairly heavy media buy. The Liberals then countered with a positive ad about Trudeau refusing to go negative;[42] and the NDP, fearful of being excluded from public attention, released their own positive ad showing Mulcair in a soft light.[43] It was not clear, however, how large the media buys were for any of these ads; expenditure numbers will not be released by Elections Canada until mid-2014. In any case, if one major party resorts to pre-writ advertising, the others will be hurt if they stand idly by.

Extensive pre-writ advertising is also becoming, if not universal, at least common in provincial politics. The NDP released their hilarious

"Christy Crunch" ad against Christy Clark as soon as she won the BC Liberal leadership race in early 2011. "Christy Crunch" was just repackaged "Campbell Crunch," according to the ad, except that it was "loaded with HST" and "artificial sweeteners," while offering zero health benefits.[44] Later that year, both Progressive Conservatives and Liberals ran pre-writ ad campaigns before the general election in Ontario. And in 2011–12, Wildrose ran three waves of ads against Alison Redford and the Progressive Conservatives before the writ was dropped on 26 March 2013.

HERE TO STAY?

The Canadian permanent campaign model, with its new emphasis on pre-writ advertising, was born of minority government, with public money serving as the midwife. Will it continue now that we have returned to the historical norm of majority government?

My tentative answer to that question is yes, though the pace will undoubtedly slow down in periods of majority government. The permanent campaign, including pre-writ advertising, has shown itself to be potent political weaponry, useful for attracting new support groups, passing legislation, questioning the opposition's policies, and undermining the image of the opposition leader – in short, for winning and holding onto power. It is a political arms race, in which competitors will have to adopt new generations of weaponry or fall irretrievably behind. As long as they can find the money to pay for it, parties will be forced to keep up in order to compete. Indeed, interim Liberal leader Bob Rae publicly vowed in July 2011 to compete with the Conservative permanent campaign. That would mean, he said, raising money to do pre-writ advertising if the Conservatives once again went after a new Liberal leader.[45]

The permanent campaign is also spreading to the provincial level, not only because it works but because seven provinces have adopted fixed election-date legislation. As opponents of such legislation always argued, it tends to encourage all parties to start campaigning before the writ is dropped. That certainly happened in Ontario in the summer of 2011 when the Progressive Conservatives and Liberals both started making policy announcements and running expensive ad campaigns building up to the election with a legislatively fixed date of 6 October 2011.

The federal jurisdiction also has fixed election-date legislation, introduced by the Harper government in 2006, but in practice it has been trumped by the exigencies of politics in a period of minority government. Harper asked for an early election in 2008 because, mistakenly, as it turned out, he thought the time was right to win a majority. Opposition parties forced another early election in 2011. Fixed election-date legislation clearly did not fulfill Peter Russell's hope that it might provide a legal framework to encourage cooperation between parties in a minority Parliament.[46] Now that majority government has returned to the federal level, a fixed election date will encourage getting an early start on the campaign, as it does at the provincial level. But of course that was already happening at the federal level as parties jockeyed for advantage in a minority Parliament.

Canadian federal parties have less money to play with since the quarterly allowances started to decline in fiscal 2012–13. But with their powerful grassroots fundraising machine, the Conservatives will certainly have plenty of money to spend on pre-writ advertising and in other ways get a head start on the election that will be called in October 2015 (assuming that Prime Minister Harper sticks to the timetable laid out in the fixed election-date legislation). To date, we have seen a lull in the Conservative permanent campaign, but we can expect a resumption leading up to October 2015. The other parties will want to compete as best they can, but their financial capacity cannot really be gauged at this time.

Over the long run, reducing the amount of public money flowing to political parties may reduce their permanent campaigning and pre-writ advertising. Another approach would be legislated spending limits for the pre-writ period, which at present is entirely unregulated. Ontario NDP leader Andrea Horwath called for such a limit in August 2011 as her two main competitors, the Liberals and Progressive Conservatives, launched expensive pre-writ campaigns.[47] Such limits, however, would arguably benefit the government in power, because it can manipulate government advertising and other forms of communication for its own advantage, while spending limits would prevent opposition parties from fighting back. Manitoba has tried to evade this dilemma by legislating an advertising limit of $250,000 in the year in which an election is called, in addition to what is spent in the writ period.[48] This limit prevents high levels of expenditure on advertising in the immediate run-up to the writ period, but leaves parties free to advertise in the years between elections. Such legislation might reduce the volume of pre-writ advertising from existing levels but would not remove it altogether.

It might also induce parties to start seeking third-party surrogates to do their pre-writ work for them, as commonly happens in the United States. The Swift Boat Veterans were able to do enormous damage to John Kerry in 2004 even though they were not officially part of the Republican campaign. On a smaller scale, organized labour in Canada has already used similar methods to assist the NDP, spending money both before and during the writ period to run "issue-based campaigns" that don't mention the NDP specifically but urge voters to support policies on which the NDP is running.[49]

In Ontario, organized labour has showed how it is possible to get around restrictive legislation, virtually hijacking the electoral process and becoming kingmaker of provincial governments.[50] In the 2011 Ontario provincial election, the law limited the Liberal and Progressive Conservatives parties to spending a little over $9 million during the writ period, of which about $5 million went to advertising. Three union entities – the Working Families Coalition, the Elementary Teachers Federation of Ontario, and the Ontario English Catholic Teachers Association – continued the major role in the electoral process that labour had also played in 2003 and 2007. Together the three spent more on advertising in the writ period than either of the main parties.[51] To use American terminology, organized labour turned itself into a Super PAC.

Individuals, corporations, and unions were legally limited to giving a maximum of $9,300 to Ontario political parties in 2011, whereas contributions to third-party entities were unlimited. The Elementary Teachers alone spent an astonishing $2.6 million on ads, almost three hundred times as much as they could have given to a party. And these numbers underestimate what the unions actually spent, because Ontario law requires reporting only during the writ and a short period before and after. The unions also spent heavily on advertising before the election was called, but since they didn't have to report such expenditures to Elections Ontario, we will never know the true extent of their electoral involvement.

This situation wouldn't matter very much if the unions had advertised for and against candidates of all parties, but in fact their activity was directed monolithically against the Progressive Conservatives and especially against PC leader Tim Hudak. The union entities ran mostly anti-PC negative ads, which of course conferred an advantage on the Liberals. Dalton McGuinty could take the high road, with positive ads showcasing his likable "Premier Dad" self. In effect, the union ads more than doubled the size of the Liberals' advertising budget, compared to what the PCs were legally allowed to spend.

For a time, it was a brilliant strategy for increasing the political power of organized labour, which, during the McGuinty years, led to bailouts of troubled industries, sweetheart contracts with public sector unions, favourable provisions in the labour code, and job-creation schemes. However, the result is a provincial deficit driven out of control, with Ontario slipping into the embarrassing category of a have-not, equalization-receiving province. It all came crashing down in 2012 when McGuinty imposed a wage freeze on teachers unions and then resigned as premier.

To limit such developments, some might want to extend Canada's present ban on third-party advertising during the writ period to cover the pre-writ period as well. Such regulatory creep, however, might be seen as posing a danger to freedom of speech. In sum, I suspect that the permanent campaign, including pre-writ advertising, is here to stay at some level, even though many observers profess not to like it. Regardless of likes and dislikes, legislative remedies seem politically difficult to enact and loaded with unintended consequences worse than the alleged evil they are supposed to ameliorate.

8

Going Negative

An election for public office entails a choice among competing candidates. It is, in a sense, an employment decision, and employers (in this case, the public) like to have as much information as they can get. Employers are not satisfied with job applicants telling them how wonderful they are; they also demand references to see if there is another side to the applicant's story. Obviously the parallel is not exact, because in the world of employment, candidates do not usually run public campaigns against each other. But the principle is clear: employers may seek both positive and negative information before deciding.

Campaigning has had its negative side as far back as we have any record. In 63 BCE, in the world's first known campaign manual, Cicero's brother is reputed to have offered this advice on attacking competitors: "Last of all, see that your whole campaign is full of show; that it is glorious and colourful, and pleasing to the people; that it has a fine appearance and dignity; furthermore, if it is by any means possible, see that your competitors are smeared with an evil reputation – which fits their characters – for crime, vice, or bribery."[1]

Negative campaigning is also coeval with the rise of democracy in modern times. A historian describes pamphlets distributed during the Adams-Jefferson presidential race of 1800 as containing "extravagant overstatement, heated defamation, polarizing excess, and threatening and divisive imagery. Their tone was unremittingly negative, harsh, and hostile, filled with fearful images. Their authors conjured monsters, the avaricious bank, the uncontrolled despot, and later the aggressive slavocracy and the rampaging abolitionist."[2]

Political conflict could be just as vicious in nineteenth-century Canada. Advertising as we now know it did not exist, but politicians' speeches were widely reprinted in partisan newspapers and pamphlets. They were the attack ads of the day. To cite only one famous example, when Liberal leader Wilfrid Laurier proposed free trade with the United States in the 1891 election campaign, John A. Macdonald accused him of "veiled treason which attempts by sordid means and mercenary proffers to lure our people from their allegiance."[3] In some ways, standards of public life have improved since then; no leader of a major party today would ever use the word "treason," veiled or otherwise, to describe an opponent's policy.

Negativity continues, however, even if the vocabulary is more veiled than in the nineteenth century. It memorably made the leap to the new medium of television advertising in the 1964 American presidential campaign. The famous "Daisy" ad showed a little girl pulling petals off a daisy as she counted them. Toward the end of the count, a military voice took over, and then there was a nuclear explosion, followed by president and Democratic candidate Lyndon Johnson repeating an approximate quote from the poet W.H. Auden, "These are the stakes! To make a world in which all of God's children can live, or to go into the dark. We must either love each other, or we must die." The ad never mentioned Republican presidential candidate Barry Goldwater, but viewers would have recalled his comment that the atom bomb was "just another weapon."[4] Although the ad was screened for only one evening, it received enormous media amplification and turned an already guaranteed Democratic victory into a rout.

Contemporary politics is filled with negativity, both in the writ period of the campaign and in the broader backdrop. Here are just a few examples from the end of the twentieth century; I will deal with the first decade of this century a little later in this chapter:

• In 1988, John Turner accused Brian Mulroney of betraying Canada with the Free Trade Agreement: "I happen to believe that you have sold us out."[5] The Liberals ran ads showing a hand erasing the 49th parallel on a map of North America.[6] The Conservatives responded by calling Turner a liar[7] and running a massive ad campaign whose most memorable line was that Turner was "out to save his job, not mine."[8]

- On 18 November 1991, Liberal MP Sheila Copps compared Reform leader Preston Manning to the Louisiana racist David Duke. Even Prime Minister Mulroney came to Manning's defence: "He is no such thing! He is just a political opponent."[9] But Copps received no rebuke from her leader, Jean Chrétien, and her slur on Manning reverberated for years as part of the Liberal attack on Manning and Reform.

- Late in the 1993 campaign, the Progressive Conservatives released a television ad showing a close-up of Jean Chrétien's face, while an off-screen voice said, "I personally would be very embarrassed if he were to become prime minister of Canada."[10] The PCs denied that they were trying to draw attention to Chrétien's partial facial paralysis, but the Liberals played it that way. Chrétien said, "They try to make fun of the way I look. God gave me a physical defect and I've accepted that since I was kid,"[11] while Liberal operatives contacted organizations of the handicapped, urging them to complain. In this instance, the Liberals came up with inspired tactics of negative ju-jitsu, using a not-very-effective Conservative ad to accuse their opponents of something that would have been truly reprehensible – attacking a handicapped man because of his handicap.

- In the fourth week of the 1997 campaign, the Reform Party released an ad that simultaneously attacked all major opponents. It showed head shots of Liberal leader Jean Chrétien, PC leader Jean Charest, BQ leader Gilles Duceppe, and former BQ leader Lucien Bouchard, each in a red circle with a slash through it. Referring back to the 1995 sovereignty referendum, the voice-over said that the constitution belonged to all Canadians, not just Quebec-based politicians. Chrétien accused Preston Manning of running "the most divisive campaign in Canadian history," Sheila Copps said he was taking Canada "down the path to war," and Charest called Manning a "bigot" appealing to "the worst in human nature." Although Reform's support went up when the ads were playing, Manning followed the original plan of pulling them after a week and switching to a more inspirational (but less effective) positive ad.[12]

- In the 2000 campaign, Joe Clark's Progressive Conservatives ran nothing but negative ads, one of which referred to a record album containing "Jean Chrétien's 101 Greatest Lies."[13] The Canadian Alliance campaign was relatively positive (and ineffective) due to Stockwell Day's "agenda of respect." But the Liberals didn't get the message. While Chrétien accused the Alliance of representing "the dark side of human nature" and Day of harbouring a "hidden agenda" to introduce two-tier health care, Liberal paid advertising reinforced the same points.[14] But the award for creative and funny negativity should go to Warren Kinsella for mocking Stockwell Day's Pentecostal religious beliefs on *Canada* AM. After Day's alleged creationism had been in the news, Kinsella pulled out a purple Barney dinosaur on camera, saying it was the only dinosaur that had ever coexisted with human beings. Then came the punch line: "*The Flintstones* was not a documentary."[15]

CONTROVERSY

Though negative messaging has always been a part of American politics, and negative TV advertising was common from 1964 onwards, it didn't really become a topic of controversy until the 1988 presidential election, when the Bush campaign deployed several highly effective ads against Democratic candidate Michael Dukakis. Their effect wasn't felt in Canada until the 1993 election, even though our own 1988 race was highly negative. Canada is usually somewhat behind the United States in picking up on trends in public discussion.

The most famous of the 1988 Bush ads, entitled "Revolving Door" but usually known as the "Willie Horton Ad," ran as follows:

Bush and Dukakis on crime. Bush supports the death penalty for first degree murderers. Dukakis not only opposes the death penalty, he allowed first degree murderers to have weekend passes from prison. One was Willie Horton, who murdered a boy in a robbery, stabbing him nineteen times. Despite a life sentence, Horton received ten weekend passes from prison. Horton fled, kidnapped a young couple, stabbing the man and repeatedly raping his girlfriend. Weekend prison passes. Dukakis on crime.[16]

The facts related in the ad were uncontested, though as usual there were debates about the broader context. But what really made "Revolving Door" controversial was that Willie Horton was black, the young people he brutalized while on furlough were white, and the ad showed Horton's picture.

Much of the criticism of "Revolving Door," as well as the other Bush ads, could be dismissed as the usual sour grapes from losers, until two academics, Stephen Ansolabehere and Shanto Iyengar, made a wider case against negative advertising, sometimes known as the "demobilization hypothesis." In their prize-winning book, *Going Negative,* they argued that negative advertising was turning people off politics, polarizing those who remained interested, and driving down turnout at elections:

> Attack advertisements resonate with the popular beliefs that government fails, that elected officials are out of touch and quite corrupt, that voting is a hollow act. The end result: lower turnout and lower trust in government, regardless of which party rules.
>
> The marginal voter – the Independent – feels the pinch of negative advertisements most sharply ... As a result negative campaigning divides the American electorate into a voting public of party loyalists and a nonvoting public of apathetics.[17]

Their line of argument was elegant. Candidates resort to negative advertising because it works, and their opponents have to fight back with other negative ads, because that is the only countermeasure ever demonstrated to have an effect. It is "a tragedy of the political commons," in which civility is destroyed.[18] One might call it "the back of the invisible hand." Pursuit of individual self-interest by politicians destroys the collective good of public support for political institutions. It is the kind of argument routinely made to justify government intervention to provide any public good – in this case, the well-being of the political system.

Lucidly written and compellingly argued, *Going Negative* was widely read and discussed. Its thesis that negative advertising depresses turnout has become conventional wisdom, both in Canada and the United States. But the authors' evidence for that thesis was actually quite skimpy, and subsequent research has called it into question.

One branch of the empirical evidence in *Going Negative* consists of experimental studies. The authors showed people both positive and negative versions of the same ads and found that "people exposed to the negative versions of the advertisements registered lower intentions to vote, expressed less confidence in the political process, and placed less value on their own participation."[19] So far, so good. But the question about experimental results in political research is always whether they carry over into the real world of politics. The authors of *Going Negative* concluded that they did, based on their study of thirty-two Senate races in 1992. They found that, after controlling for several other factors, races judged to be negative averaged 4.5 percentage points lower in turnout than races judged to be positive.[20] An interesting finding, to be sure, but a flimsy platform on which to base conclusions about negative advertising in general.

In 2007, Richard Lau and collaborators reviewed fifty-five published studies of the relationship between turnout and negative campaigning. They found that twenty-five of these studies reported findings in the direction of Ansolabehere and Iyengar's demobilization hypothesis, but twenty-nine pointed in the opposite direction: that is, that negative campaigning actually increases turnout by fostering interest in the campaign. Only three studies found large effects; the others all reported effects that were so small as to have little practical impact, even if they were statistically significant.[21] As Permanent Secretary Humphrey Applebee once said to Minister Jim Hacker in the British TV comedy series *Yes Minister*: "As far as we can see, looking at it by and large, taking one thing with another, in terms of the average ... then in the last analysis it is probably true to say that, at the end of the day, you would find, in general terms that, not to put too fine a point on it, there really was not very much in it one way or the other."[22]

It is certainly possible that in some circumstances not yet fully specified by researchers, negative campaigning might reduce turnout, just as it might increase it in others. Campaigns are open, dynamic games with many players making many moves. But it is wrong to make the generalization, as so many political observers now do, that negative campaigning always works to reduce turnout.

After a thorough review of the academic literature, Lau and Rovner offer a number of well-balanced generalizations about negative campaigning:[23]

- Negative campaigning is certainly prevalent, but there is no good evidence that it has increased in recent years. However, it may appear to have become more common because media have paid more attention to it.
- "Baseless attacks and unwarranted character assaults" may occasionally occur, but they are not the norm. Voters are capable of detecting them and usually punish those who launch such attacks.
- "The widespread concern that negative campaigns can reduce turnout appears unwarranted."
- There is more evidence that negative campaigning can reduce trust in government, but "negative campaigns also stimulate interest and learning about the candidates and issues in an election" (a finding also supported, surprisingly, by Ansolabehere and Iyengar).
- Political choice is inherently comparative, so it is a service to voters when candidates point out their opponents' weaknesses. One can expect ads to be one-sided and exaggerated, but balance emerges at the systemic level, through attack and counter-attack in an adversarial process.
- There is no need for further government regulation to reduce negativity in political advertising.

NEGATIVE ADS IN THE "PEACEABLE KINGDOM"

According to Lau and Rovner, "the literature does reflect an overall indictment of baseless attacks and unwarranted character assaults."[24] Have we seen such ads in Canada in recent years? The *Globe and Mail* columnist Jeffrey Simpson thinks so. He has decried Conservative attack ads as "nasty, personal and below-the-belt."[25] In his view, shared by many others in the media, negative ads should deal only with policy, not personal character. The *Ottawa Citizen* columnist Dan Gardner has a similar view: "[The Conservative ads were] viciously personal, sustained, and launched in the relative civility between election campaigns, they marked a new low in Canadian politics. They were also devastatingly effective."[26]

Negative advertising would indeed be unfair and harmful to political decision-making if it were based on a lie – for example, claiming that Michael Ignatieff was a junior college instructor, not a Harvard professor – or if it targeted the candidate's family members in a way that was true but unrelated to politics – for example, drawing attention to the fact that Stephen Harper's grandfather disappeared without explanation.[27] But such untrue or irrelevant ads are almost never produced because they are so obviously ineffective and would rebound badly upon whoever issued them.

The real problem with negative ads is not that they are untrue but that they are almost always exaggerated and distorted. They contain not lies but partial truths taken out of context. But the same could be said of most political communication, or indeed of most communication in an adversarial process. A lawyer pleading his client's case in court would be stupid to lie, but he is expected to make out the best possible case for his client. He won't say everything that could be said; he will emphasize those points that help his client, and he will present them in the most attractive way possible. It is up to the other side, whose presentation will be equally skewed in the other direction, to provide balance, so the judge and jury can make an informed decision. Such adversarial argumentation is obviously less than perfect, but we use it in situations of imperfect information, where the truth is not obvious and perhaps can never be known with full certainty. The best we can do is to appoint advocates for each side, ask them to do their best for their clients, and let the authorities sitting in judgment come to whatever conclusion they can.

Political campaigning is also an adversarial process. Two or more candidates, leaders, or parties are asking for voters' support. No one can say with certainty who would do a better job in office. Indeed, that question has no clear answer, because judgments of office-holders' performance in office will depend crucially on the values, opinions, and material interests of whoever is doing the judging. Candidates make the best rhetorical case they can in their own favour and against their opponents, knowing that their skewed presentations will be balanced by the skewed presentations of those opponents.

Of course negative advertising is misleading and distorted. So is positive advertising. So is all political communication. The real-world question to be answered is whether, in spite of its limitations, negative advertising communicates important information to voters, and I believe the answer is an unequivocal yes. As John Geer has shown, positive ads, which voters claim to prefer, are often devoid of solid information.[28] They usually depend on visuals, music, and poetic language to create an impression, without much reference to fact. Effective negative ads, in contrast, usually offer specific facts, often supported by precise citation of sources in the ads. They have to do this because, as Geer points out, voters are less receptive to negative ads and thus require a higher threshold of plausibility before they will pay attention.

For concrete illustrations, let's look at how the three most prominent negative advertising campaigns in recent Canadian history have conveyed information to voters. Let's start with the "Hidden Agenda" campaign that the Liberals waged against Stephen Harper and the Conservatives in the 2004 and 2006 election races. Actually, the Liberals didn't employ the term "hidden agenda" in their ads, but it was widely used to describe the portrait they were trying to create. Their efforts began just before the writ was dropped in May 2004 and ran for about ten days of TV, supplemented by some newspaper ads referring voters to a website entitled "Stephen Harper Said." Scott Reid, then Paul Martin's director of communications, recalls that this ad campaign, though small by later standards, was controversial within the Liberal Party: "Got huge blowback from caucus, internal party types who regarded negative ads in pre-writ as a terrible act. But, of course, they worked."[29]

The website site was full of quotes from Harper's days as a Reform MP, president of the National Citizens Coalition, and Canadian Alliance leader. All the quotes were accurate and carefully sourced. The general impression created was that Harper's real views, as documented in these quotations, were far more conservative than the moderate image he was now trying to convey as leader of the newly formed Conservative Party of Canada.

Was this fair game? I would say, absolutely. For the previous six months, Harper had been emphasizing that the new Conservative Party was "moderate and mainstream," but surely voters were better off for being reminded that he had taken much more conservative positions on a wide variety of issues over the past fifteen years. Referring to a hidden agenda was a typical political exaggeration, which implied that Harper was now lying to voters. Nonetheless, it dramatized the obvious truth that many of the things he was saying now were different from what he had said not long ago. The only convincing rebuttal was for Harper to demonstrate over a substantial period of time that what he was saying now would be the basis of his policies, not what he had said in previous years when he held different jobs and represented different political parties.

The Liberal approach was sound, and it certainly helped them pull out a victory in 2004. At times, however, they tended to go over the top with it. A good example was their first television attack ad in the 2004 campaign:

(*Female narrator, deliberate diction, ominous music.*) Stephen Harper would have sent our troops to Iraq. (*Stock footage of tanks and soldiers crossing desert.*)

He'd spend billions on tanks and aircraft carriers (*stock footage of ship at sea*), weaken our gun laws (*close-up of gun pointed at camera*), scrap the Kyoto Accord. (*Stock footage of industrial pollution.*)

He'd sacrifice Canadian-style health care for US-style tax cuts. (*Close-up of oxygen mask descending onto camera, cut to doctors wheeling patient on gurney.*)

He won't protect a woman's right to choose. (*Desperate teenage girl rocking on floor.*)

And he's prepared to work with the Bloc Québécois. (*Pan over Gilles Duceppe.*)

Stephen Harper says that when he's through with Canada (*zoom out on flag*), we won't recognize it.

You know what? (*Flag begins to burn and disintegrate.*) He's right. (*Fade to black.*)[30]

The visuals made the ad powerful in terms of *pathos,* but the *logos* was weak. No documentation of facts was provided, and some of the assertions were demonstrably false. Harper had never called for Canadian troops to be sent to Iraq, though he had criticized Jean Chrétien for not giving political support to the American invasion. And he had never opposed the legalization of abortion, though he had never supported "a woman's right to choose" in those explicit terms. Interestingly, the ad drew a lot of attention while it ran, but Conservative polling numbers did not go down at that time. The Liberals did more damage with less emotional but more focused ads that they ran later in the campaign, such as the ones speaking of a "$50 billion black hole" in the Conservative budgetary projections. It turned out, in fact, that the Conservative budget numbers were too optimistic. Once he did get into power, Harper increased spending at the same rate as Paul Martin had done, used up the surplus that Martin had left behind, and ended up by running deficits that peaked at more than $50 billion during the Great Recession.

Failing to learn from experience, the Liberals made very damaging errors in the suite of negative ads released toward the end of the 2006 campaign. One ad tried to play off Harper's 2002 campaign for the leadership of the Canadian Alliance:

Who paid for Stephen Harper's rise to the head of the party? We don't know. He refuses to reveal his donors. What do you suppose he's hiding? We do know he's very popular with right-wingers in the US. They have money. Maybe they helped him. We just don't know. He just won't say.[31]

In fact, there is no evidence anywhere that Harper ever accepted financial support from American donors. To do so would be illegal. As manager of that campaign, I would know if we had accepted contributions from offshore. It would have been better for the Liberals, if they wanted to go down this path, to stick with the undoubted fact that Harper in 2002 had refused to release the names of a few donors who had specifically requested confidentiality – which was legal at the time.

In short, there was nothing unfair about the basic thrust of the Liberals' "Hidden Agenda" ads, but they sometimes went too far in ignoring documentation and retailing demonstrable falsehoods. They might have stayed in power longer if they had not overplayed their hand.

A second example of negative advertising was the Conservative pre-writ onslaught on Stéphane Dion described in the preceding chapter. The first and most famous ad in this series had no documentation problem, because it consisted almost entirely of televised footage from the Liberal leadership race that Dion had won. It showed Michael Ignatieff, one of his main opponents in that race, criticizing Dion's record as minister of the environment because "We didn't get it done" (didn't live up to the Kyoto Accord), and Dion replying defensively and in not very good English, "Do you think it's easy to make priorities?" It's hard to say this was unfair when it was part of the public record of a very recent leadership campaign. The ad's conclusion ("Leaders get things done. Stéphane Dion is not a leader") was open to argument, but defensible in the light of what viewers had just seen.

My final example is perhaps more debatable. I refer to the string of ads that the Conservatives ran against Ignatieff, also described in the preceding chapter. The most prominent theme of the ads, and the most controversial, was that Ignatieff had chosen to spend twenty-eight years, from 1978 to 2006, living and working in the United Kingdom and the United States, before he came back to Canada to seek election to Parliament as a stepping stone to the Liberal leadership. "Michael Ignatieff – he didn't come back for you" was the ads' conclusion.

Remember that an election chooses people for office; it is not a referendum on policy. And I, for one, would see a candidate's twenty-eight-year absence from Canada in the prime of life as a relevant consideration. Ignatieff may have visited Canada occasionally and kept up on Canadian news in the international media, but he was absent from all the great debates of Canadian life from 1980 through 2005 – constitutional patriation, Petro-Canada, Meech Lake, Charlottetown, the rise of Reform, balancing the budget, refusing to support the invasion of Iraq (which Ignatieff in fact did support while he was at Harvard). How well would Ignatieff really understand Canadian issues after such a long absence? And how well would he understand Canadians, after so many years of not paying Canadian taxes, not watching Canadian television, not cheering for Canadian hockey teams?

In his usual entertaining way, Warren Kinsella describes Ignatieff's failure to understand what was at stake (he was working for Ignatieff when the ads first appeared):

> Harper had decided to define Ignatieff before he could define himself. Simple. Politics 101.
>
> Except when the $4 million "Just Visiting" campaign commenced, Ignatieff wasn't nearly as concerned as me or [Ian] Davey or [Paul] Zed. If anything, he was initially bemused by it all. Ignatieff, who had a tendency to regard politics as a teaching experience, simply couldn't believe Canadians could be taught he was a foreigner.
>
> Said he: "I'm a Canadian. Nobody will believe these stupid ads."
>
> "They're not trying to say you're an American, or that it's bad to be American," I said to him. "The point of their ads, Michael, is that you're not 'just visiting' Canada – you're 'just visiting' Earth. They're trying to suggest that you've never been on public transit, or worried about a mortgage payment, or lost a job. They're trying to say you don't understand the reality of the average Canadian's life." He disagreed with our suggestion that we fight fire with fire, as was his prerogative, and that was that. I went back to the real world in Toronto and, a few months later, he did likewise.[32]

In my view, Ignatieff's long absence from Canada should not have been an absolute bar to his becoming prime minister, but it certainly was something to consider along with many other factors. In a way, it was like the Liberals' charges of "Hidden Agenda" against Stephen Harper. People do change their minds, so Harper's having espoused more conservative views in the past should not be an absolute barrier against his becoming prime minister. Nevertheless, it is certainly something a voter is entitled to know about and take into consideration.

On 15 April 2013, the day after Justin Trudeau was chosen Liberal leader, the Conservatives released a suite of negative ads against him quite similar in spirit and execution to the ads they had used against Dion and Ignatieff. They used documented though sometimes out-of-context quotes, combined with unflattering pictures, to suggest that Trudeau was "in over his head" – not ready to be prime minister. Equally importantly, they suggested that Trudeau would favour Quebec to the detriment of the other provinces. That suggestion, if taken seriously, might actually help Trudeau and the Liberals to regain lost ground in Quebec at the expense of the NDP, but it would set up a barrier to their progress in the rest of Canada.

The ads, in my opinion, were just as well thought out and just as well executed as the anti-Dion and anti-Ignatieff ads. They played on Trudeau's obvious weaknesses, which had already been highlighted and widely discussed during the Liberal leadership race. Yet they did not appear to have any effect, at least in the short run. Two weeks after the ads had started to run, the Liberals had moved out to a seven-point lead over the Conservatives in a Harris-Decima poll.[33]

One possible explanation is that advertising takes time to work. Two weeks after his leadership victory, Justin Trudeau was still enjoying a typical winner's "bounce." What is more important will be the level of his popularity after months or years. Another explanation worth considering is that attacks are less effective when the target is more esteemed than the source of the attack. When the Conservatives released their ads, their party and their leader were already in a slump due to a number of factors, the most prominent of which was the long-running scandal over senators' expense claims. Even before Trudeau became Liberal leader, an Ipsos-Reid poll showed that he ranked ahead of Harper on virtually all attributes of leadership.[34] Under such circumstances, negative advertising may not work, or may even backfire.

Canadian political observers, who in general profess not to like negative advertising, seized on the seeming ineffectiveness of the anti-Trudeau ads to proclaim that a new era might be dawning. However, the unexpected victory of Christy Clark and the Liberals in British Columbia on 14 May 2013 threw cold water on the party. The Liberal campaign had featured unrelenting negative advertising, including a revival of the weathervane ad that Mike Harris had used against Dalton McGuinty in 1999.[35] The NDP, in contrast, had eschewed negative advertising until the last few days, when they sensed that their lead was slipping away. The media always love a winner, so the consensus among *punditi* after the BC election was that negative advertising does in fact work.

CANADIAN-AMERICAN DIFFERENCES

There are some important differences in negative advertising between Canada and the United States. For one thing, the sheer volume of negative advertising, indeed, of all political advertising, is much greater in the United States. Because there are no spending limits in American elections, parties and candidates spend much more on advertising, even in relation to the size of the market. Also, there is no restriction on third-party advertising in the United States. As a result, every American election is potentially like the 1988 Canadian election, when business groups, and to a lesser extent organized labour, advertised heavily around the issue of free trade, or the Ontario election of 2011, when organized labour spent more money than the Liberals in attacking PC leader Tim Hudak. But most importantly, many separate races will be running concurrently in an American election year, and each will have its own advertising campaign. Candidates for president, senator, congressman, governor, and so on run their own campaigns and deploy advertising for their own purposes. All these factors together create on American airwaves a Babel of political advertising of which Canadians have no experience in their own country.

Another difference is focus. In the United States, a candidate for office attacks the person who is running against him for the same office. In Canada, on the other hand, virtually all negative advertising is directed at the party leader, because in our system of disciplined parties, the leader is a huge factor in voters' decision-making in local races. Other figures are sometimes woven into the advertising narrative (for example, the Conservatives referred to David

Dingwall and Ralph Goodale in their 2006 negative ads); but when that happens, it is always to reinforce the case against the opposing party leader. For most voters, the leader is a more important factor than the local candidate. Also, spending limits in local races are so low that it would be impossible to mount much of an advertising campaign against your opponent. Candidates may resort to whisper campaigns or distribution of flyers to denigrate an opponent, but that is a far cry from the American practice of running as many TV attack ads as you can afford. So while a party leader in a Canadian election may carry the brunt of substantial negativity, other candidates are largely spared, unless they are singled out as examples of what's wrong with the party as a whole.

The most important and interesting difference between the two countries has to do with the existence of multi-party competition in Canada, as compared to the norm of two-party competition in the United States. When there are only two candidates, each sponsored by a different party, and the sponsoring parties are largely the same everywhere in the country, negative advertising is quite straightforward. You can attack your opponent, knowing that if you are successful you will help your own cause. Success means converting your opponent's supporter to vote for you, convincing a non-voter to vote for you, or dissuading an opponent's supporter from voting at all. The first scenario is the most favourable, because your vote total goes up one while your opponent's goes down one, for a net gain of two, whereas there is only a net gain of one in each of the other two scenarios. Yet it is always a gain: the only way in which a candidate in a two-party system can lose by negative advertising is by doing it so badly that it rebounds against him or her – not unheard of, but not the norm, either.

Things are very different in a multi-party system. Let's say Party A attacks Party B. There are now many more scenarios than the three that characterize two-party competition. It is quite possible that a successful attack by A upon B will drive some of B's supporters in the direction of Party C. A's successful attack upon B could conceivably create an even more dangerous opponent – an enlarged C.

Some observers believe that something like this happened in the 2011 Canadian general election. Starting months before the actual campaign, the Conservatives had run very effective negative ads against Michael Ignatieff, which they continued during the campaign. The ads were probably part of the reason why the Liberal vote share collapsed from 26 per cent in 2008 to 19 per cent in 2011. But the Conservative vote share increased only about 2 percentage points from 2008 to 2011 – from 37 per cent to 39 per cent. Where did all the other Liberal voters go? Many must have gone to the NDP, who increased their vote share from 19 per cent to 30 per cent. Conservative advertising contributed to destroying Ignatieff's Liberals as a viable option without doing much to increase Conservative support. That was acceptable to the Conservatives because the NDP did not increase enough to prevent the Conservatives from winning a majority government, but it illustrates how unpredictable the results of negative advertising can be in a multi-party system.

Actually, the situation was even more complicated than portrayed in the preceding paragraph. The Liberals were going full-bore negative against the Conservatives, both in advertising and in daily messaging, accusing Harper of being undemocratic. And in Quebec, the BQ were extremely negative against the Conservatives, claiming that the only way to stop Harper from winning a majority government was to vote BQ. But no one was going all out against the NDP, at least until the last days of the campaign, because at the beginning the NDP did not seem to be a serious contender. And while the NDP did make attacks on other parties, they were more humorous than degrading; and the whole tone of the NDP campaign, epitomized by Jack Layton's perpetual smile, seemed friendlier than that of the other parties. So the NDP's unpredicted late surge may be explained, at least in part, by having the least negative message while the other parties savaged each other.

A multi-party system also offers opportunities to use negative messaging, including advertising, to help one's cause by promoting strategic voting. Again, the 2011 election provides an excellent example. In the last few days of the campaign, the Conservatives turned their guns against the ascendant Jack Layton, particularly in Ontario, arguing that an NDP minority government would be a danger to Canada's fiscal status. The point was not so much to shift voters from the NDP to the Conservative column but to deter Liberals disappointed by their own party's performance from voting NDP and even to get them to vote Conservative to ward off the threat of Jack Layton as prime minister. I have not seen the effects demonstrated with hard data, but many close observers of the Ontario scene believe there was a modest shift in the closing days from the Liberals to the Conservatives, prompted by the Conservative attacks on the NDP.[36]

If this perspective is true, it is appropriate payback for what the Liberals did in 2004. In the closing days of that campaign, they went very hard against the Conservatives in Ontario, not to convert Conservatives to the Liberal cause but to scare NDP supporters into voting Liberal in order to forestall a Harper victory. That tactic almost certainly cost the Conservatives a number of ridings in Ontario and made Paul Martin's resulting minority government more viable.[37]

These differences between Canada and the United States mean that we cannot simply import into this country the results of the voluminous American research on negative advertising. The laws of politics are not like the laws of physics. A falling body accelerates at the rate of 32 feet/second/second everywhere on earth, but the impact of negative advertising will depend crucially on the context on which it is used. We need a lot more research on the effect of negative tactics, including negative advertising, in the Canadian multi-party context.

PART III

Fear and Loathing in Alberta

9

Fear and Loathing in Alberta

SOME BACKGROUND

The political party that now calls itself Wildrose is the morganatic child of the Canadian Alliance. The latter was established by Preston Manning in 2000 to broaden the appeal of the Reform Party; but when Stockwell Day won the leadership race, the Canadian Alliance became more open to religious influence than it had been under Manning. In early 2003, the founding convention of the Alberta Alliance chose Mormon businessman Randy Thorsteinson, former leader of the Social Credit Party of Alberta, as interim leader. The party's positioning was true conservative, more so than the governing Progressive Conservative Party. In the 2004 provincial election, the Alberta Alliance won 8.7 per cent of the vote and elected one member, Paul Hinman of Cardston-Taber-Warner. Hinman was a Mormon, and his riding was heavily Mormon. He went on to become leader of the Alberta Alliance in 2005. (I mention the religion of Thorsteinson and Hinman because factionalism between Mormons and others became an important subplot within the Alliance, as it had earlier been within Social Credit.)

After this promising beginning, things went downhill. The Alliance did not do well in 2006 by-elections and raised only $55,000 that year.[1] In 2007, a competing group, whose most prominent member was former *Alberta Report* editor Link Byfield, formed another further-right party, the Wildrose Party. Under the name of the Wildrose Alliance Party, the two parties merged barely in time for the 2008 election, but they were not well prepared. They could not field a full slate of candidates, and Paul Hinman, the leader and only sitting MLA, lost his seat.

After considerable soul-searching, Wildrose decided to carry on. Hinman resigned, and a leadership race was announced, with the selection to be made in October 2009. At this point events started to help the struggling party. Premier Ed Stelmach's upward revision of oil royalties was becoming ever more unpopular, particularly after the Great Recession of 2008 struck. Some people in the oil industry were starting to see Wildrose as a friendlier option than the Progressive Conservative government. And the Wildrose leadership race attracted attention with speculation that Danielle Smith would enter it.[2]

When Smith had studied English and economics at the University of Calgary, she had been part of a talented political student generation including media gadfly Ezra Levant and Calgary mayor Naheed Nenshi. After graduation, she did an internship at the Fraser Institute, then went through several jobs in the realm of public affairs, including writing editorials for the *Calgary Herald,* hosting a television show for Global TV, and serving as the Alberta director of the Canadian Federation of Independent Business. She also won a seat on the Calgary Board of Education, though that board became so mired in conflict between liberals and conservatives that Minister of Learning Lyle Oberg dissolved it and called new elections.

Articulate, gregarious, and photogenic, Smith also attracted attention because she played against type for Wildrose. She was a pro-choice libertarian who had no problems with gay marriage, whereas the party membership had a heavy representation of religious and social conservatives. She squared this circle by being candid about her own views, while also vowing to stand up for the freedom of speech of social conservatives. The formula worked well in building the party, but, as we will see, it ran into problems in the 2012 election.

By the time Smith won the Wildrose leadership on 17 October 2009, the party had developed considerable momentum. An Environics poll taken shortly after her victory put Wildrose only 3 percentage points behind the Tories, 28 to 34.[3] With Smith's backing, Paul Hinman was back in the legislature, having won a by-election in Calgary-Glenmore the previous month – a stunning defeat for the PCs. In 2010, three backbench PC MLAs crossed the floor, joining Hinman to make up a caucus of four with recognized party status, entailing some money for staff and research. Published polls throughout 2010 never had Wildrose further than six points behind the Tories, and sometimes even in the lead.

GETTING READY

I had known Danielle Smith for about twenty years, ever since she took a political science course from me on statistical research methods, and I had recommended her for an internship at the Fraser Institute. We had stayed in touch over the years and collaborated on a couple of small projects. Thinking that the PCs could use some pressure from the right, I had voted for the Alberta Alliance and Wildrose but had not been otherwise involved until Smith decided to run. Then I publicly announced my support for her and the party.

After she won the leadership, she asked me to advise her on party organization and then to help with long-range campaign planning. I was happy to become an unpaid adviser with no administrative responsibilities. I met periodically with a somewhat shifting group of Wildrosers throughout 2010 and early 2011, discussing all aspects of running a full-scale provincial campaign. It quickly became obvious that our model would be the federal Conservative campaign of 2005–06. It was ideal for us because the Conservatives had then been in opposition and had built their campaign around a substantial and detailed platform. Our party was all about policy, and our campaign had to reflect that.

In the meantime, our task shifted somewhat. We were looking forward to running against Ed Stelmach, because his oil royalty review, exploding provincial deficits, and various political missteps had made him extremely unpopular. However, he announced his resignation on 25 January 2011, after a dispute with Finance Minister Ted Morton over the budget.[4] Because of a long PC leadership race, we wouldn't find out who our new opponent would be until 2 October. While we were waiting for the Tories to hold their leadership contest, Wildrose house leader Rob Anderson took over as leader of campaign preparations; he had the time because the legislature was adjourned for seven months while the Tories held their leadership race. Anderson wrote a detailed campaign plan that we would end up following, with only a few modifications. He also worked with the caucus to produce a platform organized around "Five Pledges," in an echo of Stephen Harper's "Five Priorities" of the 2005–06 campaign:

- Balanced Budget and Savings Act – legislation to stop the sequence of deficits that the Tories had been running
- Wildrose Family Pack – a bundle of tax credits and other benefits for families with children
- Alberta Resource Dividend – annual payments to individuals after the budget had been balanced
- Alberta's Patient Wait Time Guarantee – a promise to pay for treatment out of province if it was not available in timely fashion within Alberta
- Alberta Accountability Act – a package of political reforms, including the institutions of direct democracy

It was a platform based on conviction, and for the most part it worked very well in the 2012 election campaign, with the exception of the Resource Dividend. Our opponents found it too easy to paint it as a mere cash giveaway – "Dani Dollars," just like the famous Prosperity Bonus ("Ralph Bucks") of 2006.[5] There were qualifications around the Resource Dividend – it wouldn't start until the budget was balanced, would include only a certain percentage of resource revenue, and would come after payments to the Heritage Fund – but these riders proved impossible to communicate during the heat of a campaign. We should have tested the platform more seriously with polling and focus groups, a lesson for Wildrose to heed in the future. No matter how firm your convictions, you have to adopt a platform that can be communicated effectively in the hurly-burly of a campaign, with your opponents doing their best to denigrate and distort it.

Smith formalized the campaign team in late summer 2011, appointing Cliff Fryers chairman and Rick Anderson manager. I was supposed to be an assistant to Anderson, taking some responsibility for operations while he concentrated on communications. I had to have a limited role because I was teaching full-time in fall 2011. We feared that a new PC leader might call a snap election, so I couldn't then have taken on the full responsibility of management. Anderson, however, found that he was unable to continue, so in late November, Smith asked me to take over from him. I could agree to do that because it was apparent now that there would be no election until 2013, and probably not until after the budget was approved in March. I wasn't scheduled to teach in the coming term, so I could take leave to become the manager.

But that's getting ahead of the story. As we waited for the Tories to choose their leader, we, like almost everyone else, expected front-runner Gary Mar to win. We wanted to go after him almost immediately after the expected announcement of his victory on 2 October. Rob Anderson had produced a highly effective one-minute ad we called "Trailer" (like a movie trailer), which would link Mar to the PC Party's many ethical lapses. We didn't have the money for a big media buy, but we thought if we ran the ad a few times on news broadcasts watched by journalists, we might be able to create a media echo.

Our plans were temporarily derailed when Alison Redford, not Gary Mar, won the race. We had to revise "Trailer," putting in shots of Redford instead of Mar, but the general message remained the same, that a new leader didn't mean the PC Party had changed. We got the ad up, along with a companion piece featuring our leader, on Thursday, 6 October.[6] There was in fact considerable media resonance, with screen shots of our ads in major newspapers. We also created quite a bit of controversy, with some of our own people feeling uneasy about negative ads. There hadn't been a real contest for so long in Alberta that many Albertans had forgotten what a vigorous campaign looks like.

Although we ran the ads and were pleased with the result, we felt we had to do more research on Redford. Polling and focus groups showed that she would indeed be a formidable opponent. Her unexpected victory had driven her name recognition upwards, and her image was extremely positive. People remembered two things about her leadership campaign: that she had performed with dignity and grace in the final debate, even though her mother had just died, and that she had promised to give more money to the little school-children.[7] This gave us pause, because we had seen her promise of $107 million to school boards as simple pandering to the Alberta Teachers Association, but that's not how voters saw it.

Redford herself appeared to be coated in Teflon, so we decided the right strategy was to continue to link her to the past misdeeds of the party – illegal contributions, big salary raises for MLAs and ministers, spiralling deficits. We ran two more waves of negative ads before the writ was dropped, but they didn't have the same impact as "Trailer." After "Trailer," pre-writ ads were no longer novel, so the media weren't particularly interested, and we didn't have the money for more than a token media buy.

The outlook didn't seem very optimistic toward the end of 2011. Not only did Redford test well in our research but the Tories had been rebounding in the polls after Stelmach's resignation. Ten polls published between May of 2011 and January 2012 showed an aver-age lead of twenty-three points for the Tories; indeed, a Leger poll in January showed them ahead by thirty-seven points: fifty-three to sixteen.[8] The low poll numbers certainly didn't help our fundraising. We were always in the black, but we had to be careful with money. Another nasty surprise was that no bank would extend a line of credit to us; they said they would do that only for the governing party and the official opposition.[9] We thought that with luck we might be able to fund a $1.6 million campaign, far more than any other opposition party but still much less than what we expected the PCs to spend.

One area where we cut corners was on opposition research, on our opponents as well as our own candidates. Our small legislative staff was already heavily tasked, and we didn't have the money to hire other researchers, even if we could have found the right people. Anyone seeking a Wildrose nomination had to fill out an extensive questionnaire, and our staff did a check of criminal and civil court records. But our Internet research wasn't as extensive as it ideally should have been – an omission that came back to haunt us in the "lake of fire" episode.

Though the outlook wasn't sunny and our resources were limited, we threw ourselves into the frenzy of work needed to prepare a full-scale campaign. Deputy manager William McBeath took over the recruitment of staff for the war room and leader's tour and also supervised the scripting of the tour, choosing locations to visit and matching policy announcements to locations. Because of our many connections to the federal Conservatives, McBeath was able to recruit a surprising number of experienced people to handle advance, staff the tour, and do communications and constituency liaison from the war room. He also organized worthwhile training sessions for candidates and their campaign teams.

I concentrated on keeping control of expenditures, because it was unthinkable for a Wildrose campaign to run a deficit. That meant I had to take personal charge of the largest discretionary expenditures – advertising and direct voter contact – to make sure they didn't get out of control. With the help of several consultants, McBeath and I prepared an ad campaign for the writ period. Rob Anderson updated "Trailer" for a lead-in to the campaign, and we produced five positive, policy-related ads featuring the leader – one to run concurrently with the release of each of the Five Pledges. That approach was taken straight from what the federal Conservatives had done in 2005–06, in order to amplify the effect of the platform.[10] Our writ-period advertising was mostly TV with some radio, plus a little Internet advertising directed mainly at fundraising. Maybe we were too traditional in our media buy, as the industry is definitely trending toward greater use of highly targeted ads on the Internet and social media.

We had previously done some Voter ID in connection with auto-dialler polls and electronic town halls, but the budget had no provision for live calling, which can be very expensive. I therefore contracted Matt Gelinas's small company, Blue Direct, to offer that service to those constituencies that could afford to pay for it. Gelinas was another former student of mine, young in years but with extensive campaign experience, particularly on the technical side. A few ridings signed up, but take-up was very slow in January and February, far below the number of ridings we hoped would be winnable.

That sluggishness reflected the general tightness of money and our relatively low standing in the polls.

Yet the current was starting to flow our way. After the disastrous Leger poll in January, in which we were thirty-seven points behind, five other polls released in January and February showed an average Wildrose deficit of twelve – not great, but certainly better than thirty-seven down. And things got even better in March, when the average of four polls taken before the election call on 26 March placed us only three points behind. By the time Redford made the decision to ask for an election, it was obviously turning into a horse race. But the change was not caused by our campaign team. Our underfunded pre-writ ads probably helped a little, but they couldn't possibly have moved the needle that much, and our other activities were still behind the scenes. It was the impact of events that eroded Redford's seemingly insurmountable lead. As Harold Macmillan responded when asked what he feared the most as prime minister, "Events, dear boy, events!"[11] The legacy of previous Tory misdeeds was catching up with them.

THE RACE IS ON

Bad headlines started falling like hammer blows as soon as the Legislature opened. On 6 March, the Canadian Taxpayers Federation gave a Teddy award for governmental waste to the so-called "no meet" committee, the Alberta Legislature's Standing Committee on Privileges and Elections, Standing Orders and Printing.[12] Although this body had not met since 2008, all its members had been collecting $1,000 every month. This was part of a Byzantine scheme of MLA compensation designed to prevent voters from knowing what elected members were really paid. Only a forensic accountant could penetrate the maze of tax exemptions, special allowances, and committee honoraria piled on top of salary. In practice, appointments to the "no meet" committee were used to stream a little extra money to opposition and surplus government MLAs, while preventing them from doing anything that might have an impact. After the Teddy award, members of the opposition parties volunteered to repay the money, but the government caucus could not reach a unified position, so public outrage kept growing. There was already so much concern about MLAS' pay and perks that Redford had appointed retired Supreme Court Justice Jack Major to inquire into the compensation scheme and report in May 2012, after the election was over.[13] Thus the "no meet" committee was not just an issue in itself but served to bring back the whole festering issue of MPS' pay.

Then Mar, Redford's main opponent for the PC leadership, made headlines. Redford had appointed him Alberta's trade representative in Asia, at a salary of $265,000 plus expenses for living in Hong Kong, one of the world's most expensive cities. But Mar still had a debt from his leadership race, so some of his supporters organized a fundraising dinner in Edmonton. Standard stuff, except that one version of the invitation referred to his position in Asia, leaving one to conclude that attending the dinner might lead to special treatment in trade negotiations, especially since a $20,000 trip to Hong Kong was raffled off at the event. When the news broke on 9 March, Redford immediately suspended Mar without pay until an inquiry could be conducted.[14] Again, it brought back old memories, because Redford had not only given Mar a plum job but had also appointed his erstwhile political adviser, Kelly Charlebois, executive director of the PC Party, and Charlebois was famous for having invoiced Mar for almost for $400,000 without any tangible evidence of work (maybe it was all verbal advice).[15]

In the backdrop of these major stories, there was also a steady drumbeat of reports about illegal donations to the PC Party made by public-sector authorities such as universities, colleges, school boards, and local governments. These agencies would buy tickets for their employees to attend PC leader's dinners and other fundraisers. The practice had been common for many years, but legislation passed when Redford was minister of justice prevented Elections Alberta from prosecuting the political party; only donors could be penalized. Wildrose researchers had been instrumental in using Freedom of Information requests to make some of the details public.

Beyond all these corruption stories, the government was coming in for a lot of other bad headlines. Its new budget claimed to have a projected deficit of $886 million to be covered from the rapidly depleting Sustainability Fund.[16] Critics, however, said the assumptions behind the budget were too optimistic and that the manner of presentation obscured the true transfer of revenue from the Sustainability Fund to capital projects, totalling over $3 billion.[17] Redford's cabinet ministers mused publicly about the need for tax hikes, furnishing more grist for the Wildrose mill. And the government was persisting in building two high-voltage DC power lines from northern to southern Alberta, a policy that was extremely unpopular with many Wildrose rural supporters. A campaign conducted by Keith Wilson and the Alberta Landowners Council over the lines and related issues of property rights had a great deal to do with securing our rural vote.[18]

We had only one misstep of our own during this period. On Monday, 19 March, now that our tour bus was fully wrapped, we took it out for a drive in Edmonton to show the press that we were ready to go – except that we weren't ready! The wrap had positioned the leader's head and shoulders right above the double rear tires, just where a woman's breasts would be. The "boob bus," as it was dubbed by the media, caused an immediate sensation, going viral and appearing on Jay Leno and other American television shows.[19] Lots of our people – the original designer, senior members of the campaign team, the company that produced the wrap, the people who installed it, everyone at the bus barn – had seen the wrap, but no one saw it as a "busty bus" until it encountered the dirty minds of the media. Smith herself had a lot to do with that oversight. She got so involved in reviewing the design for the bus wrap that everyone else on the team backed off, so the design didn't get as much scrutiny as it should have – an object lesson in what happens when the leader gets too involved in a secondary issue.

Anyway, Smith handled it with good humour, and the episode didn't hurt us. Indeed, it probably helped us by drawing attention to our campaign. Lots of people asked me if I had done it on purpose, and I wish I could have said yes, but in truth it was just a mistake that under some circumstances might have been fatal but in fact turned out okay. We got a new wrap produced in a few days, and the "boob bus" was never a factor in the campaign after the writ was dropped.

Not surprisingly, our poll numbers surged dramatically. Gone were the days of double-digit deficits. In the first three polls taken after the election was called on 26 March, we were ahead by an astonishing average of 11 percentage points.[20] We had always planned to be running from behind, trying to make up ground by drawing attention to our platform, yet now, largely as a result of the government's self-created problems, we seemed to have a big lead. Although it was a welcome development, we didn't really have an adequate plan for running in front, and that lack was part of what caught up with us in the final week.

For the first three weeks of the writ period, however, everything seemed to go swimmingly. Our leader's tour functioned just as we had hoped. Every day Smith revealed a new part of our platform, all organized under the Five Pledges. The announcements largely controlled the agenda of news coverage. Of course, our opponents criticized what we said, but they were forced to talk about our ideas. The tour ran smoothly, with only occasional minor timing glitches. Our leader looked happy all the time and produced great photo ops, which often found their way onto the front pages. An enormous amount of work had gone into planning the tour and scripting the events, but to observers it looked fun and effortless. The media were impressed, as no party had ever put on a federal-style tour like this in an Alberta election. The Progressive Conservatives hadn't had to bother in the past, because they had always been so far ahead, and no opposition party had ever had the money to finance a full-scale tour.

Our television advertising also seemed effective. After starting with "Trailer" to take advantage of all the PCs' ethical problems,[21] we switched to our policy-based ads as Smith rolled out the pledges.[22] Each of the ads was timed to coordinate with the news coverage of the pledge announcement to which it related. One indicator of success was the money that the ads raised. Each time we released a new ad, we put up a new "money bomb" (actually a donation thermometer) on the party's website. All ads went over the top, and collectively they raised hundreds of thousands of dollars in website donations. We took that as a vote of confidence in what we were doing and ploughed the donations back into enlarging our media buy.

Money, in fact, was rapidly ceasing to be a problem. As our campaign looked professional and smooth, and we maintained a sizable lead in the polls throughout the writ period, large donors started to come forward, thinking we had a good chance of winning. By the end of the campaign, companies that had never given us the time of the day were getting in touch to ask how they could contribute. In accord with the long Alberta tradition of cozy relations between business and government, they wanted not just to give but to be seen to be giving to the party that looked as it would form the next government. I had to tell one eager donor that, no, we wouldn't stop the tour bus for him to hand the leader an envelope – shades of Karl-Heinz Schreiber!

In the end, we reported raising $3.1 million in the writ period, against $1.6 million for the Tories.[23] But that does not mean we were able to outspend them. They probably had money in the bank before the writ was dropped, and they were also able to borrow about $3 million, whereas we borrowed nothing except for normal thirty-day commercial credit from suppliers. Thus, the PCs reported spending about $4.6 million against $3.1 million for our side. I cannot comment further on their reported numbers, but ours were a bit misleading, because the reporting period does not coincide perfectly with the fundraising and spending cycles. Because our money came flooding in late during the campaign, we were not able to spend it all. Our media buyer frankly told us in the final week that her agency could not responsibly spend the money we suddenly had available. We thus ended our campaign not in debt, which is the most common outcome for political parties, but with a cash surplus of about $600,000.[24] It was frustrating to me as a manager not to be able to spend all the money that became available at the end, but likely it was for the best. We lost the election because of messaging problems in the final week, problems that more money would not have solved. If we had spent the extra money, it would not have affected the outcome. You can't win by spending more if your message has gone off the rails.

Another reason for our financial success was the unexpected entry of Responsive Market Group (RMG) on our side. Shortly before the writ was dropped, RMG president Michael Davis called to say that he was no longer tied to the Alberta PCs and would like to work for us. As soon as we could sign a contract, we turned RMG loose on our donors. We had done some telephone fundraising before, but never with the professionalism and large phone banks that RMG could muster. The result was another stream of donations joining that produced by our direct mail, large donors, and advertising/website combination, to produce what was, by our previous standards, a veritable flood of money.

Having the services of RMG also solved our direct voter contact problem. As we stayed ahead in the polls and all other indicators remained positive, more and more ridings wanted to purchase voter ID from Blue Direct as well another local firm that we had enlisted, Pro Call Marketing. RMG was able to pick up some of the load, particularly with GOTV calling, which is very compressed in time at the end of the campaign. I also ploughed back some of the money that RMG was raising into additional voter ID and GOTV beyond what the ridings had contracted for, thinking we had the chance of a lifetime to win a majority government.

That strategy failed, however, when our support dropped suddenly in the final weekend. Ridings that looked winnable when we were ten points ahead in the polls were out of reach when we fell ten points behind on election day. Voter ID and GOTV will move the dial a bit in close races, but not twenty points. Yet the money spent on DVC was not wasted, even if it did not produce victory. It has left a legacy of hundreds of thousands of Albertans identified as having some degree of sympathy for Wildrose. Having all the data in the party's database will be an invaluable resource for fundraising and other forms of party-building in the future.

To finish off what seemed like a highly successful three weeks, our leader performed very well in the televised leaders' debate. An Ipsos-Reid poll suggested she had "won" the debate against the more experienced Redford – thirty-seven to twenty-eight.[25] Using different metrics, Return on Insight found that Smith had experienced a boost of thirteen points from the debate, whereas Redford had suffered a loss of twelve.[26] Smith is a naturally gifted debater, but her success did not come just from innate talent. We set up a strenuous debate preparation process modelled on that used by the federal Conservatives and borrowing some of the same people. When Smith went up against Redford, she had been thoroughly briefed and had survived hours of simulated debate against Calgary lawyer Laurie Livingstone playing Redford's "Black Swan" against her "White Swan."

If so many things worked well for us, the obvious question is, "Why did we lose?" To answer that, we must remember that campaigning is a game with multiple players, in which all sides have moves to make. We have to go back and look at the key moves of our major opponent, the incumbent Progressive Conservatives.

Initially, their campaign seemed to get off to a bumpy start. On the fourth day, Redford, looking shaken, announced that she had changed her mind and would require all PC caucus members to pay back the honoraria earned by being a member of the "no meet" committee since 2008.[27] Although she looked weak for having waited so long to catch up with the opposition parties, she did manage to reduce the salience of the issue, which up to then had been killing the PCs' campaign.

Almost immediately, Redford went through another ordeal when she had to apologize for the remarks of one of her employees. Amanda Wilkie, an assistant in the premier's office, had used a Tweet to mock Smith's childlessness: "If @elect Danielle likes young and growing families so much, why doesn't she have children of her own? #wrp family pack = insincere #abvote."[28] Observers called it a new low in campaigning. Wilkie, in fact, was a former Wildrose employee with a grudge against the party and the leader. To deal with it, Smith went public about the fact that she and her husband had tried to have children but discovered a medical problem that prevented her from conceiving. With public opinion swinging heavily in Smith's direction, Redford called to offer her an apology, which Smith accepted.[29] It was a low moment for the Tories, but Redford's apology did allow them to get beyond it.

On the positive side, the Conservatives made many new promises of better social services. *Calgary Herald* editor Licia Corbella nicely summarizes the main ones:

She promised to build 50 new schools and to renovate 70 more at a cost of $2.4 billion over four years. Then, in what is viewed as a slap to Alberta's hard-working doctors, she vowed to open 140 family care clinics, which will cost $3.4 billion in a model not supported by physicians.

She promised – and has since reneged – on bringing in full-day kindergarten at a cost of $200 million a year. She also immediately gave $107 million to teachers to fill a funding gap that was being blamed on former Premier Ed Stelmach.

Redford also vowed to fund oil sands research to the tune of $150 million per year for 20 years – or a whopping $3 billion – and claimed she could do all that with a budget surplus of nearly $1 billion the following year and a surplus of $5.2 billion the year after that.[30]

The PCs' budget had already taken a very optimistic view of resource revenues for the coming year, allowing them to promise only a small deficit for 2012–13 (to be covered from the Sustainability Fund) and a return to balanced budgets in 2013–14, with no cuts to social services and continuation of all capital projects, such as roads, hospitals, and schools. Wildrose attacked the budget as "Alison in Wonderland,"[31] but it would take months to show that Redford's assumptions were far too optimistic, while the campaign would be fought in the short run. Then on top of the budget came the campaign promises, such as construction of 140 new family care clinics over the next three years, costing about $3 billion.[32] Doctors didn't like the promise, and Wildrose could attack it for breaking the limits of an already unrealistic budget; but it and other promises achieved the positioning the Tories wanted. It made them the party of better social services, while they attacked our Resource Dividend as a reckless giveaway to individuals. It helped cement the support of public-sector unions, signalling that a Redford government would create even more jobs for them while protecting their earnings. It also appealed to the young families with children that we needed to attract to our coalition if we were going to win. Our Family Pack of tax credits still had some traction, but it had to go head to head with promises of social services whose unaffordability we could not demonstrate within the four weeks of a campaign.

A couple of episodes in the second week, though they did not seem to hurt us badly at the time, illustrated our underlying vulnerability that allowed the PCs to run an effective campaign of fear in the final week. The first event was an email letter from our chief administrative officer suggesting that Wildrose's direct democracy position could be used to legislate on abortion. It was an answer that the party had previously given to others asking similar questions: "The legalities of abortion fall under federal jurisdiction. We respect that Albertans view social issues differently, which is why Wildrose would immediately introduce legislation allowing citizens to put issues like abortion to a citizen initiated referendum. This open and democratic process allows Albertans to tell government what they believe is important."[33]

The legality of abortion is a Criminal Code matter over which provinces do not have jurisdiction, but Alberta could conceivably try to delist abortion from Alberta Health Care Insurance coverage – an option that has often been discussed in social conservative circles, including within the Progressive Conservative Party. Smith was forced to address this issue repeatedly in the next few days before making it clear that as premier she would not move to defund abortion.[34]

At almost exactly the same time, conscience rights also came to the fore, through an Edmonton blogger to whom Tory operatives had fed information.[35] In context, the phrase "conscience rights" refers to the right, say, of a marriage commissioner to refuse to marry a gay couple, or a medical staffer not to participate in an abortion, or a pharmacist to decline to sell the morning-after abortifacient pill. Wildrose members had voted to put conscience rights in the party's policy book, and Smith had previously defended that position as a libertarian compromise to protect everyone's freedom. In fact, conscience rights went back to Ralph Klein's government in the era of the gay marriage debate, when prominent PCs, such as Ted Morton, had defended the idea. Conscience rights constitute an interesting topic of debate but one that is much too complex for a campaign, where it is easily caricatured as homophobia. It took Smith a couple of days to arrive at the simple position that she wouldn't legislate on conscience rights.[36]

Although our poll numbers held up during the second week, these episodes illustrated some grave weaknesses in our campaign positioning and preparation. They were, in effect, a dress rehearsal for the disaster of the final week, because they showed that we were carrying a lot of unwanted baggage. We had designed the campaign around the Five Pledges in the platform, which had nothing to do with social conservative issues, but there was lots of social conservatism buried in the Wildrose policy manual adopted by the members. And it was hard for the leader to disown, even though she was not herself a social conservative, because her approach in winning the leadership of the party had been to stress her respect for social conservatives and to defend their freedom of speech. With enough thoughtful preparation, we could perhaps have devised some simple statements that could work in the heat of a campaign, but we hadn't done the homework. Mesmerized by the beauty of our own platform, we thought we could make it the centerpiece of the campaign, without anticipating how our opponents would go beyond the platform to dredge up positions that weren't Danielle Smith's but with which she could plausibly be associated.

Week 2 also allowed Redford to establish the theme of fear. On 26 March, when the campaign had begun, she had said, "I don't want this to be a campaign about fear, I want this to be a campaign about hope."[37] But on 4 April, she said that the Wildrose position on conscience rights was "frightening."[38] Voters didn't seem frightened yet, but in Week 4 fear would become the master theme leading to Tory victory.

But that was still in the future. At the end of Week 2, we felt good about our campaign, though we recognized that we faced a potential scripting problem for the final ten days. What would our message be after our platform had been fully revealed and the leaders' debate had been held? Since we were following the federal Conservative campaign model, we were conscious of problems that had plagued them in the final week of their campaigns, after the main message had run out. A group of us met at Cliff Fryers's house on Easter Sunday, 8 April, to develop what we thought was a reasonably strong plan for closing out the campaign. We would return to the theme of loathing, revealing new instances of PC ethical problems (unfortunately, we had only minor illustrations that hadn't been used before) and backing them up with new negative ads. We would also try to reinforce our platform messages with specific applications of the

Five Pledges. And we would produce an upbeat closing ad with lots of pictures of our leader amid crowds to emphasize the momentum the polls showed we had. It wasn't a bad plan, and it might have worked except for the "lake of fire" and related episodes of Week 4.

On the evening of Saturday, 14 April, I was sitting in my recliner at home, watching television and thinking of going to bed, when our deputy manager, William McBeath, called to alert me to an emergency. Our opponents were tipping off the media to a ten-month-old blog posting by our Edmonton South-West candidate, Allan Hunsperger:

Sunday, 05 June 2011 09:55
Born this Way
Written by Allan & Cindy Hunsperger
I have decided to do a sequel to Lady Gaga's CD, "Born this Way." My CD will be entitled, "Born this Way – And that's why Jesus came." The world is believing the lie that because you were "born this way" you now have a right to live this way – the way you were born. Sounds great at first except nobody is mentioning what the results will be of living the way you were born! If you were "born this way," are you going to "die this way?" Well if that is true, and it is, then you have fallen right into the trap that is as old as time. That trap is what satan wants for you – but is that what you want? You see, you can live the way you were born, and if you die the way you were born then you will suffer the rest of eternity in the lake of fire, hell, a place of eternal suffering. Now at this point I am not judging, I am just stating a fact! You may not believe me and you have that choice, but I would challenge you to seriously check it out because once you cross over, there is no turning back. It is not only Lady Gaga that doesn't understand this, it is also our educators with the Edmonton Public school board. The following is right from the public school board's website: "PHILOSOPHICAL FOUNDATION STATEMENT The Board is committed to establishing and maintaining a safe, inclusive, equitable, and welcoming learning and teaching environment for all members of the school community. This includes those students, staff, and families who identify or

are perceived as lesbian, gay, bisexual, transgender, transsexual, two-spirit, queer or questioning their sexual orientation, gender identity, or gender expression. The Board expects all members of our diverse community to be welcomed, respected, accepted, and supported in every school." Why this from our public educators? Because they believe people were "born this way" and have a right to die this way. The blind leading the blind! Now every Christian school that has come under the Edmonton Public School board will have to adopt this as well. Trapped! For years I have warned Christian educators that you can't partner with public education because public education is godless. As far as public education is concerned, there is no God. The dictionary defines godless as profane or wicked. Psalm 1:1 "Blessed is the man who does not walk in the counsel (teachings) of the wicked or stand in the way of sinners or sit in the seat of mockers." There is so much I could teach on from this point but I will stick to the subject and then all the other subjects that come out of this, I can speak to later. Back in the eighties Holy Spirit revealed to me a truth that I have never forgotten. Our family was flying from California back to Calgary and we had to make a change over in San Francisco. As we were waiting for our plane to leave, two men who were homosexuals were also waiting and we began to share in conversation. Once they found out that I was a pastor the conversation went to their lifestyle and they began to expand how we as Christians have judged them wrongly. Then one of the men said to me, "You will never understand what it is like to be born one way and have society expect to you live another." Immediately Holy Spirit dropped this in my mouth and I said, "You know, I do understand, because I was born the same way. I was born living one way and God expects me to live another way. I can't do that on my own and that's why Jesus Christ came so I could be changed." Warning people to not live the way they were born is not judgment or condemnation – it is love! Accepting people the way they are is cruel and not loving!39

Hunsperger was pastor of the House Christian Church in Tofield, not far from Edmonton; it's a Pentecostal place of worship.40 He had unsuccessfully sought a Wildrose nomination in one riding, then had been parachuted into Edmonton South-West at the last minute when our nominated candidate had to withdraw for family reasons. Hunsperger, whom I have never met, was well known to our candidate recruitment team, who thought he had integrity and would be cooperative with the campaign. And indeed he was cooperative. This was not an off-message gaffe: this was an old blog post – a church sermon, actually – that should have been picked up long before by our own opposition research. But as I noted earlier, we did not do enough opposition research, either on our own people or on our opponents.

The blog post was political dynamite because it challenged the right of gay people to be who they are. The "lake of fire" imagery from the Book of Revelation was eminently quotable. And the "lake of fire" was hard to write off as a purely personal view, because Hunsperger had explicitly linked it to the Edmonton Public Schools' foundational statement regarding gay students. McBeath and I discussed all the options, and he convinced me it would be best to cut Hunsperger loose. I said, "Let's let Danielle sleep. I'll call her first thing Sunday morning."

It was too late to remove Hunsperger's certification as a candidate. The most Smith could have done was to say that, if he was elected (of which there was no chance in Edmonton South-West), he would not be allowed to sit in the Wildrose caucus. Maybe that's what she should have done; I proposed it to her, and later there was no shortage of second-guessers to say so. But she felt that throwing Hunsperger under the "boob bus" (so to speak) would threaten party unity because it would repudiate her position that had worked so well in holding the party together – being a libertarian, but defending the freedom of speech of social conservatives. Instead she made a public statement dissociating herself from Hunsperger's views and emphasizing that he did not speak for the party.[41] He also made a statement emphasizing that these were purely personal views. It might have been good enough for the first week of a campaign, with three weeks left to recover, but it was pretty iffy for the final week. And the mischief was soon compounded by several other instances of candidates going off message.

While debate over the "lake of fire" was still raging, we had to confront a new crisis – the "Caucasian candidate." Our candidate in heavily ethnic Calgary-Greenway, Ron Leech, had this to say on a community radio broadcast: "I think, as a Caucasian, I have an advantage. When different community leaders, such as a Sikh leader or a Muslim leader speaks, they really speak to their own people in many ways. As a Caucasian I believe that I can speak to all the community."[42] Leech was a retired minister whose East Calgary church included people from about fifty countries. What he meant to say was that he wouldn't be beholden to any particular ethnic group and would work to represent them all – a big issue in his ethnically mixed riding. But his use of the outdated word "Caucasian" made him sound like a racist. Unfortunately, he hadn't followed the rule we had laid down that candidates should consult with the war room before doing media. If he had, his poorly worded statement could have been edited to make it acceptable.

Coming right after the "lake of fire," it provoked another media firestorm. Smith at first tried to downplay Leech's remarks: "I know Dr. Leech runs a private school that has a large number of people from cultural communities, he has an ethnically diverse riding, he's made great friendships and inroads with leaders of different cultural communities there, so I assume he was probably commenting on his own ability."[43] Leech also apologized for expressing himself badly.[44] But then Calgary mayor Naheed Nenshi and Edmonton mayor Stephen Mandel jumped in, saying a stronger apology was needed.[45]

Scrambling to stay in front of the story, we sent the leader to visit an east Calgary mosque and make a long statement about ethnicity, in which she expanded on her Native American heritage, which she had never kept secret but hadn't discussed much in public: "My great-grandmother Mary Crow was a member of the Cherokee Nation that had been forcibly relocated from the southeastern United States to the Oklahoma territory in the 1830s by the US government, a terrible stain on the history of America known as the Trail of Tears."[46] The campaign team put a lot of work into her speech, but it was late in the day to be taking on such a controversial topic.

"Lake of fire" and "Caucasian candidate" grabbed the most headlines because they represented the most sensitive issues, but we also experienced a rash of untimely truth-telling in the final week that alarmed certain categories of voters. In an online leaders' debate sponsored by two newspapers, Smith questioned the science of global warming: "We have always said the science isn't settled and we need to continue to monitor the debate."[47] She would have been better to stick with the difficult economics of climate change policy, as Stephen Harper has always been careful to do. On a related note, she also used inflammatory language when she talked about the possible need to "break contracts" for carbon capture and storage. This possibility was always implicit in our policy, but talking about breaking contracts needlessly alarmed people in the business community. Somewhat similarly, our health critic, Heather Forsyth, raised alarm when she spoke about a possible wage freeze in the public sector. Caucus members, including the leader, had repeatedly talked about this issue at the time of the budget debate, but it wasn't a good closing theme in the late phase of an election campaign.

Another unwanted visitor in the last week of the campaign was my "Firewall" letter of January 2001, which I had written under different circumstances ten years before, collaborating with Stephen Harper. It was an open letter addressed to Premier Ralph Klein, urging him to make full use of Alberta's constitutional jurisdiction to run social programs and reject interference from Ottawa. Smith made a public statement endorsing the "firewall" ideas of considering an Alberta Pension Plan to replace the Canada Pension Plan, and an Alberta Provincial Police Force to replace the RCMP in the province.[48] Both ideas have merit, and both had been adopted by member resolution at earlier conventions. But they had nothing to do with our platform and should have been left in the closet during the campaign.

In short, we lost control of the agenda in the final week. We found ourselves talking about almost everything except the platform that had been so well received in the first three weeks. There were multiple causes: lack of a powerful script for the final week, inadequate opposition research on our own candidates, candidates not consulting the war room before talking to the media, leader and candidates being overeager to answer questions that should have been deflected. Whatever the precise weight of these causes, they came

Table 9.1
Summary of published polls during the writ period, Alberta provincial election, 2012*

Week	Number of Polls	Average Wildrose Lead
1	3	11
2	7	9
3	5	12
4	7	8

*Compiled from Internet sources.

together to produce a catastrophic breakdown of message discipline in the final week.

As I tried to play whack-a-mole with these emerging problems, I worried that our support would collapse. Table 9.1 provides a summary of published polls for the four weeks of the writ period. Seven polls were published in the final week, conducted by six different companies using a variety of methodologies. Each showed us in the lead between 6 and 10 percentage points, with an average of 8. These published figures were consistent with a very large push-button poll (almost 20,000 respondents) that we did at the end of the third week in order to target our GOTV efforts on ridings that seemed winnable. Every day there was more good news, so I began to think that, maybe, somehow, we would escape the consequences of losing control over our message. But it was not to be.

The morning of election day, Monday, 23 April, I learned of a Forum poll showing that our lead had shrunk to 2 percentage points.[49] It had been conducted too late on Sunday, 22 April, for the results to be published in the mainstream media, but they had been posted on the Internet late that night. All day Monday I had a case of the jitters, which turned to deep depression when the votes were counted Monday evening. It was obvious from the very first returns that we would finish behind the Tories, and far behind what every poll taken during the campaign had predicted.

READING THE TEA LEAVES

Table 9.2 contains the election results. As always, the data can generate a number of stories. In historical context, the two biggest stories

Table 9.2
2012 Alberta election results

Party	Seats	2012 Vote Share (%)	2008 Vote Share (%)
PC	61	44.0	52.7
Wildrose	17	34.3	6.8
Liberal	5	9.9	26.4
NDP	4	9.8	8.5

Table 9.3
New parties, new leaders

Year	Juris.	Party	Leader	No. Seats	% Pop. Vote
1952	BC	Social Credit	W.A.C. Bennett	19/48	27.2*
1962	Can.	NDP	Tommy Douglas	19/265	13.6
1967	AB	PC	Peter Lougheed	6/65	11.1
1970	QC	Parti Québécois	René Lévesque	7/108	23.1
1993	Can.	Reform	Preston Manning	52/295	18.7
2004	Can.	Conservative	Stephen Harper	99/308	29.6
2012	AB	Wildrose	Danielle Smith	17/87	34.3

*This is the percentage obtained by Social Credit on the first count. The 1952 BC results are not really comparable because a preferential ballot was used, and Bennett did not become the official leader until after the campaign. Bennett was able to form a minority government with the support of a Labour member of the legislature.

were the rise of Wildrose, adding 26 percentage points of vote share and becoming the official opposition, and the fall of the Liberals, losing 16 percentage points of vote share along with official opposition status. The PCs went down a bit, and the NDP went up, but these were much smaller changes than what happened to Wildrose and the Liberals.

In historical perspective, Wildrose did quite well. Danielle Smith was a new leader, seeking a seat in the legislature for the first time, and Wildrose was essentially a new party. The last time that a new party with a new leader actually won an election in Canada was in 1952, when W.A.C. Bennett led Social Credit to a narrow victory in British Columbia. Prior to that was the Alberta victory of Social Credit, led by William Aberhart, in 1935. Table 9.3 shows some major examples of electoral results of new parties with new leaders. Each case is unique, so I wouldn't push comparisons too far, but arguably Danielle Smith did at least as well in her first outing as some of the giants of Canadian political history – Tommy Douglas, Peter Lougheed, René Lévesque, Preston Manning, and Stephen Harper. And yet, on election night, the results seemed like a bitter defeat, not a triumph, because the polls had led us to expect to win at least a plurality of seats in the legislature, and quite possibly a majority.

What happened? Seven companies published the results of twenty-two polls during the writ period, and Wildrose led in every one. Each company had its own sampling frame, and all three major methods of data collection were employed at one time or another – live calling, Internet panel, and auto-dialling. It is hard to believe that all these polls were simply wrong. A more plausible explanation is that there was a last-minute shift as voters digested the events of the final week. Our own post-election poll found that 36 per cent of voters did not make up their mind until the last weekend, or even on election day, and of these late deciders, 50 per cent went to the PCs. The one-day Forum poll conducted on the Sunday before the election, which showed our lead down to 2 percentage points, apparently was a snapshot taken in the middle of this gigantic vote swing.

By aggregating the results of several questions, our post-election pollster Hamish Marshall was able to decompose the victorious PC/Redford coalition into three distinct blocs:

· PC loyalists (17.4 percentage points)
· soft PCs (15.1 percentage points)
· left-wingers (11.4 percentage points)

"PC loyalists" were voters who had supported the PCs in the past and stuck with them this time. "Soft PCs" were voters with a history of voting PC who had considered switching to Wildrose during the campaign but drew back at the end. People like this were our main growth target; if we had got their support, we would have won the election. "Left-wingers" were those who would have preferred to vote NDP, Evergreen, Liberal, or Alberta Party, but switched to the PCs because they saw Wildrose as too radical and a danger to their values. They were particularly upset by the "lake of fire" and "Caucasian candidate" episodes. This group consisted mainly of former Liberals; remember that the party lost 16 percentage points of vote share in this election. They were strategic voters who saw the PCs as a less bad option. Wildrose didn't "lose" these votes: we were never going to get them. But we also couldn't win unless voters felt able to support their genuine first choice – Liberal or another party of the left.

We did further qualitative research with a couple of focus groups composed of "soft PCs" from Calgary. We had to learn more about their views, because it was people like them, open to our message and situated in our geographical base of southern Alberta, who really cost us the election. If we could have retained their support to the end, we could have formed at least a minority government.

The focus group participants confirmed that the events of the final week caused them to draw back from voting Wildrose. They weren't particularly exercised about the intolerance supposedly symbolized by the "lake of fire" and the "Caucasian candidate." Several seemed much more concerned about bread-and-butter issues, such as the pay packets of public-sector workers. They saw the missteps of the last week as demonstrating that Wildrose wasn't ready to govern. They saw them as reflecting the immaturity of the party. Interestingly, they still had a high opinion of Danielle Smith. Half of them (and remember, these were all people who had voted PC) even said they would have preferred her as premier. They all said they would consider voting Wildrose in the next election.

Our post-election research sent two very clear messages to Wildrose if it hopes to win a future election. First, stop scaring the left. Stop flirting with issues such as abortion and gay marriage, over which past generations of social conservatives have done battle and lost. Those battles are over, and voters don't want to hear about them again. The same is true of radical-sounding ideas such an Alberta pension plan and an Alberta police force. They may have been interesting topics of discussion ten years ago, when Alberta was facing a hostile Liberal government in Ottawa, but not with a Conservative federal government in Ottawa. Wildrose can't expect ever to get many votes from the left, but it can work to liberate voters of the left, especially Liberals, to support their true first choice. If the Redford PCs were to lose the 11.4 percentage points of "left-wingers" who ran to them in this election out of fear of Wildrose, their days as a governing party would be over.

The second message for Wildrose is to maintain focus and discipline. The Wildrose universe of voters – those who would consider voting for the party – want a provincial government that balances its budget, keeps taxes low, and efficiently provides necessary public services. In any campaign, Wildrose should talk about those issues and no others. It shouldn't comment on issues under federal jurisdiction, such as abortion and gay marriage, or on issues that aren't under any government's jurisdiction, such as the science of global warming. It should keep the focus on how Wildrose will restore the Alberta Advantage by balancing the budget, keeping taxes low, and providing essential services. In that way the party will communicate the impression of discipline and organizational competence needed to attract the "soft PCs" who will ultimately determine the future of Wildrose.

10

Applying the Principles

In this chapter, we see how the principles of campaigning developed in chapters 1 to 8 apply to the 2012 Alberta election campaign.

RHETORIC

The Progressive Conservatives and Wildrose each presented to voters their own powerfully persuasive combination of ethos, pathos, and logos. Though the views espoused by the two parties were different, there was a kind of symmetry between them.

Ethos

Both parties made a positive case for their own character and that of their leaders. The PCs wanted to be seen as experienced and reliable, albeit with a reform-minded new leader. Wildrose portrayed itself as fresh and populist, with an energetic and intelligent new leader. This part of the battle was pretty much a standoff, as voters, other than confirmed partisans, don't put a lot of trust in any political party, and both leaders seemed intelligent and articulate. Smith may have been more personable, but Redford was more experienced in public life. Overall, it was pretty much an even choice for uncommitted voters. Neither party had much negative to say about the ethos of the other party's leader; instead, they each attacked the ethos of the other party, at which point pathos took over.

Pathos

The PCs tried to make voters fear the alleged extremism and incompetence of Wildrose, while Wildrose tried to make voters loathe the "culture of corruption" of the PCs. Each party's case worked best when it was substantiated by headline news. For the PCs, that happened in the last week of the campaign, when Wildrose was making news every day for all the wrong reasons. For Wildrose, their case against the PC ethos worked best in the run-up to the campaign, when the "no meet" committee and Gary Mar's suspension dominated the news. In the end, fear trumped loathing, and the PCs won the election, but that outcome may have been an artifact of timing, in that the fear issues became prominent just before votes were cast. While loathing might, with different timing, have trumped fear, timing was largely out of the control of each party when it was on the attack. Wildrose had contributed to the loathing stories with its research on illegal contributions, but the furor over the "no meet" committee and Gary Mar came from elsewhere. Similarly, although the PCs helped put some of the final-week Wildrose stories in the news, mostly it was a case of Wildrose damaging itself.

Logos

In spite of the importance of ethos and pathos, voters also got a choice in terms of policy or logos. The PCs emphasized enhancement of services in education and health care while maintaining a balanced budget. Wildrose emphasized balancing the budget, but also promised an enticing menu of tax credits and dividends to be implemented once balance was achieved. Behind the arguments over the state of provincial finances and fiscal responsibility loomed the typical difference between right and left in contemporary Canadian politics. The left prefers to woo voters with state-delivered services; the right prefers to offer cash to citizens so they can make their own choices. Of course, both approaches depend on the public treasury being full, which seems unlikely in Alberta for the next few years.

THE RULES OF THE GAME

Like all contemporary elections of senior governments in Canada, the 2012 Alberta election was conducted as a single-member-majority or first-past-the-post exercise, which had an important effect on the result. One of the major causes of the Progressive Conservative victory was the collapse of the Liberal vote from 26 per cent to 10 per cent, and the transfer of many of those Liberal votes to the PCs. It was a massive exercise in strategic voting, as many Liberals (and smaller numbers from other left-wing parties) voted PC to stop Wildrose from winning. Strategic voting is particularly encouraged by the all-or-nothing rules of the single-member-majority system. If your first choice can't win, you can still vote negatively to try to block your last choice from winning. In a system of proportional representation, on the other hand, strategic voting is much less common. Almost all voters will support their sincere first choice and hope that that party, even if it only wins a few seats, will be able to participate in the governing coalition that will be negotiated after the election. Strategic voting would make sense only if your first-choice party was so weak that it was unlikely to surmount the threshold for winning any seats at all, in which case your vote would be wasted if you stuck with your first choice.

Liberal leader Raj Sherman did not seem to grasp what was going on. He repeatedly scaremongered against Wildrose with a line of which he seemed quite proud: "This is Alberta, not Alabama."[1] It didn't seem to occur to him that, if Liberal voters were paying attention, he was driving them to vote PC by painting Wildrose in such frightening terms, because it was obvious that the Liberals had no chance to win. If Sherman had been able to hold the Liberal vote at anything close to its historic level (25 per cent or more of the total), his party would have won more seats, as would Wildrose, and probably no party would have earned a majority. Under those circumstances, Sherman would have been in the driver's seat. Both Redford and Smith would have come calling for his support, and he could have played queen-maker. He could have supported Redford and the PCs because they were closer to the Liberals on many economic and social issues, or he could have supported Smith and Wildrose

in return for reforms of the political system on which the two parties largely agreed. In particular, he might have got some reforms to
party funding to rescue the Liberals from their chronic poverty and
indebtedness.

As it was, the Liberals got nothing, and fell to third place in the
legislative assembly, losing their status of official opposition and all
the funding and other perks that go with it. Wildrose is now the
official opposition, with dozens of staff members and millions of
dollars to spend developing its profile in anticipation of the next
election. Wildrose didn't win first prize, to be sure, but the second
prize – official opposition – may turn out to be an important mile-
stone on the road to power.

STRATEGIC POSITIONING

Like Reform in 1993, Wildrose tried to play "invasion from the margin," peeling off the more conservative voters from the former PC
coalition. It was a strategic choice, to be sure, but it was also based
on conviction. The Wildrose leader, activists, and supporters almost
all had a prior history of having been conservative-leaning PCs or
having supported parties even further to the right, such as Social
Credit. To the right of the current PCs was where they wanted to be.

Invasion from the margin worked for Reform, though success
took ten years to achieve. Starting in 1993, Reform won large numbers of former PC seats and eventually pushed that party to the
brink, leading them to accept a merger offer in 2003. With Stephen
Harper winning the leadership race of the new Conservative Party of
Canada, the merger was pretty close to a Reform/Canadian Alliance
takeover. The strategy of crowding the federal Progressive Conservatives from the right eventually worked because they had nowhere
else to go, being blocked on the left by a strong and united Liberal
Party.

Wildrose hoped to imitate Reform's success but to do so much
faster, winning power in one election. The dream seemed feasible
for a while but fell apart because, in the Alberta case, the Progressive Conservatives were not blocked on the left. The Alberta Liberals
were too weak to defend their own turf, and Redford moved in on

them, co-opting traditional Liberal supporters such as teachers and other public-sector union members. With no money to run a proper campaign, demoralized by factional infighting and leadership contests, and with a leader who didn't understand what was happening, Liberals were easily seduced by PC alarmism about Wildrose, validated by Wildrose missteps in the final week.

The Wildrose invasion from the margin worked up to a point, securing the support of a large number of more conservative PCs. But the PC Party under Redford's leadership was able to make good those losses by recruiting erstwhile voters from the Liberals and other smaller parties of the left. Further progress for Wildrose will probably require these leftist voters to go back to where they really would prefer to be. Wildrose can't cause this to happen, but it can assist the process by making itself less scary to the left, severing all connections with the lost causes of social conservatism.

Regardless of the ultimate outcome, this election offers a valuable lesson in political strategy. Those who want to play invasion from the margin, from either the right or the left, must consider the position not only of their principal opponent but also of their opponent's opponents on the other side of the spectrum. If your main opponent faces little resistance from the other side, your onslaught may indeed attract many of its erstwhile supporters, but it may find new reservoirs of support by moving away from you – essentially what Redford's party accomplished in this election.

COALITION BUILDING

Politically, Wildrose largely succeeded in attracting the more conservative-minded voters away from the Progressive Conservatives. One way of looking at it is that Wildrose got the support of about half the people who reported having voted for the federal Conservatives in 2011 (66.8 per cent). Wildrose and the PCs would have fought to a draw except that the PCs were able to add an additional 11 percentage points of vote share from former left-wing voters, mainly Liberals. Wildrose solidified its core political support during the campaign but did not add much to it, while the PCs were able to add a large bloc of new voters.

A look at the map shows how Wildrose did in terms of its projected geographic coalition. It won every rural seat south of Red Deer except for Banff–Cochrane, but it failed to carry Red Deer and Lethbridge and won only two seats in Calgary. Failure to carry southern urban seats made the difference in the results. Wildrose never really expected to win seats in Edmonton, but right up to the end it was hoping for much better results in Calgary and Lethbridge.

Demographically, Wildrose did well with men, winning about half the votes of men over thirty-five. But support was much weaker among women, particularly older women. Wildrose did better than the Tories among lower-middle-class voters, to whom the Resource Dividend seemed like an appreciable amount of money, but it fell off badly among higher-income voters, who were more likely to see the Dividend as an improvident giveaway. As in the geographical analysis, Wildrose kept its core demographic support in the election but did not succeed in adding the target voters it needed to win. Or, to put it another way, it had these target voters on side for most of the campaign but lost them in the final weekend.

What happened to the PC coalition in this election is extremely interesting. Historically, the Alberta PC Party has always been balanced between Blue Tory and Red Tory wings, with the Red Tories ascendant under Peter Lougheed and Don Getty, and the Blue Tories under Ralph Klein. In this election, most of the Blue Tory wing migrated to Wildrose, to be replaced by voters whose natural tendencies lie more to the left. The Alberta PC Party now looks very much like a centre or even centre-left party, drawing heavy support from those dependent on the state, such as single women and public-sector workers, who usually vote Liberal or NDP. The future of Wildrose depends largely on how stable this new PC coalition will be in the long run. State-client voting groups may return to left-wing parties if the PC government, in its attempt to cope with shortfalls in petroleum revenues, makes substantial cuts to the services and grants on which they depend. But if the government does not make those cuts, or raises taxes to make up the shortfall, some of its remaining conservative supporters may go over to Wildrose. Borrowing money can allow a centrist party to avoid making hard choices for some period of time: Dalton McGuinty put Ontario deeply into debt while keeping his electoral coalition, which strongly resembled Redford's, together for nine years. Alberta's credit rating is AAA, so Redford's government can certainly keep borrowing if it wants to (it has already started). But the political culture of Alberta is averse to public debt, as Don Getty found out. No one can predict the future, but one can foresee the forces at play and the battle of coalitions that will emerge in the 2016 Alberta election.

COMMUNICATIONS TECHNOLOGY

Both the PCs and Wildrose mounted full-scale leader's tours to get their message out. This was a new development in Alberta, to have competing tours, because in recent elections only the PCs had the money to put one on, and they hardly had to bother. A provincial tour is far less expensive and cumbersome than a national tour for several reasons, including much smaller distances, many fewer big cities to visit, and no need for bilingualism. Hence, no one in Alberta has put forward the kind of critique of leader's tours that emerged nationally after the 2011 election. Indeed, media observers seemed pleased to have genuine leader's tours to cover. They did not, however, travel much with the tours, preferring rather to meet them when they stopped for an event. That approach is not practical in a national election but can work in a single province.

The two major contestants made full use of conventional media, including lawn and boulevard signs, radio and television advertising, and websites for displaying the campaign platform and news releases. Both also used social media as a sort of extension of conventional media. For example, Tweets were used as miniature press releases, to point reporters to larger stories and to joust with opponents. But neither party used social media in the more expansive way that has come to characterize American campaigns, especially those of Barack Obama – raising money, recruiting volunteers, facilitating local grassroots activities. In the Canadian tradition of centralized, disciplined parties, social media and the Internet remained under tight control.[2]

Be that as it may, it must be admitted that PC advertising was more nimble than Wildrose's in the closing phase of the campaign.

The PCs placed a print ad entitled "Not Your Father's PC Party" in alternative newspapers, and it garnered quite a bit of commentary on the Internet as well as in the mainstream media.[3] They had realized by this time that, in order to win, they would have to attract previous left-wing voters to their cause. Even stronger in the same direction was a video entitled "I Never Thought I'd Vote PC," which circulated widely on YouTube in the final days.[4] When I checked the total on 21 February 2013, it was 93,140 views, most of which must have taken place during the campaign – considerable for a video of that type. In comparison, Wildrose campaign policy ads have each had about 15,000 views on YouTube. The NDP tried to fight back with its own video, but the Liberals did nothing to protect their vote – nor did Wildrose at this stage, misled by the false confidence inspired by high poll numbers.

"I Never Thought I'd Vote PC" showed hip young people, not traditional supporters, advocating strategic voting because Wildrose was so dangerous. It didn't show any authorization from the PC Party, and who made and distributed it was never explained, but it's hard to believe the Tory campaign had no hand in it. The creative, production, and distribution strategies were all perfectly designed to meet the Tories' need of bringing left-wing voters on side. So give the PCs full marks for imagination in desperate circumstances. Wildrose, on the other hand, led by polls to believe it was ahead, didn't try anything adventurous in the final week.

PARTY FINANCE

Alberta's electoral finance laws are the fiscal foundation of the one-party system that has existed since 1971. To level the political playing field and remove suspicions of undue influence, all other jurisdictions in Canada have adopted some combination of strict limits on the size of personal donations, prohibition of corporate and union contributions, campaign spending limits, and campaign rebates plus other subsidies to political parties.

The only such measure that Alberta has adopted is a limit of $15,000 a year for personal and corporate contributions, raised to $30,000 in election years. And this "limit" is interpreted loosely, so that donors can give the maximum not only in their own names but also through any or all companies that they control. Late in the campaign, Edmonton Oilers owner Daryl Katz wrote a single cheque to the PCs for $430,000, which was then divided up for reporting purposes among his companies and family members. After an investigation, Elections Alberta found the donation to be legal.[5]

The Progressive Conservatives' deliberate failure to adopt modern regulations for political party financing underpins Alberta's one-party state. As the governing party, the PCs have had virtually unlimited access to corporate and high-end personal donations. Prior to 2012, they always outspent all other parties together by a large margin. Meanwhile, the opposition parties would borrow whatever they could to run under-financed campaigns, then spend the next four years trying to climb out of debt, without the assistance of campaign rebates or other public support.

In 2012, however, Wildrose broke the PCs' financial monopoly by combining appeals to the business community with unprecedented (for Alberta) efforts at attracting small donors, raising twice as much as the PCs during the campaign period. Yet the effects of the past could not be erased. The Tories had so much money in the bank before the election started, or perhaps such a good credit rating, that they could still outspend Wildrose by 50 per cent – $4.7 to $3.1 million.

Even more importantly, the PCs kept themselves in power by siphoning support from the Alberta Liberals, whose vote share dropped from 26 per cent in 2008 to 10 per cent in 2012. Many factors were involved in the Liberals' collapse, but lack of money was surely an important one. Weakened from years of indebtedness, the Alberta Liberal Party spent only $150,000 in the 2012 election campaign – a fringe-party total, hardly what one would expect from a party that had been the official opposition when the writ was dropped.[6]

Even though one opposition party, Wildrose, was able to play in 2012 on an almost level field with the Tories, the latter survived, at least in part, because of the weakness of the other opposition parties, who had been systematically deprived of financial resources for decades. Alberta's regime of election financing continued to prop up the one-party state.[7] But if Wildrose can maintain its financial independence, it will have chances in the future to break the PCs' monopoly of power.

PERMANENT CAMPAIGN

The one aspect of the permanent campaign to figure in this election was Wildrose's decision to release three waves of negative ads against Alison Redford in the pre-writ period, starting a week after she was chosen PC leader on 2 October 2012, which was almost six months before the writ was dropped on 26 March 2013. This tactic was consciously inspired by the federal Conservatives' success in using pre-writ advertising against new Liberal leaders Stéphane Dion and Michael Ignatieff. Wildrose, however, did not have nearly as much money to spend as the federal Conservatives, so the results of their pre-writ advertising were limited. The first wave did, indeed, create considerable buzz in the mainstream media because it was so unprecedented in the Alberta context, earning free media that was worth several times more than the relatively puny paid media buy of about $40,000. But the other two waves had less impact, even though they were useful in helping the members of the newly constituted Wildrose campaign team learn how to work together. It still seems to be true that successful permanent campaigning in Canada requires lots of money, more than Wildrose had at the time.

GOING NEGATIVE

Both Wildrose and the PCs used negative campaigning in 2013, albeit in different ways, thereby creating the dialectic of fear and loathing. Wildrose repeatedly used paid advertising in an attempt to link Redford to the "culture of corruption" associated with the PC Party before she became leader. After saying she wanted the campaign to be about hope rather than fear, Redford then repeatedly emphasized, both personally and through surrogates, how frightening Wildrose was.

In my opinion, the negative campaigns were hard-hitting but not unfair. The PCs had engaged in a lot of sleazy transactions in their forty years in power. And Wildrose did have unresolved social conservative issues lingering from an earlier period when gay marriage was still a debated question.

In fact, there were greater questions about the truth of the two parties' positive campaigns than about the negative side. At the time of writing (spring 2013), it is now clear to everyone that the PCS' 2012–13 budget and their spring campaign were based on wildly over-optimistic revenue projections. Their promises of offering expensive new programs while balancing the budget and starting to rebuild the Heritage Fund, if they were sincere, were based on gross self-deception. Wildrose's financial projections were more sober, but the platform was not forthcoming about the steps required to balance the budget. Like all conservative parties running on a platform of balancing the budget, Wildrose tried to give the impression that the job could be accomplished by eliminating waste and thinning the ranks of senior management in the public service. Heather Forsyth's statement about wage freezes was a gaffe only in the sense of American TV personality Michael Kinsley's definition: "A gaffe is when a politician tells the truth."[8] As several authors have suggested is usually the case, the negative side of the campaign probably had a higher intellectual content than the positive side.

FINAL REFLECTIONS

The 2012 Alberta provincial election campaign resembled in many ways a lot of other recent election campaigns in Canada. It was vigorously fought, with the main contenders using every possible channel of communications to persuade voters. There were unexpected surges in the polls, with Wildrose forging ahead at the beginning and the PCS recovering for victory at the end. An existing old party – the Liberals – suffered a cataclysmic decline in support, while a new party – Wildrose – won the second prize by becoming the official opposition.

As in other campaigns, there was exaggeration and distortion. Wildrose exaggerated the Tories' ethical lapses, while the PCS exaggerated the danger that Wildrose might pose to minorities. The biggest issue now facing Albertans – budget deficits arising from a combination of excessive spending and resource revenues falling below projections – did not come through clearly in the campaign. Wildrose said there was a problem, but by offering a program of positive benefits, such the Family Pack and the Resource Dividend, obscured its magnitude. For their part, the Tories denied the fiscal problem and depicted a future characterized by both balanced budgets and lavish new spending programs.

So the campaign wasn't a good seminar – but then campaigns rarely are. A campaign is just a moment in an endless political process. It doesn't solve all problems; it merely determines who will govern for the next few years. After denying the existence of a major fiscal problem, the PCs now have to try to solve it. Poetic justice indeed.

As a campaign manager, I was bitterly disappointed to lose, especially after thinking throughout the campaign that Wildrose was ahead. There is only one way to play politics, and that is to win. Losing sucks. But as a political scientist, I can't criticize the outcome. Wildrose was in effect a new party. Danielle Smith was not only a new leader but she had also never served in the Legislature and had never even held elective office, except for a brief and tempestuous period as a public school trustee. She had at the time some odd ideas about how a cabinet government could be conducted, though I imagine she's learned better since being elected to the Legislature. Voters were justified in being cautious. Though the result was not intended – some voters wanted Wildrose to win, others did not – the effect of the aggregated decision was to give Wildrose a big promotion, to the status of official opposition, without turning over government to this inexperienced crew.

The official opposition is actually part of the government, because parliamentary democracy internalizes opposition toward the ends of subjecting the elected government to criticism and preparing an alternative government should the government of the day prove inadequate. Wildrose now has the honour of being on probation as a future government – a status that the Liberals used to have but to which they did not measure up. The election earned Wildrose four years to learn how Alberta's government works and how they might do a better job of running it. So they didn't win the prize they wanted, but they won a prize worth having, and perhaps that was all they could reasonably expect so early in the life of a new party.

The Calgary Centre By-Election: A Clash of Campaign Models

With Ryan Pike

Some literature exists on Canadian by-elections,[1] but not on campaign strategies in by-elections. This appendix is a first step in that direction. I hope it will make by-elections more comprehensible to observers and perhaps assist campaigners in choosing an appropriate strategy when they run in by-elections. In a larger context, this appendix fits one of the main themes of the book, namely, the arrival of the permanent campaign in Canada. Students of campaigning have to broaden their focus from the writ period to include all the other essential activities that take place before and between elections. By-elections are an important part of total strategy for the permanent campaign.

Since 2004, the Conservative Party of Canada has developed a standard model for fighting by-elections, based on the way that Conservative candidates are trained to run in general elections. The first rule is for the candidate not to spend too much time in the public eye. Don't worry about getting featured in the media, especially the national media, which might want to torque their coverage to suit objectives outside the local race. Don't get drawn into too many candidate forums. One or two might be all right, but remember that most people who attend are committed voters who have already made up their minds. Even worse, the forum might be organized by an unfriendly organization that will stack the audience with hostile partisans.

Rather than seek public attention and media coverage, the candidate should spend as much time as possible door-knocking, not

Table A.1
Federal by-election results, 2005–13

	Conservatives	Liberals	NDP	BQ
Pick-up	5	2	1	0
Hold	3	5	2	3
Fail to gain	12	11	16	0
Lose	1	3	1	2

just to meet voters personally (although that is certainly important), but to identify supporters who can be driven to the polls with an intensive GOTV campaign. For ridings considered winnable, the candidate's personal efforts will be backed up by an extensive telephone voter ID and GOTV campaign, financially assisted by the national party if necessary. The emphasis on voter ID and GOTV is especially powerful in low-turnout elections, as is typical of by-elections. Indeed, the national party spent a total of about $1.1 million on recent by-elections, for an average of about $58,000 per race, far exceeding what any other party has spent.[2] If you can get your supporters to vote while most people are staying home, your chances of winning are enhanced. The Conservative model is tailor-made for low-turnout elections, which Canadian by-elections usually are.

The Conservative by-election model has been quite successful thus far. In the twenty-one by-elections held from 2005 through 2013, the Conservatives picked up five seats previously held by other parties, held onto three of their own, and lost only one – a record far superior to that of their competitors. Table A.1 gives an overview of these results:

Conservative by-election successes played a significant role in the party's progress from official opposition in 2004 to majority government in 2011. Each of the five times that the Conservatives took a seat away from another party, it helped to build momentum and to position the party for improvements in the next general election. The one Conservative loss took place on 13 May 2013, when the Liberals took back Labrador from the Conservatives. The Conservative candidate Peter Penashue had won the riding in 2011 but then resigned to run again after disclosure of financial irregularities in his 2011 campaign. The Labrador by-election was thus not typical because Penashue was a severely damaged candidate, and the riding itself, with its sparse and heavily aboriginal population, does not lend itself well to Conservative DVC techniques.

In more typical contests, the Conservative by-election model is obviously effective, but, like all human strategies, it is not invulnerable and may be beaten under certain conditions. One weak point is the cone of media silence under which the candidate operates. This is not such a big problem in national elections because the leader's tour generates daily news stories while paid advertising also fills the media. The party's message becomes the candidate's message, releasing the candidate to concentrate on meeting voters. But in a by-election there is no leader's tour and no paid advertising to create a media presence for the Conservative candidate, leaving a vacuum that opposing candidates may try to fill. The Conservative candidate may be accused of running in a bubble, dodging the media, and avoiding election forums, thus giving rise to negative stories that in a national campaign are largely drowned out by all the noise surrounding the leader's tour, platform release, and advertising.

On 26 November 2012, the Conservative by-election model was put to a severe test in Calgary Centre. It passed the test, but not by a very large margin, suggesting a certain vulnerability that might be exploited by future opponents.

During the run-up to the by-election, Calgary Centre was sometimes portrayed in the media as a Conservative fortress, but the truth is more complicated. The riding is demographically mixed. It has large tracts of middle-income single-family housing, which are indeed Conservative strongholds, but there is also an important area of high-income housing in which the Liberals are relatively strong (think of Rosedale in Toronto or Kerrisdale in Vancouver). In addition there is an inner-city apartment area populated mainly by young, single people, who are likely to tilt Liberal, NDP, or Green, if they choose to vote.

Calgary Centre also has a complicated political history. Held by PC Harvie Andre during the Mulroney years, it went Reform in 1993 and 1997 but returned to the PC fold in 2000, when the Liberal vote in the riding migrated to former Prime Minister Joe Clark. It then went Conservative in 2004, 2006, 2008, and 2011, when the candidate was Lee Richardson, a former Progressive Conservative who had once been executive assistant to Peter Lougheed. Richardson was very popular in the riding because he could call on his PC history while still remaining loyal to Conservative leader Stephen Harper.

Calgary Centre includes the entire provincial riding of Calgary–Elbow, which has been represented by Alberta premiers Ralph Klein and Alison Redford. But Calgary–Elbow also went Liberal in a 2007 by-election after Klein retired. Moreover, the tensions between Reform/Alliance Conservatives and Progressive Conservatives, which continue to bubble underground in the federal party, have now become explicit in Alberta provincial politics, with Wildrose looking much like a reincarnation of the Reform Party.

It was thus quite significant that the Conservative nominee in Calgary Centre, former *Calgary Herald* editor and television pundit Joan Crockatt, was commonly painted as a Wildrose supporter. Even though Lee Richardson and Alison Redford publicly threw their support behind Crockatt,[3] the stage was set for many provincial PCs to sit on their hands, not bother to vote, or even vote for another party in this federal contest. Due to its demographic composition and political history, Calgary Centre can never be taken for granted, and this inherent unpredictability was exacerbated by nomination of a Wildrose supporter so soon after Wildrose had made a spirited effort to turn the provincial PCs and Premier Alison Redford out of office.

Liberal candidate Harvey Locke was perfectly suited to bring out that party's core vote and also appeal to *bien-pensant* Progressive Conservatives who might find Joan Crockatt too right wing. He is the scion of a well-established Calgary family, bilingual, a former downtown lawyer, and president of the Alberta Liberal Party as well as of the Canadian Parks and Wilderness Society, now a full-time conservationist, photographer, and author. But the real wild card was Green nominee Chris Turner. Not yet forty years old, Turner was a successful journalist, appearing often in *Shift* magazine, and an author of several prize-winning books.[4] He was well positioned to galvanize younger voters who would never vote Conservative or Liberal and are turned off by the NDP's alliance with organized labour.

Crockatt was now faced with two opponents who were accomplished authors, well known to the media and at home in that environment. Moreover, Turner's campaign attracted many of the young people who had helped propel Naheed Nenshi to the mayor's office in his 2010 insurgent campaign. By an "insurgent" campaign, I mean one in which a candidate largely unknown to the public (Nenshi was polling about 1 per cent when he started) comes out of nowhere to become a serious contender and even win. Recent successful examples in Alberta include Nenshi's race for mayor of Calgary in 2010 and Alison Redford's selection as leader of the Progressive Conservative Party in 2011. In both of those victories, Calgary consultant Stephen Carter played an important advisory role.

By definition, an insurgent campaign begins with limited resources of money and manpower, and faces much better established opponents who have far more supporters and money. The insurgent has to run as an outsider, challenging the accepted patterns of politics as usual, calling for institutional or procedural reform. With little money to spend initially, the insurgent has to create buzz in inexpensive social media, including blogging, Facebook, Twitter, and YouTube. With success at that level, money and volunteers will start to appear, and the campaign can progress to using as much conventional media as it can pay for, including lawn and boulevard signs, pamphlets, even radio and TV advertising. Throughout, however, the insurgent must remain the outsider, the challenger, because the strategic goal is to mobilize voters who would not usually vote in such an election. For Nenshi's mayoralty race, it was young, particularly ethnic voters; for Redford's PC Party leadership race, it was public sector unionists, especially teachers, nurses, and other medical workers.

During the summer of 2012, Crockatt enjoyed a lead of more than 20 percentage points over Locke, with Turner and NDP candidate Dan Meades even further behind, vying for third place. But by autumn, Crockatt had dropped to just a small lead over Locke, while Turner had surged to make it a three-way race, and the NDP candidate had fallen to single digits.[5] Crockatt's opponents kept challenging her to appear at candidate forums, and Mayor Nenshi jumped in by organizing his own forum, in which Crockatt declined to take part.[6]

Table A.2
Calgary Centre results, general election 2011 and by-election 2012

Party	% Vote 2011	% Vote 2012
Conservative	57.7	36.9
Liberal	17.5	32.7
NDP	14.9	3.8
Green	9.9	25.7

Locke, however, lost his momentum late in the campaign due to events outside his control. On 21 November, federal Liberal natural resources critic David McGuinty commented on Alberta MPs, "They are national legislators with a national responsibility, but they come across as very, very small-p provincial individuals who are jealously guarding one industrial sector, picking the fossil fuel business and the oil sands business specifically, as one that they're going to fight to the death for."[7] Liberal Leader Bob Rae tried to contain the damage by removing McGuinty from his critic's position, but then the Conservatives compounded the damage by releasing to *Sun Media* an old Justin Trudeau video clip containing colourful remarks about Albertans: "Canada isn't doing well right now because it's Albertans who control our community and socio-democratic agenda. It doesn't work."[8] A chill descended on the doorsteps of Calgary Centre just as Locke was making his final GOTV push.

There was considerable media speculation in the later stages of the campaign that Crockatt might lose. However, she scraped through on 26 November, as shown in Table A.2.

The Conservative vote share dropped by 20.8 points between 2011 and 2012, and the NDP share fell by 11.1, while the Liberal and Green shares went up by 15.2 and 15.8 points, respectively. In terms of vote totals rather than vote shares, Joan Crockatt received 18,000 votes fewer than Lee Richardson got in 2011, while both the Liberal and Green candidates attracted more voters to the polls in 2012 than in 2011. Crockatt survived because the Conservatives started with such a huge advantage, but in this instance the Conservative by-election model failed to galvanize voters, while the Liberals and Greens seemed to grow at the expense of the NDP.

Table A.3
Poll-level correlations of party vote percentages between general election 2011 and by-election 2012

	Con 2011	Lib 2011	NDP 2011	Green 2011
Con 2012	.79*	−.49*	−.60*	−.53*
Lib 2012	−.36*	.58*	.13	.06
NDP 2012	−.36*	.04	.50*	.08
Green 2012	−.50*	.10	.41*	.55*

* Statistically significant at the .01 level or better (two-tailed test). Ryan Pike, a graduate student in political science at the University of Calgary, downloaded the data from Elections Canada and generated the correlation matrix.

The correlation matrix presented in Table A.3 offers a more refined version of this impressionistic interpretation.

Except for some differences in aggregation and reporting, poll boundaries were the same in Calgary Centre in 2011 and 2012, so we can use correlation coefficients to explore geographical tendencies in the distribution of the vote in the two elections. To read the table, look first at the main diagonal (running down and to the right). The diagonal presents the correlation of each party's vote percentage with itself in the two different years. Not surprisingly, all four correlations are large, positive, and highly significant statistically. In simple language, all parties, and especially the Conservatives, tended to do well (or poorly) in 2012 in the same polling districts in which they had done well (or poorly) in 2011. Of course, many fewer votes were cast in 2012 than in 2011, but the *relative* patterns of strength remained similar, even if the *absolute* numbers were smaller.

Now look vertically down the third column, which shows the correlations between the 2011 NDP vote and the 2012 votes for all parties. The correlation between the 2011 NDP vote and the 2012 Conservative vote is strong and negative (−.60), which is to be expected. But the correlation between the 2011 NDP vote and the 2012 Green vote is moderately positive (.41), indeed almost as high as the correlation of the NDP with itself in the two different elections (.50). No other party shows this pattern. In plain language, the conclusion is that many traditional NDP voters must have defected to the Greens in 2012, whereas the other parties were hanging onto traditional supporters.

This conclusion is corroborated by what one of my graduate students told me during the campaign. Knowing that she was left wing in her views and politically engaged, I asked her if she was working for anyone in the by-election. "Chris Turner [Green Party]," she said, "… and Dan Meades [NDP]. I just wish Dan hadn't run." In the end, the Greens did well by poaching the NDP vote, but even if they had got all of that relatively small pool, it wouldn't have been enough to win. Ultimately, Joan Crockatt was saved by the reality of vote-splitting on the left. The NDP and Greens got together under Green auspices, but the Liberals put on their own strong showing with an excellent candidate, thus allowing Crockatt to slip through in spite of internal divisions among the Wildrose and Progressive Conservative tribes that now make up the federal Conservative coalition in Alberta.

Two big stories were in play in this by-election. One concerned the divided left and the need to get together if they were going to defeat the Conservative candidate. They took a step in that direction, but it was not big enough. The other story concerned campaign strategy. Events showed that the Conservative keep-your-head-down-and-door-knock strategy might be vulnerable to challenge by an insurgent campaign. Crockatt's initial high level of support sank dramatically as her insurgent opponents dominated the media. If there had just been one strong insurgent challenger, she might today be back looking for work in the media instead of sitting in the House of Commons. But she faced two powerful insurgent campaigns, thus allowing her to claw out a victory under Canada's SMP voting rules.

Notes

INTRODUCTION

1 "Elections Canada Due for an 'Upgrade' Running Elections," *Hill Times Online*, 12 July 2012.
2 Yaroslav Baran, "Social Media in Campaign 2011," *Policy Options* 32 (June–July 2011): 82.

CHAPTER ONE

1 Frans de Waal, *Chimpanzee Politics: Power and Sex among Apes* (Baltimore: Johns Hopkins University Press, 1982).
2 Thomas Hobbes, *Leviathan*, part 1, ch. 11.
3 Jane Goodall, *Through a Window: My Thirty Years with the Chimpanzees of Gombe* (New York: Houghton Mifflin, 1990), 114–29.
4 Christopher Boehm, *Moral Origins: The Evolution of Virtue, Altruism, and Shame (New York: Basic Books, 2012),* 96.
5 Aristotle, *Politics*, 1253a1–3.
6 "Campaign," *Oxford English Dictionary.*
7 Aristotle, *Rhetoric*, 1356a, in *The Basic Works of Aristotle* edited by Richard McKeon (New York: Random House, 1941), 1329–30.
8 David Hume, *A Treatise of Human Nature*, 2.3.3.4, http://www.gutenberg.org/files/4705/4705-h/4705-h.htm#2H_4_0075.
9 Richard D. Alexander, *The Biology of Moral Systems* (New York: Aldine de Gruyter, 1987); Robert Wright, *The Moral Animal: Evolutionary Psychology and Everyday Life* (New York: Vintage Books, 1994); Christopher

Boehm, *Moral Origins: The Evolution of Virtue, Altruism, and Shame* (New York: Basic Books, 2012).

10 Jonathan Haidt, *The Righteous Mind: Why Good People Are Divided by Politics and Religion* (New York: Pantheon, 2012).

11 Rick Hillier, *A Soldier First: Bullets, Bureaucrats and the Politics of War* (Toronto: HarperCollins, 2009), 401.

12 Matthew 4:19.

13 Two English translations are available. D.W. Taylor and J. Murrell published a translation entitled *A Short Guide to Electioneering* (London: London Association of Classical Teachers, 1968; 2nd ed. 1994), and republished it with some other material in *Cicero's Consulship Campaign* (London: London Association of Classical Teachers, 2009). Another translation is by Philip Freeman, *How to Win an Election: An Ancient Guide for Modern Politicians* (Princeton: Princeton University Press, 2012). I have quoted the Taylor-Murrell translation because it is closer to the original Latin, though the Freeman translation is far more enjoyable for modern readers.

CHAPTER TWO

1 For a similar analysis, see Ted Morton, "Leadership Selection in Alberta, 1992–2011: A Personal Perspective," *Canadian Parliamentary Review* (Summer 2013): 31–8.

2 David K. Stewart and Keith Archer, *Parties and Leadership Selection in Alberta* (Vancouver: UBC Press, 2000), 62.

3 Morton, "Leadership Selection," 34.

4 David K. Stewart and Anthony M. Sayers, "Leadership Change in a Dominant Party: The Alberta Progressive Conservatives, 2006," *Canadian Political Science Review* 3 (2009): 100, http://ojs.unbc.ca/index.php/cpsr/article/view/188/253.

5 "Mar Leads Race for Alberta PC Leadership: Poll," *National Post*, 13 September 2011.

6 Quoted in David K. Stewart and Anthony M. Sayers, "Responding to Challenge: An Analysis of the 2011 Alberta Progressive Conservative Leadership Election" (Canadian Political Science Association, 2012), 7.

7 Ibid., 8.

8 Stewart and Sayers, "Leadership Change."

9   Dave Dorner, "Alberta Tories Vote to Change Leadership Rules at Annual General Meeting," *Calgary Sun*, 10 November 2012.

10   Morton, "Leadership Selection," 36–8.

11   Sasha Issenberg, *The Victory Lab: The Secret Science of Winning Campaigns* (New York: Random House, 2012).

12   Elections Canada, "Final Election Expenses Limits for Registered Political Parties," http://www.elections.ca/content.aspx?section=ele&document=index&dir=pas/41ge/limpol&lang=e.

13   Tom Flanagan, "Organized Labour Is Now a Super PAC," *Globe and Mail*, 16 July 2012.

14   http://www.youtube.com/watch?v=RJls9nQouvQ.

CHAPTER THREE

1   Anthony Downs, *An Economic Theory of Democracy* (New York: Harper and Row, 1957).

2   Kenneth A. Shepsle and Mark S. Bonchek, *Analyzing Politics: Rationality, Behavior, and Institutions* (New York: W.W. Norton, 1997), 88–91.

3   Britain, Canada, and the United States use the first-past-the-post system. Australia's alternative ballot is not that much different in practice except that it has promoted a two-party coalition (Liberal/National) on the right. New Zealand adopted a form of proportional representation in 1993, but it was not actually used until the election of 1996.

4   Fan-Yee Suen, "NDP Votes to Drop 'Socialism' from Its Constitution," CTV website, 14 April 2013, http://www.ctvnews.ca/politics/ndp-votes-to-drop-socialism-from-its-constitution-1.1237369.

5   Patrick Donleavy, *Democracy, Bureaucracy and Public Choice* (New York: Prentice-Hall, 1991), 132–5.

6   Tom Flanagan, *Waiting for the Wave: The Reform Party and the Conservative Movement,* 2nd ed. (Montreal: McGill-Queen's University Press, 2009), 223.

7   Réjean Landry, "Incentives Created by the Institutions of Representative Democracy," in *Representation, Integration and Political Parties in Canada,* edited by Herman Bakvis (Toronto: Dundurn, 1991), 446–8; Steven J. Brams, *Rational Politics*: Decisions, Games, and Strategy (Washington, DC: CQ Press, 1985), 32–6.

8   Flanagan, *Waiting for the Wave,* 224.

9   Downs, *Economic Theory of Democracy*, 131.

10 http://quotes.yourdictionary.com/hurry.

11 Flanagan, *Harper's Team: Behind the Scenes in the Conservative Rise to Power*, 2nd ed. (Montreal: McGill-Queen's University Press, 2009), 186–7.

12 "World's Smallest Political Quiz," http://www.theadvocates.org/quiz.

13 Shepsle and Boncheck, *Analyzing Politics*, 101–2.

14 Mark O. Dickerson, Thomas Flanagan, and Brenda O'Neill, *An Introduction to Government and Politics: A Conceptual Approach*, 9th ed. (Toronto: Nelson, 2013), 337.

15 Arend Lijphart, *Democracies: Patterns of Majoritarian and Consensus Government in Twenty-One Countries* (New Haven: Yale University Press, 1984), 127–49.

16 William H. Riker, *Liberalism against Populism: A Confrontation between the Theory of Democracy and the Theory of Social Choice* (Prospect Heights, IL: Waveland Press, 1988), 197–232.

17 William H. Riker, *The Art of Political Manipulation* (New Haven: Yale University Press, 1986), ix–xi.

18 Antonia Maioni, "Grits: Be Bold, or Get Lost," *Globe and Mail*, 1 September 2011.

CHAPTER FOUR

1   Quoted in Milan Vego, "Clausewitz's Schwerpunkt: Mistranslated from German – Misunderstood in English," *Military Review*, http://findarticles.com/p/articles/mi_mopbz/is_/ai_n27135952.

2   Tom Flanagan, *Harper's Team: Behind the Scenes in the Conservative Rise to Power*, 2nd ed. (Montreal: McGill-Queen's University Press, 2009), 137–62.

3   This chapter is adapted from Tom Flanagan, "Campaign Strategy: Triage and the Concentration of Resources," in *Election*, edited by Heather MacIvor (Toronto: Emond Montgomery, 2010), 155–72.

4   Carl von Clausewitz, *On War*, translated by Michael Howard and Peter Paret (Princeton, NJ: Princeton University Press, 1976), 595.

5   Thomas Flanagan, *Game Theory and Canadian Politics* (Toronto: University of Toronto Press, 1998), 74–92.

6 Steven Hobbs, "Direct Voter Contact: Its Effectiveness in the 2004 and 2006 Conservative Party of Canada's Election Campaigns" (MA thesis, University of Calgary, 2008), 63.

7 Daniel LeBlanc, "Tories Target Specific Ethnic Voters," *Globe and Mail*, 16 October 2007.

8 Tom Flanagan, "The Emerging Conservative Coalition," *Policy Options* 32 (June–July 2011): 104–8.

9 Flanagan, *Harper's Team*, 224.

10 Anthony Downs, *An Economic Theory of Democracy* (New York: Harper & Row, 1957).

11 Flanagan, *Harper's Team*, 226.

12 Margaret Thatcher, speech to the Conservative Party Conference, Brighton, 8 October 1976, quoted in Claire Berlinski, *There Is No Alternative* (New York: Basic Books, 2008), 69.

13 George Panagiotou, "Bringing SWOT into Focus," *Business Strategy Review* 14, no. 2 (2003): 8–10; David W. Pickton and Sheila Wright, "What's SWOT in Strategic Analysis?" *Strategic Change* 7 (1998): 101–9.

14 Flanagan, *Harper's Team*, 231.

15 Ibid., 314–15.

CHAPTER FIVE

1 "Political Campaign," *Canadian Encyclopedia,* http://www.thecanadian encyclopedia.com/index.cfm?PgNm=TCE&Params=A1ARTA0006368.

2 J.M. Beck, *Pendulum of Power: Canada's Federal Elections* (Scarborough: Prentice-Hall of Canada, 1968), 382.

3 Marjory LeBreton, "Thirty-Seven Days 'in the Bubble' with the National Media," *Policy Options* 32 (June–July 2011), 38.

4 Ibid., 81.

5 http://en.wikipedia.org/wiki/Front_porch_campaign.

6 Warren Kinsella, *The War Room* (Toronto: Dundurn, 2007), 43.

7 Patrice Dutil and David McKenzie, *Canada 1911: The Decisive Election that Shaped the Country* (Toronto: Dundurn, 2011), 242.

8 http://books.google.com/books?id=pggbAAAAYAAJ&pg=PA251&lpg= PA251&dq=silver+tongued+laurier&source=bl&ots=_gGibxBwjc&sig= NRAtCFZJOQIUdmAnao2dhnphRmk&hl=en&ei=vfJ4TqnyCOzxiALE9

PHNAQ&sa=x&oi=book_result&ct=result&resnum=9&sqi=2&ved=
OCECQ6AEWCA#v=onepage&q=silver%20tongued%20laurier&f=false.

9   Dick Morris, *Power Plays: Win or Lose – How History's Great Political
    Leaders Play the Game* (New York: Harper Collins, 2002), 249.

10 "The Branding Irons of the Antichrist," in *Aberhart: Outpourings and
    Replies,* edited by David R. Elliott (Calgary: Historical Society of Alberta,
    1991), 1–41. It is not on YouTube, but a version is advertised on
    IMDb.

11 Pierre Elliott Trudeau, *Memoirs* (Toronto: McClelland & Stewart, 1993),
    105–6.

12 David Carr, "How Obama Tapped into Social Networks' Power," *New
    York Times,* 9 November 2008.

13 http://www.youtube.com/watch?v=molwTfv8TYw.

14 http://www.youtube.com/watch?v=gvcTdbemaVY.

15 http://en.wikipedia.org/wiki/Yes_We_Can.

16 Ron Strand, "How Social Media Worked for Calgary's New Mayor,"
    http://ezinearticles.com/?How-Social-Media-Worked-for-Calgarys-New-
    Mayor&id=5240470.

17 *Globe and Mail,* 24 October 2010, reprinted http://ismailimail.wordpress.
    com/2010/10/24/cowtown-no-more-why-calgary- chose-naheed-nenshi-
    the-globe-and-mail.

18 Yaroslav Baran, "Social Media in Campaign 2011: A Noncanonical Take
    on the Twitter Effect," *Policy Options* 32 (June–July 2011), 85.

CHAPTER SIX

1   Tom Flanagan and Harold J. Jansen, "Election Campaigns under Canada's
    Party Finance Laws," in *The Canadian Federal Election of 2008,* edited
    by Jon H. Pammett and Christopher Dornan (Toronto: Dundurn, 2009),
    194–5.

2   A legislated formula imposes a cap on national campaign expenditures
    (about $21 million in 2011 for a party that ran candidates in every con-
    stituency). After the election, parties can apply to Elections Canada for a
    rebate of 50 per cent of documented expenses.

3   Flanagan and Jansen, "Election Campaigns," 195–6.

4   Ibid., 197.

5   Ibid., 4.

6   Ibid., 5. This increase in revenue was complemented by campaign rebates of 60 per cent in 2004 and 50 per cent thereafter, compared with 22.5 per cent between 2000 and 2003. I did not add revenue from campaign rebates to the quarterly allowances, however, because the former depends on the frequency of campaigns. There have been four elections since 2004, so rebate revenue has been high in recent years; at the same time, of course, the parties have also had higher expenses from waging election battles.

7   Eddie Goldenberg, *The Way It Works: Inside Ottawa* (Toronto: McClelland & Stewart, 2006), 383.

8   Mark Milke, "What Saved the Parti Québécois in the 2008 Election: Public Money" (Winnipeg: Frontier Centre for Public Policy, 2008), http://www.fcpp.org/images/publications/FB066%20What%20Saved%20the%20Bloq%20Quebecois.pdf.

9   John Laschinger and Geoffrey Stevens, *Leaders and Lesser Mortals: Backroom Politics in Canada* (Toronto: Key Porter Books, 1992), 164–70.

10 Tom Flanagan, "Database Party: The 2002 Leadership Campaign for the Canadian Alliance," *Canadian Parliamentary Review* 26 (Spring 2003): 8–11.

11 2010 Conservative financial report, Elections Canada website, http://elections.ca/fin/pol/asset/2010/conservative_2010.pdf.

12 Milton Friedman, *Capitalism and Freedom* (Chicago: University of Chicago Press, 1962), 135. Friedman argued against all charitable contributions by corporations.

13 Tom Flanagan and David Coletto, "Replacing Allowances for Canadian National Political Parties?" University of Calgary School of Public Policy Briefing Papers (January 2010).

14 Conservative Party of Canada, *Demanding Better* (2004 platform), 11.

15 Federal Election Commission, "Public Funding of Presidential Elections," http://www.fec.gov/pages/brochures/pubfund.shtml.

16 Frederika Schouten, "Taxpayers Elect Not to Pay for Campaigns," *USA Today,* 17 April 2007, http://www.usatoday.com/news/washington/2007-04-17-preztax_N.htm?csp=34).

17 IRS Data Book, 2007. http://www.irs.gov/taxstats/article/0,,id=171961,00.html.

18 Tom Cole, "Taxpayers Shouldn't Fund Conventions," *U.S. News and World Report*, 27 August 2012, http://www.usnews.com/opinion/articles/2012/08/27/taxpayers-shouldnt-fund-conventions.

CHAPTER SEVEN

1   John Ivison, "Expect Cabinet Shuffle and Election Agenda As Harper Gets Set to Switch Back into Constant Campaign Mode," *National Post*, 14 February 2013.

2   Norman Ornstein and Thomas Mann, eds., *The Permanent Campaign and Its Future* (Washington: American Enterprise Institute and the Brookings Institute, 2000); Corey Cook, "The Contemporary Presidency: The Permanence of 'The Permanent Campaign': George W. Bush's Public Presidency," *Presidential Studies Quarterly* 32 (2os02): 753–64; Catherine Needham, "Brand Leaders: Clinton, Blair and the Limitations of the Permanent Campaign," *Political Studies* 53 (2005): 343–61; Peter van Onselen and Wayne Errington, "The Democratic State as a Marketing Tool: The Permanent Campaign in Australia," *Commonwealth & Comparative Politics* 45 (2007): 78–94.

3   Fear Factory is a heavy-metal rock group (http://www.fearfactory.com). *Fear Factor* is an NBC TV show about overcoming scary challenges (http://www.nbc.com/Fear_Factor).

4   "Conservatives Show Off Election War Room," *Guelph Daily Mercury*, 3 April 2007.

5   Glen McGregor, "Tories Sued for Back Rent on Former 'Fear Factory' Campaign Headquarters," *Ottawa Citizen*, 3 January 2013.

6   Peter Kuitenbrouwer, "Fuel Use of Liberal Campaign Jet under Attack," *National Post*, 8 September 2008.

7   Campbell Clark and Josh Wingrove, "Liberals Left in Dark As Plane Grounded in Montreal," *Globe and Mail*, 17 September 2008.

8   Flanagan, *Harper's Team: Behind the Scenes in the Conservative Rise to Power*, 2nd ed. (Montreal: McGill-Queen's University Press, 2009), 320 (index references to "direct voter contact").

9   Tamsin McMahon, "Fantino Wins in Vaughan While Liberals and Tories Split Manitoba Ridings," *National Post*, 29 November 2010.

10 Bill Curry, "Attack Ads Signal Campaign Start," *Windsor Star*, 19 May 2004.

11 Tom Flanagan, *Harper's Team*, 201–2.

12 Ibid., 222–3.

13 Ibid., 229.

14 Canadian Press, "Anti-Dion Ads Producing Laughs, Not Votes; Poll Shows Majority Believe Conservative TV Advertisements Attacking Liberal Leader Are Unfair," *Guelph Daily Mercury*, 8 February 2007.

15 http://www.ctv.ca/servlet/ArticleNews/story/CTVNews/20070410/ses_poll_070410?s_name=&no_ads=.

16 http://www.conservative.ca/EN/1091/80381.

17 http://www.ctv.ca/servlet/ArticleNews/story/CTVNews/20080609/carbon_plan_080609?s_name=&no_ads=.

18 Juliet O'Neill, "Green Shift Support Declining, Poll Shows Liberals' Carbon Tax Proposal Not Enough to Beat Tories: Pollster," *Ottawa Citizen*, 2 September 2008.

19 http://www.conservative.ca, accessed 10 September 2008.

20 Fleishman Hilliard poll tracker, http://election08.fleishman.ca, accessed 10 September 2008.

21 Joan Bryden, "Tory TV Ads a Success, Poll Shows: Barrage of Sweater-Clad Harper Ads Help Tories Win Air War," *Canadian Press*, 13 September 2008.

22 "Tories Begin Battle against Coalition," http://www.cbc.ca/canada/story/2008/12/02/harper-coalition.html.

23 Rob Silver, "The Future of the Liberal Party: E-Mail Exchange with Scott Reid," *Globe and Mail*, 17 October 2008. Accessed online 18 October 2008.

24 http://ignatieff.me.

25 "Hypocrisy," http://ignatieff.me.

26 The Conservatives reported spending $4.3 million on television advertising in 2009. See http://elections.ca/fin/pol/asset/2010/conservative_2010.pdf.

27 Juliet O'Neill and Janice Tibbets, "Ignatieff to Harper: Time Is Up," *National Post*, 2 September 2009.

28 Andrew Potter, "It's the Stupid Leadership, Stupid (Nanos Poll)," 14 November 2009, http://www2.macleans.ca/2009/11/14/its-the-stupid-leadership-stupid-nanos-poll.

29 "MP Niki Ashton: Vote to Scrap the Long-Gun Registry," 26 October 2009, http://www.conservative.ca/EN/5439/111099.

30 Jane Taber, "Ignatieff Cracks Whip on Gun Registry," *Globe and Mail*, 19 April 2010.

31   "Ignatieff Threatening to Roll Dice?" *Winnipeg Free Press,* 20 December 2010.

32   Jane Taber, "Ignatieff's Numbers Plummet As Tories Unleash Another Attack Ad," *Globe and Mail,* 10 March 2011.

33   See, for example, the time series in the Ekos poll of 27 April 2011, http://www.ekospolitics.com/wp-content/uploads/full_report_april_27_2011.pdf. All published polls showed the same tendency for Conservative numbers to rise and Liberal numbers to drop in the first quarter of 2011.

34   Warren Kinsella, *The War Room: Political Strategies for Business, NGOs, and Anyone Who Wants to Win* (Toronto: Dundurn, 2007), 111.

35   Meagan Fitzpatrick, "NDP Unveils Radio Ads Decrying Ignatieff," *Canwest News Service,* 29 January 29, http://www.canada.com/news/story.html?id=1231593.

36   Les Whittington, "Liberals' Soft Ad Approach Questioned," *Toronto Star,* 26 September 2009.

37   http://www.youtube.com/watch?v=NZ2ixKkwljI.

38   http://www.liberal.ca/en/newsroom/liberal-tv.

39   John Ibbitson, "Bob Rae Attack Ad Shows It's a Liberal Revival the Tories Fear Most," *Globe and Mail,* 21 March 2012; John Ivison, "Conservative Ads Attacking NDP Leader Thomas Mulcair Miss Their Mark," *National Post,* 11 November 2012.

40   Jessica Bruno, "NDP Dishes Out $1.9-Million on Advertising to Define Mulcair, Outspends Tories Last Year," *Hill Times Online,* 15 July 2013, http:// http://www.hilltimes.com/news/news/2013/07/15/ndp-dishes-out-$19-million-on-advertising-to-define-mulcair-outspends-tories-last/35319.

41   http://www.youtube.com/watch?v=sGwuN3zVuxU.

42   http://www.youtube.com/watch?v=ILBWN_Ut_pM.

43   Gloria Galloway, "New NDP Ads to Bring Mulcair Back into Spotlight," *Globe and Mail,* 21 May 2013.

44   http://bc.ctvnews.ca/christy-crunch-ad-takes-aim-at-b-c-premier-1.624067.

45   Susan Delacourt, "Liberals Ready to Wage Ad War with Conservatives," *Toronto Star,* 6 July 2011.

46   Peter H. Russell, *Two Cheers for Minority Government* (Toronto: Emond Montgomery, 2008), 134–42.

47   Tanya Talaga, "NDP Calls for Tough Pre-Election Ad Rules," *Toronto Star,* 19 August 2011.

48 "Annual Advertising Expense Limit," http://www.electionsmanitoba.ca/en/
    Political_Financing/annual_limit.html.

49 Harold J. Jansen and Lisa Young, "Solidarity Forever? The NDP, Organ-
    ized Labour, and the Changing Face of Party Finance in Canada," *Can-
    adian Journal of Political Science* 42 (2009): 672–4.

50 Tom Flanagan, "Organized Labour Is Now a Super-PAC," *Globe and Mail*,
    16 July 2012.

51 All Expenditure Statistics Are Taken from Elections Ontario, "Third Party
    Reports," 2011, http://www.elections.on.ca/en-CA/Tools/Financial
    StatementsandContributions/FilingStatus/2011Third+Party+Reports.htm.

CHAPTER EIGHT

1   Quintus Tullius Cicero, *A Short Guide to Electioneering*, Lactor series
    (London Association of Classical Teachers, 1970), para. 52.

2   Joel Silbey, *The American Party Battle* (1999), quoted in John C. Geer, *In
    Defense of Negativity: Attack Ads in Presidential Campaigns* (Chicago:
    University of Chicago Press, 2006), 9.

3   Cited in J.M. Beck, *Pendulum of Power: Canada's Federal Elections* (Scar-
    borough: Prentice Hall of Canada, 1968), 63.

4   Warren Kinsella, *"The War Room": Political Strategies for Business, NGOs,
    and Anyone Who Wants to Win* (Toronto: Dundurn, 2007), 108–10.

5   Richard Johnston, André Blais, Henry Brady, and Jean Crête, *Letting the
    People Decide: Dynamics of a Canadian Election* (Montreal: McGill-
    Queen's University Press, 1992), 27.

6   http://www.youtube.com/watch?v=jKQPw9vmGo4.

7   Robert Mason Lee, *One Hundred Monkeys* (Toronto: Macfarlane Walter
    and Ross, 1989), 215.

8   Johnston et al., *Letting the People Decide*, 131.

9   Tom Flanagan, *Waiting for the Wave: The Reform Party and Preston Man-
    ning* (Toronto: Stoddard, 1995) 94.

10 Stephen Clarkson, *The Big Red Machine: How the Liberal Party Domin-
    ates Canadian Politics* (Vancouver: UBC Press, 2005), 173.

11 Ibid., 174.

12 Preston Manning, *Think Big: My Adventures in Life and Democracy*
    (Toronto: McClelland & Stewart, 2002), 176–8.

13 Peter Woolstencroft, "Some Battles Won: War Lost," in *The Canadian General Election of 2000*, edited by Jon H. Pammett and Christopher Dornan (Toronto: Dundurn, 2001), 100.

14 Faron Ellis, "The More Things Change ... The Alliance Campaign," in *The Canadian General Election of 2000*, edited by Jon H. Pammett and Christopher Dornan (Toronto: Dundurn, 2001), 79.

15 "Barney, Ten Years later," http://warrenkinsella.com/2010/11/barney-ten-years-later/.

16 Geer, *In Defense of Negativity*, 122. The ad can be seen at http://www.youtube.com/watch?v=Io9KMSSEZOY.

17 Stephen Ansolabehere and Shanto Iyengar, *Going Negative: How Political Advertisements Shrink and Polarize the Electorate* (New York: Free Press, 1995), 147–8.

18 Ibid., 146.

19 Ibid., 103–4.

20 Ibid., 108.

21 Richard R. Lau and Ivy Brown Rovner, "Negative Campaigning," *Annual Review of Political Science* 12 (2009): 299.

22 http://moksheungming.tripod.com/yes.html.

23 Lau and Rovner, "Negative Campaigning," 304.

24 Ibid., 304.

25 Jeffrey Simpson, "Attack the Policies, Not Person," *Globe and Mail,* 21 January 2011.

26 Dan Gardner, "Canadians Are Fine with Politics as Usual," *Ottawa Citizen,* 31 August 2011.

27 William Johnson, *Stephen Harper and the Future of Canada* (Toronto: McClelland & Stewart, 2005), 3–4.

28 Geer, *In Defense of Negativity*.

29 Email from Scott Reid to author, 8 September 2011.

30 Paul Attalah, "Television and the Canadian Federal Election of 2004," in *Canadian General Election of 2004,* edited by Pammett and Dornan (Toronto: Dundurn, 2009), 271.

31 Chris Cobb, "Liberals Launch Attack," *National Post,* 11 January 2006.

32 Warren Kinsella, "Iggy Schooled on Being Canuck," *Ottawa Sun,* 3 July 2011.

33 Joan Bryden, "Trudeau Liberals Jump to Seven-Point Lead over Tories: Poll," *Globe and Mail,* 2 May 2013.

34 Mark Kennedy, "Trudeau Would Be Prime Minister If Election Was Held Today, Poll Finds," *National Post,* 5 April 2013.

35 *Vancouver Sun,* 9 May 2013. http://www.vancouversun.com/Video+Liberals+Weathervane/8362576/story.html.

36 Brian Topp, "Two Down, One to Go," *Policy Options* 32 (June–July 2011): 68.

37 Tom Flanagan, *Harper's Team: Behind the Scenes in the Conservative Rise to Power,* 2nd ed. (Montreal: McGill-Queen's University Press, 2009), 186–7.

CHAPTER NINE

1 http://www.elections.ab.ca/Public%20Website/files/Reports/2006_ANNUAL_REPORT_FINAL_DRAFT.pdf.

2 http://albertadiary.ca/2009/04/danielle-smith-to-lead-wildrose.html.

3 Chris Varcoe, "New Poll Shows Tories on Top but Losing Ground," *Calgary Herald,* 5 November 2009.

4 Josh Wingrove et al., "Conservative Showdown Prompts Stelmach's Resignation," *Globe and Mail,* 25 January 2011.

5 http://thealbertaardvark.blogspot.ca/2006/02/ralph-bucks.html.

6 "Wildrose Launches Anti-Redford Campaign-Style Ads," *Calgary Sun,* 6 October 2012.

7 http://www.stephentaylor.ca/2011/10/how-did-alison-redford-win.

8 Dave Climenhaga, "Alberta Diary," http://rabble.ca/blogs/bloggers/djclimenhaga/2012/01/latest-alberta-poll-shows-redford-conservatives-commanding-lead.

9 One bank finally offered a fully secured line of credit – that is, we had to raise the money in the form of loans from supporters and deposit it in advance with the bank. I wrote a cheque for $15,000 to start the process, and deeper-pocketed business supporters put up much more. In the event, however, we didn't have to use the loans we succeeded in getting.

10 Tom Flanagan, *Harper's Team: Behind the Scenes in the Conservative Rise to Power,* 2nd ed. (Montreal: McGill-Queen's University Press, 2009), 249.

11 http://www.katenashassociates.com/disabled-employee-networks/news/blog/events-dear-boy-events.

12 http://taxpayer.com/federal/14th-annual-%E2%80%9Cteddy%E2%80%9D-government-waste-awards-winners.

13 http://www.mlacompensationreview-alberta.ca.

14 CBC News, "Mar Denies Wrongdoing As Redford Suspends Asian Envoy," 13 March 2012, http://www.cbc.ca/news/canada/edmonton/story/2012/ 03/13/calgary-mar-redford-ethics.html.

15 Jackie L. Larson, "Charlebois Named Top PC in Alberta," *Sun News*, 13 July 2012, http://www.sunnewsnetwork.ca/sunnews/politics/archives/ 2012/07/20120713-164603.html.

16 http://budget2012.alberta.ca/highlights/index.html.

17 http://edmonton.ctvnews.ca/budget-2012-big-spending-ongoing-deficit-1.766203.

18 http://www.albertalandownerscouncil.com/apps/links.

19 CBC News, "Jay Leno Pokes Fun at Wildrose Bus Blunder," 27 March 2012, http://www.cbc.ca/news/canada/albertavotes2012/story/2012/03/27/ albertavotes2012-leno-wildrose-bus.html.

20 My calculation from Internet reports of various polls.

21 http://www.youtube.com/watch?v=nGF4nYnwKU4.

22 For an example, see http://www.youtube.com/watch?v=pizPcykxgkU.

23 Keith Gerein, "Wildrose Bested Tories in Fundraising Battle during Alberta Election," *Calgary Herald,* 25 October 2012.

24 The precise number is hard to calculate because it depends upon accounting assumptions about accounts receivable and payable.

25 http://www.ipsos-na.com/news-polls/pressrelease.aspx?id=5587. Return on Insight used a different metric but came to a similar conclusion. http:// www.cbc.ca/news/canada/albertavotes2012/story/2012/04/16/albertavotes 2012-leader-debate-fallout-roi-poll.html.

26 CBC News, "PC's Redford Fared the Worst in Leaders' Debate, Finds Poll: Alberta Election Poll Suggests Wildrose Leader Danielle Smith Benefitted Most from the Debate," 16 April 2012, http://www.cbc.ca/news/canada/ calgary/story/2012/04/16/albertavotes2012-leader-debate-fallout-roi-poll. html.

27 Karen Kleiss, "Tory MLAs to Pay Back 'Every Penny' Earned from No-Meet Committee," *Edmonton Journal*, 29 March 2012.

28 http://www.thestar.com/news/canada/2012/03/31/alberta_tory_aide_ resigns_after_mocking_wildrose_leader_over_not_having_children.html.

29 David Akin, blog, "Redford Staffer Resigns over Inappropriate Twitter Attack on Smith," 31 March 2012, http://blogs.canoe.ca/davidakin/ politics/redford-staffer-resigns-over-inappropriate-twitter-attack-on-smith.

30 Licia Corbella, "Posh Promises and Bad Budgeting Lead to a Mess," *Calgary Herald,* 20 February 2013.

31 Wildrose media release, 9 February 2012, http://www.wildrose.ca/feature/budget-2012-alison-in-wonderland.

32 James Wood, "Alison Redford Promises 140 Family Care Clinics for Alberta," *Calgary Herald,* 3 April 2012.

33 Quoted in Drew Anderson, "Fast Forward Weekly," 6 April 2012, http://www.ffwdweekly.com/calgary-blogs/politics/2012/04/05/wildrose-and-abortion-referendum-1020.

34 For example, Keith Gerein, "Smith Denies Abortion Agenda," *Edmonton Journal,* 6 April 2012.

35 http://www.kikkiplanet.com/pruned-bush-confessions-of-a-wilted-wild-rose.

36 Keith Gerein and Kelly Cryderman, "'Conscience Rights' Discussion Puts Wildrose's Smith on Hot Seat (with Video)," *Calgary Herald,* 13 April 2012.

37 Karen Kleiss, "On the Redford Bus: 'I Don't Want This to Be a Campaign about Fear,'" *Edmonton Journal,* 26 March 2012.

38 Josh Wingrove, "Alberta Tories Label Wildrose Position on Conscience Rights 'Frightening,'" *Globe and Mail,* 4 April 2012.

39 Re-posted on Dave Cournoyer's blog, 16 April 2012, http://daveberta.ca/2012/04/allan-hunsperger-wildrose-candidate.

40 http://www.thehousetoday.com.

41 James Wood, "Wildrose Candidate Tells Gays in Lady Gaga-Inspired Blog Post: 'You Will Suffer the Rest of Eternity in the Lake of Fire, Hell,'" *National Post,* 15 April 2012.

42 http://www.cbc.ca/news/canada/albertavotes2012/story/2012/04/17/albertavotes2012-wildrose-leech-advantage-white.html.

43 http://news.nationalpost.com/2012/04/17/ron-leech-wildrose.

44 CBC News, "Wildrose Candidate Apologizes for White Advantage Comment," 17 April 2012, http://www.cbc.ca/news/canada/albertavotes2012/story/2012/04/17/albertavotes2012-wildrose-leech-advantage-white.html. Read 546 comments546

45 Staff, "Mayors Decry Wildrose Candidates' Race and Homosexuality Comments, Demand Danielle Smith Takes Action," *National Post,* 19 April 2012.

46 http://www.wildrose.ca/blog/danielle-speaks-about-mondays-election.

47   http://www.huffingtonpost.ca/2012/04/16/danielle-smith-climate-change_n_1429850.html.

48   James Wood, "Wildrose Renews Idea of Alberta 'Firewall' within Canada," *National Post,* 14 April 2012.

49   http://www.forumresearch.com/forms/News%20Archives/News%20 Releases/40010_Alberta_Issues_Poll_(Forum_Research)_(20120422).pdf.

CHAPTER TEN

1   Licia Corbella, "We're Doing OK for a Bunch of Rednecks," *Calgary Herald,* 14 April 2012.

2   Tamara A. Small, "E-ttack Politics: Negativity, the Internet, and Canadian Political Parties," in *How Canadians Communicate IV,* edited by David Tara and Christopher Waddell (Edmonton: Athabasca University Press, 2012) 169–88.

3   http://daveberta.ca/2012/04/communications-problems.

4   http://www.youtube.com/watch?v=rPR84Gn1d9I.

5   Dawn Walton and Josh Wingrove, "Katz Group's $430,000 'Bulk Donation' to Redford's Tories Cleared by Elections Alberta," *Globe and Mail,* 1 May 2013.

6   http://efpublic.elections.ab.ca/afEFUploadView.cfm?&ACID=10001.

7   This section is adapted from Tom Flanagan, "Fiscal Foundations of the One-Party State," *Globe and Mail,* 10 November 2012.

8   http://politicaldictionary.com/words/gaffe/.

APPENDIX

1   Peter John Loewen and Frédérick Bastien, "(In)significant Elections? Federal By-Elections in Canada, 1963–2008," *Canadian Journal of Political Science* 43 (2010): 87–105.

2   Tim Nametz, "Conservatives Have Spent $1.1 Million on Federal Byelections Since 2006: Elections Canada," *Hill Times Online,* 26 September 2013, http://www.hilltimes.com/politics/2013/09/25/conservatives= have= spent=%2411=million=on=federal=byelections=since=2006=36033.

3   Jen Gerson, "Wildrose and 'Progressive' Conservatives Divided over Nominee for Calgary Federal Riding," *National Post,* 12 November 2008.

4   http://en.wikipedia.org/wiki/Chris_Turner_ (author).

5 http://daveberta.ca/2012/11/calgary-centre-byelection-poll.

6 CBC News, "Nenshi Calls Crockatt's Absence 'Elephant Not in the
   Room,'" 18 November 2012, http://www.cbc.ca/news/canada/calgary/
   story/2012/11/18/calgary-byelection-forum.html.

7 Daniel Proussalidis, "David McGuinty to Tories: Go Back to Alberta,"
   Toronto Sun, 20 November 2012.

8 Tiffany Crawford and Lee Berthiaume, "Justin Trudeau Apologizes for
   Controversial Anti-Alberta Remarks," *National Post,* 23 November 2012.

Index